KEY TO THE BIBLE

VOLUME 2

> *"I am convinced that modern scholarship has opened the Bible to us in a marvelous manner, and my sole desire is to place that key in the hands of those who seek it."*

The words of Wilfrid Harrington, O.P.—eminent Scripture scholar and author of this acclaimed theological work. According to Fr. Harrington, the majority of people who read the Bible find it difficult to understand. Many are discouraged and give up Bible reading altogether. They need a guide to help them understand it and to get the most out of their Scripture reading. *Key to the Bible* is the answer to their problem; it helps them enjoy it and benefit from it.

After publication of the first volume of this three-volume series came these raves from other noted contemporary scholars:

"Record of Revelation is a very readable and interestingly written general introduction which I should be happy to recommend to anyone."   —*Bruce Vawter, C.M.*

"In *Record of Revelation* Father Harrington extends . . . his gift for simplified clarifying of issues that are still in ferment."   —*Robert North, S.J.*

". . . up-to-date in its factual information, admirable in its clarity of expression, and sure of its grasp of basic theological issues."   —*W. L. Moran, S.J.*

And about the other volumes, critics have applauded:

". . . an excellent work . . . should serve a useful purpose."   —*Emmanuel*

"The reader who lacks any special preparation, but who wishes to make a study which will give him a grasp of what the Bible is and what it contains, should welcome this work."   —*Our Sunday Visitor*

". . . is useful as an introductory survey along the lines of mainstream academic biblical criticism and as an example of where contemporary Catholicism stands."

—*Christianity Today*

KEY TO THE
BIBLE

Wilfrid J. Harrington, O.P.

VOLUME 2

THE OLD TESTAMENT
RECORD OF THE PROMISE

IMAGE BOOKS
A Division of Doubleday & Company, Inc.
GARDEN CITY, NEW YORK

Image edition by special arrangement with
    Alba House Communications
Image Book edition published September 1976

NIHIL OBSTAT: *Very Rev. Gilbert J. Graham, O.P.*
                        Censor Librorum

IMPRIMATUR: ✠ *Most Rev. Cletus F. O'Donnell, J.C.D.*
                        Administrator, Archdiocese of Chicago

The Bible text in this publication is from the
Revised Standard Version of the Holy Bible,
*copyrighted 1946 and 1952 by the Division of
Christian Education, National Council of Churches,
and used by permission.*

ISBN: 0-385-12206-3
© *Copyright* 1974 *by* Alba House Communications,
Canfield, Ohio 44406
PRINTED IN THE UNITED STATES OF AMERICA

PREFACE

In the Preface to *Record of Revelation: The Bible* I indicated the scope of this work: it is planned as a textbook for the student of Sacred Scripture, but it is also aimed at the interested layman. I feel that the student will not regret the prospect of a wider audience, for it has led me to avoid technicalities that might have awaited the elucidation of his professor. As it is, my care has been to make the book as self-explanatory as possible. This, in turn, accounts for its length; an overbrief exposition would have left too many questions unanswered.

Not that I imagine that all the problems of the Old Testament have been faced. Indeed, it is best not to speak of "problems." What I have tried to do is to approach the Old Testament in a positive fashion and to present it illuminated by modern biblical scholarship. I have (with rare exceptions) refrained from giving a series of more or less conflicting views; rather, I have chosen, in each case, the position that seems to me the most satisfactory. This is not to say that I put forward merely personal views; the choice is personal, but the position I adopt is always solidly supported by outstanding scholars. I believe that this procedure is justified. The important thing is to lead the student to an appreciation of the Bible, an object that is not achieved by a medley of opinions—some of them dated and ill-founded. The student, guided by his professor and helped by his reading, will gradually become aware of other views; then he will make his own informed choice and find that his knowledge of Scripture has grown and deepened.

I have consistently sought to bring out the religious significance of each biblical writing—after all, this is the ultimate purpose of our study of Scripture. It will be seen, however, that the religious message can be grasped only when the book is properly understood; this is why literary analysis looms so large throughout. And though I have developed some theological ideas at greater length, the work does not cease to be an *introduction* to the Bible, and makes no claim to be also a manual of biblical theology. It is meant to introduce the student to the Old Testament and to help him to read it intelligently. I am convinced that modern scholarship has indeed opened the Bible to us in a marvelous manner and my sole desire is to place that key in the hands of those who seek it. If they find that the key does turn in the lock they will soon learn to appreciate the Old Testament as a literary achievement of God's people and to savor it as God's own word; and they will find themselves not only witnesses of the unfolding stages of God's saving history but also, by faith, participants in that history.

Once again my sincere thanks are due to my colleagues, Father Liam G. Walsh, O.P. and Father Thomas P. McInerney, O.P., who have so patiently read through my typescript. I have profited from their shrewd observations and helpful criticism and I have been greatly encouraged by their fraternal interest in the progress of the work.

W. J. H.

CONTENTS

Abbreviations

THE BOOKS OF THE BIBLE

Gn.: Genesis	Wis.: Wisdom	Mk.: Mark
Ex.: Exodus	Sir.: Sirach	Lk.: Luke
Lv.: Leviticus	(Ecclesiasticus)	Jn.: John
Nm.: Numbers	Is.: Isaiah	Acts: Acts
Dt.: Deuteronomy	Jer.: Jeremiah	Rm.: Romans
Jos.: Joshua	Lam.: Lamentations	1,2 Cor.: 1,2
Jgs.: Judges	Bar.: Baruch	Corinthians
Ru.: Ruth	Ezek.: Ezekiel	Gal.: Galatians
1,2 Sm.: 1,2 Samuel	Dn.: Daniel	Eph.: Ephesians
1,2 Kgs.: 1,2 Kings	Hos.: Hosea	Phil.: Philippians
1,2 Chr.: 1,2	Jl.: Joel	Col.: Colossians
Chronicles	Am.: Amos	1,2 Thes.: 1,2
Ez.: Ezra	Obad.: Obadiah	Thessalonians
Neh.: Nehemiah	Jon.: Jonah	1,2 Tm.: 1,2
Tb.: Tobit	Mi.: Micah	Timothy
Jdt.: Judith	Na.: Nahum	Ti.: Titus
Est.: Esther	Hb.: Habakkuk	Phm.: Philemon
Jb.: Job	Zeph.: Zephaniah	Heb.: Hebrews
Ps.: Psalms	Hag.: Haggai	Jas.: James
Prv.: Proverbs	Zech.: Zechariah	1,2 Pt.: 1,2 Peter
Qoh.: Qoheleth	Mal.: Malachi	1,2,3 Jn.: 1,2,3 John
(Ecclesiastes)	1,2 Mc.: 1,2	Jude: Jude
Ct.: Canticle of	Maccabees	Ap.: Apocalypse
Canticles	Mt.: Matthew	(Revelation)

WORKS OF REFERENCE

ANEP: *The Ancient Near East in Pictures*
ANET: *Ancient Near Eastern Texts*
Atlante Biblico: Atlante Storico della Bibbia
BJ: *Bible de Jérusalem*
(BJ): A separate fascicle of the *Bible de Jérusalem*
BW: *Bibeltheologisches Wörterbuch*
DBS: *Dictionnaire de la Bible* (Supplement)
EB: *Enchiridion Biblicum*
IB: *Introduction à la Bible*
PCB: *Peake's Commentary on the Bible*
RB: *Revue Biblique*
VTB: *Vocabulaire de Théologie Biblique*

ONE

THE PENTATEUCH

1. THE PENTATEUCH AS A WHOLE

In form the Pentateuch appears as a series of legal texts in a historical framework. It is primarily as the Law of the Chosen People that the book was accepted and recognized as obligatory; it was *Torah,* "Law," not only for Jews but for Samaritans. This Torah makes known to us the constitution of the people of God and the conditions of the divine choice. The different elements of narrative and laws are unified by the theme of the divine plan whose object is the setting up of the people of Israel as a theocratic nation, with Palestine as fatherland and the Mosaic Law as charter.

The central plan and unifying idea of the Pentateuch is summed up in a little credo which the Israelite recited at the offering of the first fruits in the sanctuary:

A wandering Aramean was my father; and he went down into Egypt and sojourned there, few in number; and there he became a nation, great, mighty and populous. And the Egyptians treated us harshly, and afflicted us, and laid upon us hard bondage. Then we cried to the Lord the God of our fathers, and the Lord heard our voice, and saw our affliction, our toil and our oppression; and the Lord brought us out of

Egypt with a mighty hand and an outstretched arm, with great terror, with signs and wonders; and he brought us into this place and gave us this land, a land flowing with milk and honey (Dt. 26:5-9; cf. 6:20-24; Jos. 24:2-13).

Here we learn that God had chosen Abraham and his descendants and had promised them the land of Canaan. Then, when the whole plan seemed to have come to naught in Egyptian bondage, Yahweh intervened again and delivered his people; he made a Covenant with them and brought them into the Promised Land. These facts underlie the different traditions; the ultimate structuring of the material into a great synthesis was guided by the very same facts. Hence the Pentateuch, in its basic facts, in the units which variously reflect these facts, and in its final shape is built around the ideas of election and efficacious intervention and covenant.

2. THE ORIGIN OF THE PENTATEUCH[1]

Literary analysis of the Pentateuch has uncovered different strata and has shown, beyond doubt, that it is a composite work. A four-document hypothesis has long been widely accepted: the Pentateuch is an amalgam of four documents —J (Yahwistic), E (Elohistic), D (Deuteronomy) and P (Priestly). However, the classic documentary theory is no longer accepted without question.

The efforts to make it more precise have led to arbitrary and subjective divisions of the text. The literary problem of the date and edition of the text in its final form is taking second place to the *historical* question of the *origin* of the "documents"; and these latter are being considered in a less rigid fashion, in a way more consistent with real life.

It is clear that the origin of the "documents" must be put at a very early date. Archaeology and the history of Near-Eastern peoples have shown that many of the laws and institutions of the Pentateuch have extrabiblical parallels that are much earlier than the date attributed to the "documents." Furthermore many narratives in the Pentateuch presuppose a milieu that is not that of the "documents," but is very much older. The problem of the Pentateuch, however, remains and must be faced. There must be some explanation of the doublets, the repetitions, the disagreements that abound in the Pentateuch, and which strike the reader from the first page of Gn. We cannot really explain these facts by a compilation of "documents" which had been largely fixed in writing, and which were dismembered and regrouped by a mechanical procedure of literary composition. On the other hand, these facts denote at the very least certain "traditions" which were originally connected with the sanctuaries and recited there. They were formed into cycles in a given atmosphere and under the influence of a dominant personality. Eventually they were incorporated into the Pentateuch. Thus, instead of "documents" JEDP, we should speak of *traditions*: the yahwistic, elohistic, and priestly traditions of the first four books of the Pentateuch. Dt. and the "deuteronomical tradition" form a distinct problem.

THE FOUR TRADITIONS 1. *The Yahwistic Tradition.* It is called "Yahwistic" because it employs the name Yahweh right from the creation narrative. It has a special vocabulary, a vivid and colorful style, and a delicate psychological perception. In a simple and figurative form it gives a profound solution to the grave problems that torment every man. The history of the Fall and of human depravity is transformed into the history of salvation— both by striking interventions of God and by the hidden workings of divine Providence (for example, in saving Noah, leading Abraham to Canaan, bringing back Jacob, exalting Joseph, freeing Israel from Egypt, and guiding the people in the desert). The only legislative material belonging to this tradition is the so-called "Yahwistic" code of Ex. 34.

2. *The Elohistic Tradition.* It uses the name Elohim, for, according to this tradition, the name Yahweh was first revealed to Moses on Sinai. It has a distinctive vocabulary

and sober style. The relations of God with men are less intimate. The divine manifestations are on a less material plane and anthropomorphism is avoided. God remains invisible; he speaks from the midst of fire or cloud; frequently he speaks in dreams; more often still he acts through the medium of angels. The "elohistic" Covenant code (Ex. 21-23) is attributed to this tradition.

3. *The Priestly Tradition.* This tradition is especially interested in the organization of the sanctuary, in the sacrifices and feasts, and in the persons and religious functions of Aaron and his sons. All the legislation in Exodus (except the two Covenant codes), in Leviticus, and in Numbers is to be attributed to this tradition. But even the narrative has a legalistic and liturgical bias. It is not easy to fit the various "priestly" narrative sections into a single continuous narrative. Yet it is the priestly tradition that gave its definitive form to the Pentateuch.

4. *The Deuteronomical Tradition.* This tradition is limited to the last book of the Pentateuch. Deuteronomy is largely a recapitulation of the foregoing history from Horeb onwards; it also repeats the laws in part. The recapitulation is prompted and marked by a distinctive idea: History reflects the love of Yahweh for his Chosen People. Yahweh freely chose Israel for his own people, and the people must acknowledge him as its only God and offer him cult in his one sanctuary. This doctrine is put forward in a special oratorical, exhortatory style that is recognizable even in the legislation. The deuteronomical tradition does not affect the other traditions, which in turn have no influence on Dt. (It is perhaps true to say that Dt. *may,* here and there, have slightly changed the first two traditions in a deuteronomical sense.) The same doctrine and style are to be found in Joshua, Judges, Samuel, and Kings, which with Dt. make up a homogeneous literary corpus.

SUMMARY   The *yahwistic* tradition is found especially in Gn. (from chapter 2 onwards), and in Ex. and Nm.

The *elohistic* tradition is found in the same three books, beginning at Gn. 20. (According to some Gn. 15:1-5 is also elohistic.)

The *priestly* tradition begins in Gn. 1 and runs right through the book; it continues through Ex. and Nm. and entirely accounts for Lv.

Briefly, then:

Gn., Ex., Nm.: Mixture of yahwistic, elohistic, and priestly traditions.

Leviticus: priestly tradition only.

Deuteronomy: deuteronomical tradition only.

3. THE FORMATION OF THE TRADITIONS

If we regard the Pentateuch as being formed of various parallel "traditions" which had evolved in the course of time, then we cannot hope to fix with any exactitude the date at which any of the traditions was formed. But we may venture an approximation. We must begin with Deuteronomy which, undoubtedly, was connected with the reform of Josiah towards the close of the seventh century B.C. The kernel of our Dt., especially the deuteronomical code, represents the customs of the North brought to Jerusalem by the Levites after the fall of the kingdom of Israel (721 B.C.). This law, found in the Temple in the time of Josiah, was promulgated in the framework of a discourse of Moses. A new edition, with additions in the same spirit, was made at the beginning of the Exile.

The *priestly* tradition is later than Dt. It was formed during the Exile and afterwards joined to the two traditions that are older than Dt.: the *yahwistic*, which had taken shape about the reign of Solomon; and the *elohistic*, which is a little later.

It is more important to know *where* these traditions were formed. It seems natural to think of the sanctuaries which were the meeting places of the Israelites. There were related the wonders wrought by God, his benevolence towards the people he had chosen; there too, the great deeds of the ancestors were extolled. These epic narratives formed the commentary at the feasts which commemorated the interventions of God in the history of the people. It is still more natural to imagine that the codes of laws took shape at the sanctuaries. First of all there were the liturgical laws and cult prescriptions governing the priestly offices. Then, too, the people must have turned to the priests for juridical decisions and moral directives.

The *yahwistic* tradition is undoubtedly of Judaean origin: much of the narrative centers around Hebron; and in the story of Joseph, Judah is shown in a favorable light.

The *elohistic* tradition is generally held to be of Northern origin: it speaks of the activities of the patriarchs in Bethel and Shechem; in the story of Joseph, Reuben and Ephraim figure largely.

The *priestly* tradition is that of the priests of the Temple.

The *deuteronomical* code appears to represent the traditions of the Northern Kingdom brought to Jerusalem by the Levites after the fall of Israel.

Briefly, then:

Yahwistic tradition: Reign of Solomon—10th cent. B.C. (Judah).

Elohistic tradition: Somewhat later—9th cent. B.C. (Israel).

Deuteronomical tradition: Code formed before 721 B.C.; promulgated during reign of Josiah (640-609 B.C.); enlarged edition at the beginning of the Exile (587-538 B.C.) (Israel).

Priestly tradition: Formed during the Exile; took its final shape most likely after the Exile (Jerusalem).

4. THE FORMATION OF THE PENTATEUCH

The Yahwistic and Elohistic traditions had taken final shape and had been combined in a single narrative (JE) shortly after 721 B.C. Deuteronomy (built around the earlier code) began to take shape in the time of Josiah and received its final form during the Exile. The priestly tradition grew up contemporaneously with Deuteronomy. Eventually, a priestly writer edited the whole corpus. He took the JE epic as his basis and built into it, at various points, the material, mostly legislative, of the Temple tradition. He detached Dt. from the deuteronomical history and inserted it as a fitting epilogue to the story of Moses. Most of this editing was done during the Exile, but the work was not finished before 538 B.C. Since it seems very likely that the "book of the Law of Moses" brought to Jerusalem by Ezra in 428 B.C. (Neh. 8:1) was the Torah, it may be assumed that the Pentateuch had taken final shape in the fifth century B.C.; the ultimate work marked the close of a long and involved process that had begun in the Mosaic age. This process may be represented graphically:

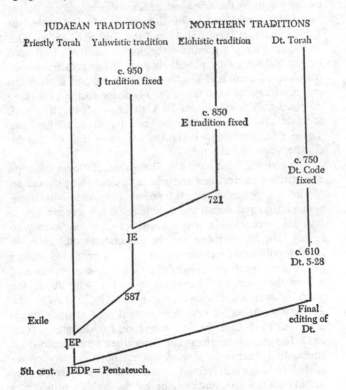

JUDAEAN TRADITIONS   NORTHERN TRADITIONS

Priestly Torah Yahwistic tradition Elohistic tradition Dt. Torah

c. 950
J tradition fixed

c. 850
E tradition fixed

c. 750
Dt. Code fixed

721

JE

c. 610
Dt. 5-28

587

Exile   Final editing of Dt.

JEP

5th cent. JEDP = Pentateuch.

5. THE CHARACTERISTICS OF THE TRADITIONS

1) *The Yahwist*

The work of the Yahwist is a synthesis, both in form and in substance; yet this writer is one of the most creative literary artists of Israel. He gathered together the traditions of the tribes and of the sanctuaries and reworked them in order to make the old relevant to the new. Many of these old narratives are aetiologies, that is, their purpose was to explain, in a popular way, some facts in tribal history, or the names of places, or certain aspects of the cult. The Yahwist combined these different materials in a new literary structure, a great epic extending from the creation of the world to the conquest of Transjordan. Some of the individual stories, taken by themselves (for example, the angel marriages [Gn. 6:1-4] and the Tower of Babel [Gn. 11:1-9]), betray a primitive theological outlook; but, used by the Yahwist, they play their part in the presentation of his elevated theology. The fact that he did not write as an independent author, but limited his scope to the reworking of older traditions, should be kept in mind—together with the fact that we no longer possess the whole of his epic. These facts explain a certain unevenness and certain inconsistencies in his work.

The style of the Yahwist is distinctive. He loves concrete and striking expressions and excels in describing character, for he is a penetrating psychologist. He writes with liveliness, clarity, and polish and is able to sketch a scene with a few bold strokes. He wears his theological proficiency so lightly that his purpose can be misunderstood. Thus, in images, with apparent naïveté, he gives a profound answer to the grave problems which are raised by the presence of evil in the good world created by God: Why death, the pains of woman, the sweat of man (Gn. 3)? Why the dispersion of peoples and their mutual lack of understanding (Gn. 11)? Can the just intercede for the guilty (Gn. 18)? The moral development (or rather retrogression) of humanity is traced in gloomy colors, but the story of repeated falls is transformed into a history of salvation by striking divine interventions, or by the hidden providence of God who saves Noah, leads out Abraham, brings back Jacob, raises Joseph, delivers the people from Egypt, and guides them in the desert. Intimate, concrete relations unite man to God who appears in human form, acts in a human manner, and feels human sentiments: Yahweh shapes man as a potter would; he walks in the garden during the cool of the evening; he accepts the hospitality of Abraham and converses with him; he is sorry and he is angry. But these anthropomorphisms[2] clothe a very elevated idea of God, who always remains the master of his creature, who does not lower himself by his care for that creature, who maintains, unimpaired, his essential holiness.

The Yahwist is keenly aware of the forces of evil at work in the world; he has no illusions about humanity and he unpityingly exposes human weakness, but he is an optimist at heart. He has confidence in nature and her laws, which will not be disrupted by another deluge. He shows the persistence and expansion of life, the good fortune of the sons of Jacob, Israel delivered from slavery, the twelve tribes on their way to a land flowing with milk and honey. This optimism is based on a knowledge of Yahweh, on confidence in his plan and in his power. Yahweh is transcendent, but draws near to men; and this nearness is expressed in bold anthropomorphisms. He demands of men faith, courage, and confidence in the traditions and in the life of the nation.[3]

The Yahwist regards Yahweh as the national God. By revealing himself to Abraham, by delivering the heirs of Abraham from slavery, and by giving them his law he has become *their* God. He does not cease to be the God of all peoples, for his choice of this people is universalist in its ultimate scope: all the nations of the earth will bless themselves by Abraham. But the future belongs to Israel, for Yahweh, her God, alone has power on earth. God gives a share in this power, a part in his plan, to whom he wills; the author emphasizes the absolute freedom of God's choice by contesting the automatic right of the first born. Thus the prayer of Abel is heard in preference to that of Cain, Isaac is chosen instead of Ishmael, Jacob instead of Esau, Judah instead of his three older brothers. In this context it may be noted that the messianic prophecies of the Pentateuch occur in the Yahwist's epic: Gn. 3:15, which promises salvation by the seed of the woman; the prophecy of Jacob regarding Judah (Gn. 49:10); Balaam's prophecy of the star coming forth from Jacob (Nm. 24:17).

The Yahwist's epic falls into three parts: primeval history; the patriarchal tradition; the Mosaic tradition.

PRIMEVAL   The primeval history, constructed from ele-
HISTORY   ments of very different kinds, proclaims that
all evil comes from sin and testifies to a growth in evil.
Yet the widening chasm between God and man remains
spanned by a bridge of mercy and is matched by an in-
creasing power of grace. In the call of Abraham (Gn.
12:1-3) primeval history is linked with sacred history and
finds its meaning in this link.

THE PATRIARCHAL   The Yahwist continues his theological
TRADITION   synthesis by utilizing the patriarchal
traditions. In his eyes, Abraham is the model patriarch.
Yet the promises of God are destined not for him but for
his posterity. By linking the cycle of Abraham to the cycle
of Isaac the author intended to mark the unity of the cult
of the *Elohim* of Abraham, honored at Hebron, and of
the *El 'Olam* ("God anciently honored") worshiped at
Beersheba and in the Negeb. The further joining of the
cycle of Jacob extends the cultic unity to Bethel and to
the shrines of the North. Right through the patriarchal
epoch runs the cult of the same God (the "God of the
fathers") and the participation of successive generations
in the same divine promises. Important sections of the
cycle of Joseph are due to the Yahwist. Joseph is a providential instrument and the hero of this story, but he is not
the heir of the promises. Thus the Yahwist closes with
Jacob and his blessing and the assurance that the monarchy
will be the inheritance of Judah.

THE MOSAIC   For the Yahwist, Moses is the last of the
TRADITION   patriarchs, and again the cultic identity is
stressed. The God who revealed himself to Moses in the
burning bush is the "God of the fathers" (Ex. 3:16).
Yahweh is the God who has delivered Israel, his first-born
son, at the cost of the first born of Egypt (Ex. 4:22 f.).
This God set his people free and established the Pasch as
the national feast of liberation. He wills that pilgrimage
should be made to his holy mountain (Ex. 24:1 f., 9-11)

and there Israel receives from him the commandments in the form of a ritual decalogue (Ex. 34). The union between the Israelite and his God will be maintained by the rite of national pilgrimage to the seasonal feasts (Ex. 34:18,22 f.).

2) The Elohist

The Elohist begins with the call of Abraham and therefore does not have a primeval history; in this he lacks the universal scope of the Yahwist. Similarly the Elohist does not show the theological depth, much less the literary artistry, of the Yahwist. However, in comparing the work of both authors, it is well to keep in mind that circumstances have been unkind to the Elohist. Both J and E (from Abraham onwards) cover much the same ground, and the Judaean editors who combined the Northern and Southern traditions after the fall of Samaria in 721 B.C. understandably gave preference to the Yahwist's epic. It is not possible to reconstruct the E narrative as a continuous account and its impact suffers as a result.

Yet what the Elohist loses in vividness and brilliance he gains somewhat in moral sensibility. His sense of sin is more refined than that of the Yahwist. For instance, he avoids the impression that Abraham had lied to Abimelech by stating explicitly that Sarah was the patriarch's half-sister (Gn. 20:12). Jacob's flock increased not by trickery on his part but because God did not permit Laban to harm him (Gn. 31:3-13, 36-42). For him the law is more moral than cultic. The basis of it, as it finds expression in the Decalogue, concerns man's duties towards God and towards his neighbor. These duties are made more explicit in the Covenant Code (Gn. 20:22—23:19) where the respect of one's neighbor and of his goods is regulated by customs and precepts that have been sanctioned by God.

The Elohist tends to emphasize the distance of God from men, at least in comparison with the Yahwist's approach. Anthropomorphism is restricted: God does not come to walk among men (cf. Gn. 3:8; 18:1 ff.), but speaks from heaven (Gn. 21:17) or in dreams (Gn. 15:1;

20:3,6; 28:12). Indeed, it is stated explicitly: "Let not God speak to us, lest we die" (Ex. 20:19). Dreams figure largely in the story of Joseph and, as one would expect, the narrative which treats of this ancestor of the Northern tribes of Ephraim and Manasseh is more developed than in the Yahwist tradition. Here, too, the moral perception of the Elohist brings out the religious significance of the events: "As for you, you meant evil against me; but God meant it for good, to bring it about that many people should be kept alive, as they are today" (Gn. 50:20).

Perhaps, after all, the loss of immediacy with God and with his revealed word in E does not have the force it seems to have at first sight. It certainly serves to throw into prominence the special status of Moses, and it was calculated to produce this effect. To Moses the name of God, *Yahweh,* was revealed. He alone could speak to Yahweh "mouth to mouth" and could "behold the form of the Lord" (Nm. 12:8). Even more strikingly it is said of him: "The Lord used to speak to Moses face to face, as a man speaks to his friend" (Ex. 33:11); and he reflected the radiance of the divine glory (Ex. 34:29-35). He is the Prophet *par excellence,* filled with the spirit of God which he communicates to the elders (Nm. 11:10-30). Hosea can comment: "By a prophet the Lord brought Israel up from Egypt and by a prophet it was preserved" (Hos. 12:13). Likewise, Abraham is called a prophet (Gn. 20:7) and Miriam a prophetess (Ex. 15:20). The significance given to the prophet and his office must mean that E has influenced the development of prophecy in Israel.

3) *The Deuteronomist*

The kernel of Deuteronomy is the legal code (Dt. 12:1–26:15) of Northern origin, going back ultimately to the Mosaic age; the narrative part, the three discourses of Moses, are much later, from just before and after the Exile. The second discourse is especially fitting in the mouth of the great leader, because the essential purpose of Dt. is a revival of Mosaic teaching as it was understood in the seventh century B.C.; it is a reform program, not an innovation. Hence the appeal for Covenant renewal, made with urgency, the repetition of "this day," the here and now of the divine election, and the involvement of the present generation of Israel in the Covenant made at Horeb.[4] The law of the one sanctuary (Dt. 12:1-12) is inspired by the same reforming spirit: to preserve the purified cult of Yahweh from all contamination.

The style of the deuteronomist is distinctive. (We shall see that deuteronomical passages in the history Jos.-Kgs. are readily discernible.) In the discourses, characteristic turns of phrase keep cropping up. God is always "the Lord thy God" or "the Lord your God." Canaan is described as "a land flowing with milk and honey," and, in order that they might possess it, God had delivered his people from Egypt "with a mighty hand and an outstretched arm." This is why the people are admonished to "hear the voice of the Lord your God" and to "keep his statutes and his commandments and ordinances" and to "fear the Lord your God." Above all, they are exhorted: "You shall love the Lord your God with all your heart, and with all your soul and with all your might." And throughout there is the frequent reminder that faithful observance of the commandments of Yahweh will insure a blessing, and the warning that neglect of the commandments will bring upon them the anger of a loving but just God.

This warning should have been unnecessary, for these "statutes, commandments, and ordinances" are not a heavy burden imposed from without, but are intimate, interior: "For this commandment which I command you this day is not too hard for you, neither is it far off. . . . The word is very near you; it is in your mouth and in your heart, so that you can do it" (Dt. 30:11,14). Yahweh is a Father who gives his life-giving Word to Israel, the Word that brings happiness and long life. It is the Word that reveals: "The secret things belong to the Lord our God; but the things that are revealed belong to us and to our children forever, that we may do all the word of this law" (Dt. 29:29). A theology of the people of God, and a theology of the life-giving Word, it is also a theology of Revelation.[5]

Another characteristic of Dt., and one which witnesses

to the Northern origin of the tradition, is the influence of Hosea. That Prophet, too, looked back to the Exodus as to the happy honeymoon period of Israel's religion. None more fittingly than he has painted the undying love of Yahweh for his faithless spouse, because he drew his colors from life, from his own unhappy experience. It is significant that "love" is a key word of Dt. (for example, Dt. 7:8; 10:15; 26:6; 30:6-20). Indeed, together with the whole deuteronomical history, it becomes a commentary on chapter eleven of Hosea: "When Israel was a child I loved him, and out of Egypt I called my son. But the more I called them the further they departed from me. . . . How can I give you up, O Ephraim" (11:1-2,8).

Hosea is not the only prophet whose influence is evident. Jeremiah (chapter 31) had foreseen a deliverance, a return, a new Covenant; it was in this spirit that Dt. was completed. And in its final chapters, too, our book joins Second Isaiah, who described the new journey across the desert and the victory over the nations now summoned to adore the God of Israel, the only true God. Other images are borrowed from Ezekiel who also described the return from the Exile and the new division of the holy land around the new sanctuary (Ezek. 37; 40-48; cf. Dt. 3:12-17). Thus inspired by the prophetical books, Deuteronomy, in its final edition, is a witness to a crucial stage in religious history when a Monarchy yielded place to a Church.[6]

4) The Priestly Tradition

The broad spirit of Deuteronomy did not appeal to the conservative-minded clergy of Jerusalem. These took their stand on the transcendence of Yahweh: instead of bringing God, and the word of God, near to men they sought rather to raise man to God by fidelity to the traditional laws and prescriptions. Their rule was the command: "You shall be holy; for I the Lord your God am holy" (Lv. 19:2).

At much the same time that the deuteronomical code took shape in the North, the traditions of the Jerusalem priests were compiled in the Holiness Code (Lv. 17-26). Like the deuteronomical code, it opens with the law of one sanctuary and then gives several series of prescriptions regarding morality, marriage, the priests, the sacrifices, and the feasts; it closes like Dt. with blessings and curses (Lv. 26). Israel is conceived as an *'edah,* a worshiping community, ruled by the priests. The date of the Holiness Code is uncertain; it may well have been edited during the reign of Josiah, shortly before the fall of the nation, but it certainly contains many much older laws.

During the Exile the deported priests, cut off from the elaborate, ritual worship of Yahweh in his Temple, saw that their duty was to organize the religious life of the community in these different surroundings and circumstances. It seemed to them that the foundations on which this religious life might be built must be a common national origin, common traditions, and an authentic priesthood. Thus the priestly history took shape. The religious institutions of Israel were authorized and given greater force by being set in a historical framework; by projecting all these institutions back into the Mosaic age, it is dramatically emphasized that they had their beginning at Sinai. The whole presentation is pervaded by a theology of the divine presence and by the demands of a God of holiness.

It is relatively easy to isolate the P material of the Pentateuch. Since much of the priestly work is editorial, this material does not form a unified structure; but it is possible to discern, and present coherently, the priestly view of Israel's history. God's revelation is conceived as following a systematic plan which unfolds in four successive eras or dispensations: Creation; the Covenant with Noah; the Covenant with Abraham; the Sinai Covenant. Each stage is marked by different privileges and duties and different divine names are employed: *'Elohim* in the first two stages; *'El Shaddai* for the patriarchs; and *Yahweh* for the time of Moses.

Though the dry, technical style of P is readily recognizable, the priestly writer can sometimes reach sublime heights; his masterpiece is the creation story (Gn. 1—2:4a). While its form and rhythm point to liturgical use, and while the rearrangement of eight works into a six-day week points to pre-existing traditional material, it was surely one author who gave final form to the story. The understanding, or misunderstanding, of this creation story depends on the answer to the question: What does the author of the story teach us? The plain answer is that he teaches two facts: 1) God made all things.[7] 2) The sabbath is of divine institution. These two things he wishes to drive home. He believed that God created the world, but he understood no more than we (much less indeed) how it was created. He might have stated his belief bluntly, but he judged it much more effective to parcel out the work and so emphasize the fact that God made *everything*. The result of it all is that the writer's assertion, "In the beginning God created heaven and earth," is true, divinely true, but that the description of the work of creation is a product of his imagination.

For the creation story is, from the literary viewpoint, patently an artificial composition. We find that the work of the six days is so distributed that there is a close correspondence between the first day and the fourth, between the second and the fifth, between the third and the sixth. We also find that the author shares the ideas of his own time and not those of the scientific twentieth century. The people for whom he wrote—and he himself for that matter—were quite unable to grasp an abstract notion of creation (not because of lack of intelligence, but simply because of their Semitic mentality), but they did understand work; hence he presents the Creator as a Workman who completed his work in six days and then took a rest. The climax of this work is the creation of man and woman in the image and according to the resemblance of God, and their dominion over the whole material and animal world. The terms of this creation imply a state of friendship with God. It is taught that God instituted marriage and sanctified it. When all was finished, "God blessed the seventh day and sanctified it, because on it God rested from all his work of creation" (Gn. 2:3). Thus, very neatly, the story of creation is rounded off by the declaration that it was God himself who has begun the sabbath rest: the Chosen People can do no better than imitate their God.[8]

If we look again at the priestly history as a whole, we

see it as the fruit of a theological reflection on the ancient liturgical tradition and customs preserved by the Jerusalem priests. Fidelity to these traditions is the only guarantee of a life in union with God, the only means of bringing about the fulfillment of God's purpose for Israel. This follows from a consideration of that plan as it gradually unfolded.

6. THE MESSAGE OF THE PENTATEUCH[9]

The religion of the Old Testament, like that of the New, is a historical religion: it is based on the revelation made by God to certain men in given times and places and on the interventions of God at certain determined moments. The Pentateuch, which traces the history of these relations of God with the world, is the foundation of the Jewish religion, its sacred book *par excellence,* its Law. In it the Israelite found the explanation of his own destiny and a way of life.

The Pentateuch is drawn into a unity by the threads of promise and election, of covenant and law which run through it. To Adam and Eve, after the Fall, God gives the assurance of salvation in the distant future; after the Flood he reassures Noah that the earth will never again be so disastrously stricken. Abraham is the man of promises —for himself and for his posterity and through them for all mankind. In God's free choice of Abraham the election of Israel is foreseen and included. The Pentateuch is also the book of covenants: tacit with Adam; explicit with Noah, Abraham, and Moses. Each covenant is a free exercise of divine initiative, an act of benevolence; God demands in return fidelity and obedience. The Law which he gives will make explicit the divine demands and prepare the way for the fulfillment of the promises.

The unifying themes of the Pentateuch continue into the rest of the Old Testament, for the Pentateuch is not complete in itself. It tells of the promise but not of its fulfillment and it closes before the entry into the Promised Land. But even when the Conquest is achieved the fulfillment is not yet, for the promise looks ultimately to Christ, to the new Covenant and to his new Commandment.

7. DOCTRINAL ASPECTS OF THE PENTATEUCH

1) *The Theology of Primeval History*[10]

If we are to understand the first eleven chapters of Genesis we must be aware of two factors. First, these chapters combine two of the four distinct traditions that make up the Pentateuch—the earliest and the latest. A second factor, already suggested in the case of the Yahwistic tradition, is that we are dealing with theology—not in the scholastic sense of course—but theology nevertheless. The greater part of these chapters is due to the Yahwist; a study of his contribution and method is especially rewarding. We shall see how he and the priestly writer have quarried their material in varied quarters and how, from ancient and weathered stuff, they have built a fabric that was altogether new.

THE PRIESTLY   Seeing that the priestly writer had the
PRIMEVAL HISTORY   final say in the formation of the Pentateuch it is not unexpected that Genesis should open with a priestly passage. The characteristic style is in evidence from the first. Already in these early chapters we find the unfolding of a plan that stands out clearly in Genesis. From the priestly point of view God's revelation follows a pre-arranged design that manifests itself in four successive eras or dispensations: Creation; and the Covenants with Noah, with Abraham, and with Moses.[11]

The priestly creation story (Gn. 1:1–2:4a) is not, and is not meant to be, a scientific treatise on the origin of the world and man's beginning; rather it declares that the existence of all things and their meaning lie in God's hands. The world and everything in it has come from him, but the formation of man is his masterpiece, the pride of his creation. He is made "in the image of God" and set apart from the animals. Man was blessed, that he might increase and multiply, but with the blessing there went a prohibition: he may eat of fruit and vegetables only; he must be a vegetarian. The priestly narrative ends with the observance of the sabbath: God rested from his creative work. Straightway the interest is switched to Israel and her observance of the sabbath. This basic institution of Israel is given depth and meaning when it is thus brought into contact with God's creative work and attached to the Creator himself.

Mention of the sabbath observance is an anticipation of the call of Israel, and the priestly writer employs genealogies to demonstrate how, in fact, that choice was made. He uses the device to step quickly from creation to the second stage of the divine plan, the Covenant with Noah; thus we find that Gn. 5 takes us from Adam to Noah. An extraordinary longevity is attributed to the antediluvian patriarchs because it was imagined that the duration of human life had diminished from one world epoch to the next: it will be no more than 600-200 years in the period between Noah and Abraham and from 200 to 100 years from the time of the Hebrew patriarchs.[12]

We must remember that the priestly tradition has no story of the Fall, but here we have something more or less corresponding to that story. Hence we must understand man's diminishing life span as a steady deterioration seen in relation to the progress of evil, for a long life is a blessing from God (Prv. 10:27) and will be one of the blessings of the messianic age (Is. 65:20). In other words, the ages attributed to these patriarchs have a symbolic value only. Ancient Babylonian traditions knew a list of ten kings with fantastically long reigns, who lived before the deluge. The biblical writer uses a similar ancient tradition for his own purpose.

According to the priestly writer the Flood came as a result of the corruption of mankind: Noah alone was found righteous. The waters of God's judgment destroyed all living things, except those that had found shelter in the ark. Gn. 6-9 is a blend of priestly and Yahwistic narratives, but these can be isolated rather easily and then each story presents the characteristic style and outlook of its original setting. Here again an ancient and widespread tradition has been pressed into the service of religious teaching.

The climax of the story is God's Covenant with Noah, and the divine promise never again to devastate the earth. A new privilege was granted: animal flesh might be eaten provided the animal had been properly slaughtered. This involved a practical recognition of God's absolute authority over life, symbolized by blood, and was seen as the origin of sacrifice, another basic religious institution (Gn. 9:1-5). Once again there was an accompanying prohibition: the blood of man—he who, despite his corruption, is still "in the image of God" (Gn. 9:6)—must not be shed. The delightful closing touch is that the "bow in the clouds," every shining rainbow after a storm, will stand as a reassuring pledge of the Covenant between God and man (Gn. 9:8-17). From this Covenant with all men, the priestly writer, by means of a genealogy (Gn. 11:10-32) moves to the man who is the center of the next stage. But this third dispensation, the Covenant with Abraham, and the later Covenant with Moses at Sinai, fall outside our present scope.

THE YAHWIST'S   The Yahwist was the first theologian
PRIMEVAL HISTORY   and one of the greatest writers of Israel. He wrote in the tenth century B.C., during the peaceful reign of Solomon; thus, long before the priestly writer, and more strikingly, he presented the choice of Israel in the perspective of God's purpose for all mankind. With true theological insight he perceived that God's dealings with Israel must have a wider issue, and he linked that particular history to general human history and began at the beginning. He constructed his primeval history from elements of very different kinds, but its main lines were of stark simplicity. On the one hand he testified that all evil, a growing corruption, came from sin, and on the other hand that this growth was matched by the active presence of God's mercy.[13]

The opening verses (Gn. 2:4b-6) of the Yahwistic creation narrative serve as an introduction to the real purpose of the account, the formation of man; a setting has been provided but all the interest is centered on this one creature. Thus the plants and trees of Gn. 2:9-17 are those of the garden of Eden which is the home of man, and the formation of the animals (vv. 19 f.) is not related for its own sake but as an introduction to the formation of woman. The Yahwist has nothing to say about the creation of the world apart from the simple statement that Yahweh made the earth and the heavens.

In the formation of man, the Workman of the priestly narrative has given place to a Potter. The "dust from the ground" is fine potter's clay and God shaped it into a human form; then he breathed into that lifeless figure a breath of life and the figure became a man. But "it is not good for man to be alone": the writer has in mind something more specific than man's gregarious instinct; he is thinking, rather, of man's deep-felt need of another being like himself, one of the same nature as he, yet not quite himself. Then follows the charming description of the parade of animals before man. He imposes names on them; thus, at one and the same time, manifesting his knowledge of their nature and expressing his dominion over them. Though all these creatures have been formed, as he was, from clay, he is unable to find one among them that can share his life, that can hold converse with him—for he alone has been livened by the divine breath.

The seemingly artless description of the formation of woman presents a viewpoint that is nothing less than revolutionary. There was a universal tendency to regard woman as a chattel and to consider her as a being decidedly inferior to man. By describing her—in figurative terms—as made from man, the Yahwist presents her as a being of the same nature as man, his equal; a truth which man is made to acknowledge openly. She is, therefore, in the fullest sense, his helper, one entirely suited to him, particularly by her union with him in marriage.

Man, the creature, exists in dependence on God and in relation to another human being; but in this world the man finds temptation. The tempter, in the form of a serpent, prevails on him to rebel against his dependence. Therefore, immediately after his account of the creation of the first man and woman, the author describes the entry of sin into the world. The first sin is not a sin of mankind in the abstract, for mankind exists only in individual men and women; it is the common sin of the first human couple. Essentially it was the transgression of a divine com-

mand, figuratively described as the prohibition to eat a
certain fruit. The tempter insinuates that they will become
"like divine beings, knowing good and evil" (Gn. 3:5).
The "knowledge of good and evil" which would be theirs
means that they would have arrogated to themselves the
right of deciding between good and evil, of being a law
unto themselves in the moral order. So, in effect, they
would have become independent of God. They were
tempted to deny their creaturehood in the hope of tran-
scending that condition.

While the first sin was not sexual in nature it does follow that man-woman relations were involved in the process
of the sin and suffered the consequences of the Fall.
Woman was given to man as "a helper fit for him" (Gn.
2:18), but she became his seductress and led him into evil.
Man, created before woman, was by nature her leader; yet,
yielding to her seduction, he weakly followed her. In place
of communion in one flesh (Gn. 2:24) they find com-
plicity in crime. And when the crime had been committed,
that harmony that had formerly marked their relations was
shattered: Adam sought to cast all the blame on Eve (Gn.
3:12). But even before this they had already felt that something had gone wrong: "The eyes of both were opened
and they knew that they were naked" (Gn. 3:7). This is
obviously meant to be seen in sharp contrast to Gn. 2:25:
"Both were naked, the man and his wife, and they were
not ashamed the one before the other." A shadow had
fallen on sex; though good in itself, it can henceforth easily
aggravate the relations between man and woman. The sentence of God: "You shall crave to have your husband and
he shall lord it over you" (Gn. 3:16b) further underlines
the disharmony that had been introduced. The domination
of man and degradation of woman will replace the perfect
union in mutual love that would have marked their relations, while fruitfulness, a normal sequel to sexual union,
is set in a context of suffering: "I will greatly multiply your
pain in childbearing, in pain you shall bring forth children"
(Gn. 3:16a). The misery of woman's travail at birth is
matched by man's travail on the soil. Finally, both are ban-
ished from the happiness of the garden. All this is nothing

more than the actual condition of the human couple; man and woman, essentially good, have been wounded by sin and stand in need of redemption.

The present state of man, subject to suffering and death, is therefore the work not of God but of man himself, and follows on the sin of the first man; all men are born into this state. But man has not been definitively vanquished and is not hopelessly subjected to the forces of evil. The Yahwist attaches to maternity a hope based on God himself (Gn. 3:15). It is probable that he saw in the saving motherhood of Eve the prototype of the royal motherhood (cf. Is. 7:14; Mi. 5:2 [3] and the care taken in Kgs. to name the queen-mothers of Judah), and therefore of the messianic motherhood. In this sense, the text is not only messianic but takes its place in Marian theology. But even apart from this, the gesture of Yahweh in providing clothes for the unhappy couple (Gn. 3:21) is a touching indication of his care for them.

The following chapters are closely linked to the story of the Fall because they serve to illustrate the alarming proliferation of sin; we move quickly to the first murder. Cain is really the ancestor of the Kenites (Nm. 24:21 f.) and the Yahwist is obviously intrigued by the fate of that strange tribe.[14] Though they, like the Israelites, were worshipers of Yahweh (Nm. 10:29; Jgs. 1:16), they never really achieved a sedentary life, but wandered restlessly on the limits of the cultivated land (1 Chr. 2:55). However, Gn. 4:1-16 no longer relates the story of a tribe, nor does it any longer reflect the traditional animosity between farmer and nomad; now it belongs to primeval history, to the beginning of human history. We are shown what happened when mankind had fallen from obedience to God: the man who associates with sin has become its slave. Yet, despite his crime and his subsequent separation from God, Cain remains under God's protection (Gn. 4:15 f.). Again the mercy of Yahweh accompanies his just punishment.

The genealogy of the Kenites (Gn. 4:17-26) opens with the statement that Cain (a murderer) built the first city. This was an unpromising start to civilization and the song of Lamech shows that cultural advance was accompanied by violence. Originally a savage desert chant, it is used to mark a further progress in evil: the execution of vengeance which God had reserved to himself (Gn. 4:15) is claimed by man and exercised arbitrarily and without limit. In keeping with his universalist outlook the Yahwist notes briefly that from the time of Enosh, that is, almost from the beginning, "men began to call upon the name of the Lord" (Gn. 4:26). He is not seeking to deny the certain tradition that the divine name was first revealed to Moses (Ex. 3:14); rather he wishes to show that the worship of the true God was the primeval religion of mankind.

The inexorable growth of sin comes to a climax in the story of the angel marriages (Gn. 6:1-4). This story was originally an aetiology designed to explain the origin of the legendary Nephilim (cf. Nm. 13:33; Dt. 2:10), a race of giants: they were the children of a marriage of heavenly beings with human women. But under the Yahwist's pen it has become a dramatic illustration not only of man's general corruption but of a more widespread deterioration. And, at last, God's patience is exhausted at this final proof that "every imagination of the thoughts of man's heart was only evil continually" (Gn. 6:5). Yahweh was "sorry," "grieved to the heart" that he had ever created man: he will utterly destroy man and all living things. But at once his mercy steps in: "Noah found favor in the eyes of the Lord" (Gn. 6:8).

By means of the ancient popular tradition of the Flood the Yahwist presents God's judgment on sin. In a true sense it is the Last Judgment and hence, more emphatically than in the other episodes, the saving will of God is manifest. The ark in which Noah's family and the pairs of animals found refuge was a sign of Yahweh's intention to deliver a remnant, and with it to make a new beginning in history. But at this point too appears the naked mystery of the contrast between God's punishing anger and his forbearing grace. Yahweh had seen that man's inclinations were evil and had decided on the Flood (Gn. 6:5); now he declares that, though man is unchanged—"the imagination of man's heart is evil from his youth" (Gn. 8:21; cf. 6:8)—he will never again destroy all living creatures as he had done. The constant rhythm of seasons will be a lasting sign of his promise (Gn. 8:22).

And, indeed, the course of evil, temporarily checked by the Flood, soon gathers momentum again. The story of Noah's drunkenness (Gn. 9:18-27) makes this point; but it also marks a polemic against agricultural Canaan with its wine-drinking and sexual license. The unsuspecting Noah, like the Israelites coming in from the desert (cf. Nm. 25:1-3), was taken unawares by the potent taste of Canaanite civilization; when he realized how he had been overcome he pronounced a curse on Canaan.[15] No doubt the story of Noah's curse was seen as the explanation of the defeat of the Canaanites by the invading Israelites. As usual, the Yahwist has used the story for his own ends.

Another aetiology, typically divorced from its original purpose, rounds off the primeval history. For it is obvious that the story of the Tower of Babel was a popular answer to the problem of the origin of nations and languages, and a popular explanation of the name "Babel" (Babylon). But the Yahwist is not interested in these matters; in his eyes the story shows how men, in their striving for fame, unity, and political development, set themselves against God. And it illustrates how, once again, as at the beginning, the pride-inspired rebellion ended in hopeless confusion. This time the word of judgment seems to be the final word.

However, the Yahwist is still master of the situation, for at this point he knits together primeval history and sacred history. We were left with a welter of nations scattered over the face of the earth (Gn. 11:9); now Abraham is called from the multitude of nations "that in him all the families of the earth shall be blessed" (Gn. 12:1-3). The transition is dramatic. Hitherto the narrative concerned humanity as a whole; now God chooses one man and makes him the beginning of a new nation and the recipient of an unconditional promise of salvation. That promise goes beyond Abraham, beyond the nation which he fathers, to all generations. The primeval history has not ended in unrelieved gloom, but in the most impressive manifestation of God's saving grace. Already at the beginning of sacred history—

the *Heilsgeschichte*—the end is vaguely seen; and this firm link between primeval and sacred history is the first link in the chain of messianic development. The promise of Gn. 12:1-3 finds its fulfillment in the Son of Abraham who crushed the head of the serpent and who draws all men to him (Jn. 12:32).

2) *The Exodus*

Biblical history—God's saving history (*Heilsgeschichte*)—begins with Abraham—more precisely with God's choice of Abraham. Yet the decisive event in Israel's history was several centuries later than the Patriarch: this was the Exodus. The term "Exodus" signifies the going out of the Hebrews from Egypt; or, in a wider and more usual sense, the whole complex of events between the deliverance from Egypt and the entry into the Promised Land (Ex. 3:7-10). This great event became, in Jewish and Christian thought, the type and the guarantee of all other interventions of God on behalf of his people.[16]

The Exodus marked the beginning of the people of God, for then it was that God brought forth Israel (Dt. 32:5-10) and established a father relationship, full of love and solicitude (Hos. 11:1; Jer. 31:9; Is. 63:16; 64:7). Since it is a sign of the divine love, the Exodus, by that very fact, is a gage of salvation: the God who had delivered his people from the bondage of Egypt will again save that people in the hour of danger, when it is threatened by Assyria (Is. 10:25 ff.; Mi. 7:14 f.) or by Babylonia (Jer. 16:14 f.; Is. 63-64). Alas, Israel responded with ingratitude to the divine care (Am. 2:10; Mi. 6:3 ff.; Jer. 2:1-8; Dt. 32), proving unfaithful to the love of the desert days (Hos. 2:16; Jer. 2:2 f.).

Throughout the Old Testament the Exodus remained the central moment in Israel's history and in her memory, and that saving event reverberates in the New Testament.

In the Old Testament, prophet and priest, psalmist and historian alike look back to the Red Sea and Mt. Sinai, and when Jesus talked with Moses and Elijah on the mountain of Transfiguration, their subject was his *exodus*—the Greek for "departure" (Lk. 9:31)— which he had to accomplish at Jerusalem; so inwoven was that event into the texture of God's dealings with men. The Exodus is for the Old Testament and Judaism what the life, death, and resurrection of Christ are for the New Testament and Christianity. And for Christians, what Jesus brought to fulfillment was the purpose of the Exodus.[17]

3) *The Covenants*

To express the nature of the link which exists between God and his people the Old Testament uses the word *berith* (rendered in Greek by *diathēkē* and in Latin by *testamentum*). In English it is generally translated as "covenant." The term "covenant," which in its technical theological sense concerns the relations of men with God, was borrowed from the social experience of men, from the fact of treaties and alliances between peoples and individuals. In practice, the religious use of the term regards a special type of covenant, that in which one partner takes the initiative and imposes the conditions. Therefore God lays down the terms, demanding of his people that it should keep the Covenant (Gn. 17:9; 19:5)—while he binds himself by promise. The Pentateuch (P tradition) describes three Covenants made by God with men.

1. THE COVENANT WITH NOAH   Coming after the era of creation, the Covenant with Noah is, for the priestly writer, the second stage of the divine plan; following on the catastrophe of the Flood it was a new beginning, a Covenant with all mankind. In this immediate context of the Flood, too, the sign of this Covenant, the rainbow, is meaningful. "The Hebrew word that we translate 'rainbow' usually means in the Old Testament 'the bow of war.' The beauty of the ancient conception thus becomes apparent: God shows the world that he has put aside his bow."[18] God promised Noah that he would never again destroy the earth. A new privilege was introduced:

animal meat might be eaten provided it was bloodless, for blood, symbolizing life, was sacred to God. There was an accompanying prohibition against the wanton shedding of blood.

2. THE COVENANT WITH   The third stage of the divine
ABRAHAM (GN. 17:1-14)   plan was a Covenant with
Abraham. It involved the divine promise that Abraham would be the father of many nations. This Covenant, however, was made not only with Abraham, but with his descendants too: to him and to them the land of Canaan will be granted as an everlasting possession. This Covenant was unconditional and could not fail—unlike the Sinai Covenant which could and did fail. The sign of the Covenant was circumcision, and the individual Israelite who did not observe this rite did not belong to the Covenant community. The J version (Gn. 15:1-21) refers to an ancient covenant ceremony well known to many ancient peoples: certain animals and birds were halved and laid opposite each other and the partners to the treaty walked between the pieces, thus sealing the treaty and invoking a curse upon themselves if the treaty should be broken; hence the term used of covenant-making is *karath berith*, literally, "to cut a treaty." In this passage we are told that Yahweh, in the shape of a flaming torch, performed the rite and passed between the parts of the victims.

3. THE COVENANT   At Sinai the people, delivered from
AT SINAI   Egyptian bondage, entered into a
Covenant with Yahweh, and the cult of Yahweh was established as the national religion. A study of Hittite treaties has shed light on the nature of this Covenant.[19] Two types of treaty may be distinguished: the parity pact and the suzerainty pact. In a parity covenant both parties, standing on equal terms, bound themselves by bilateral obligations. The suzerainty covenant, on the other hand, was made between a king and his vassal and was unilateral. The suzerain "gave" a covenant and the vassal was obliged to accept and obey the conditions of the suzerain. Yet such a covenant was not just an assertion of power and authority on the part of the suzerain: it was explicitly regarded and

presented as an act of benevolence, and the vassal accepted the obligations in a sense of gratitude. In keeping with this conception the covenant was couched in an "I-Thou" dialogue form. The Sinai Covenant followed this pattern exactly.

At the vision of the burning bush Yahweh revealed to Moses both his name and his plan for Israel: he willed to deliver Israel from Egypt and to install his people in the land of Canaan (Ex. 3:7-10,16 f.). This plan presupposed that Israel was the object of his choice and the recipient of a promise; the Exodus demonstrated that God was capable of imposing his will ("You have seen how I bore you on eagles' wings and brought you to myself" [Ex. 19:4]) and the people responded by faith (Ex. 14:31). Then God revealed the terms of the Covenant: "If you will obey my voice and keep my covenant, you shall be my own possession among all peoples; for all the earth is mine, and you shall be to me a kingdom of priests and a holy nation" (Ex. 19:5 f.). Israel will henceforth be his kingdom, his people which will render him due cult.[20] In return, God will "tabernacle" in the midst of his people: "They shall know that I am the Lord their God, who brought them forth out of the land of Egypt that I might dwell among them" (Ex. 29:46). The Sinai Covenant, however, was conditional. In granting this Covenant to Israel and in making promises, God imposed conditions which Israel must observe. But these laws and institutions were laid down and established in order that Israel should be a holy people; they are an expression of divine benevolence, even though failure to observe them will entail a curse (Lv. 26:14-39).

The ceremony of the making of the Covenant is described in Ex. 24. Moses built an altar at the foot of Sinai and set up twelve pillars to represent the twelve tribes. Victims were sacrificed; half the blood was collected and kept in basins and half of it was thrown against the altar as a sign of Yahweh's participation in the rite. Moses read the "book of the Covenant" and the people pledged themselves to accept and obey Yahweh's ordinances. Then he cast the rest of the blood on the people, saying: "Behold the blood of the Covenant which the Lord has made with you in accordance with all these words" (v. 8).

The Covenant of Sinai revealed in a definitive manner an essential aspect of the plan of salvation: God had willed to join himself to men by establishing a cultic community dedicated to his service, ruled by his law, the recipient of his promises; the New Testament will fully realize this divine project. Though the Covenant was God's free gift to Israel it became enmeshed in the historical destiny of Israel to such an extent that salvation tended to be regarded as the reward of human fidelity to the law. Its limitation to one nation tended to obscure the universal scope of God's plan, while the promises of temporal rewards could cause men to lose sight of the religious object of the Covenant: the establishment of the kingship of God over Israel and through Israel over the whole world. Nonetheless the Covenant of Sinai dominated Israel's history and the development of revelation.[21]

4) _The Law_

The Hebrew term _tôrah_ has a wider signification, one less strictly juridical, than the _nomos_ of the Septuagint (LXX) or the English "law"; it is a "teaching" given by God to men in order to regulate their conduct. This is why the whole Pentateuch, and not only the legislation, is called the Torah. In fact, framed in a narrative setting, the Pentateuch contains the ensemble of prescriptions which ruled the moral, social, and religious life of the people. All of these prescriptions—moral, juridical, and cultic—have a religious character, and the whole corpus is presented as the charter of a Covenant with Yahweh and is linked with the narrative of happenings in the desert where the Covenant was made.

While it remains true that the basis of the legislation goes back to the time of Moses, the present form of the Pentateuch includes many laws of later ages. It is simply not conceivable that a legal code, drawn up for a small nomad people in the thirteenth century B.C., would have remained unchanged for over a thousand years while that people became successively an agricultural community, a monarchy, and a Church. Laws are made to be applied and must necessarily be adapted to changing conditions. For instance, much of the priestly legislation found in Ex. 25-31; 35-40, bears the stamp of later times. The Covenant Code (Ex. 20:22—23:19) is the law of a pastoral and agricultural society and met the conditions of an Israel already settled in Palestine. The ritual laws of Ex. 34:14-26 date from the same time but show some influence of Dt. Leviticus took its final shape after the Exile, in the Second Temple, but the basis of it goes back to the primitive ritual of the desert. The Law of Holiness (Lv. 17-26) seems to have been codified towards the end of the monarchy. The deuteronomical code (Dt. 12-26) is earlier than the fall of Samaria in 721 B.C., and though it shows a development that is influenced by an appreciation of the love of Yahweh for his people and of Israel's consequent obligation to act as he would act, it is basically a reinterpretation and a new presentation of earlier laws.

It seems possible to identify some of the earlier laws of the Pentateuch on the basis of form. Two general types are readily noted: casuistic (or hypothetical) law; and apodictic (or categorical) law. Both types are well represented in Ex. 22: the hypothetical type in verses 1-17 ("If . . ." with the provision in the third person); and the apodictic form in verses 18, 21 f. ("Thou shalt not . . ." with the injunction in the second person). Hypothetical law was common throughout the ancient world, especially in Mesopotamia and among the Hittites, and is best represented by the Code of Hammurabi.[22] Apodictic law is peculiar to Israel. This fact powerfully strengthens the argument that the Decalogue (to take a striking example) goes back to Moses. The Ten Commandments (in Hebrew the "Ten Words") are given twice (Ex. 20:2-17; Dt. 5:6-18); both versions are in apodictic form—though several of the commandments have been expanded in later times—and both go back to a common primitive form set out in sharp, terse language. In general, it may be said that the apodictic laws are early and may very well represent a nucleus that originated with Moses.

Throughout the Old Testament the Law is everywhere present and it directly or indirectly influences the thought of the sacred writers.[23] The priests are *ex officio* guardians of the Torah and specialists in its interpretation (Hos. 5:1; Jer. 18:18; Ezek. 7:26) and it is their duty to teach the people (Dt. 33:10; Hos. 4:6; Jer. 5:4 f.). Under their authority the Torah developed and was compiled. The prophets recognized the authority of this Torah (Hos. 9:12; 4:1 f.; Jer. 11:1-12; Ezek. 22:1-16,26). Their high moral doctrine was nothing more than a profound understanding of the demands of the Mosaic Law. The historians of Israel clearly saw the birth of the nation in the Covenant of Sinai. Among them, the Deuteronomist judged events in the light of the deuteronomical code, while the Chronicler was guided in his work by a completed Pentateuch. The wisdom of the sages is enlightened by the Torah, and Sirach states explicitly that the true Wisdom is nothing other than the Law (Sir. 24:23 f.). The psalmists extol the Law (cf. Ps. 19 [18]:7-14; 119 [118]). Finally, Ezra set the Torah as the authoritative rule for the faith and practice of the postexilic community and as the center of its life. Attachment to the Law inspired the Maccabaean revolt and supported the martyrs and heroes of that rising.

Yet this devotion to the Law had its dangers, and the tragedy of Judaism is that it succumbed to these dangers. The first mistake was to set all precepts, religious and moral, civil and cultic, on the same plane instead of ordering them, in correct hierarchy, around the one precept that would give meaning and life to all of them (Dt. 6:4). As a result, the Law became the preserve of casuists and became so overladen with minutiae that it turned into an insupportable burden (Mt. 23:4; Acts 15:10). The second danger, and a more insidious one, was to base man's justification on a meticulous observance of the Law rather than to visualize it as the work of divine grace, freely bestowed; it meant that man could justify himself. It needed the forceful teaching of St. Paul to make clear, once and for all, that man is not justified by the works of the Law—but by faith in Jesus Christ (Gal. 2:16; Rom. 3:28).

1 See Roland de Vaux, *La Genèse* (BJ), pp. 13-17.

2 An anthropomorphism (or "manlikeness") is a manner of describing God or of speaking of him in human terms. It is something we cannot avoid altogether if we are to speak of him at all. Thus, though we know that he is a Spirit, we can speak of the "hand of God" and of God "hearing" our prayers. If the Yahwist makes very free use of anthropomorphisms this does not indicate a primitive notion of God, but is the expression of faith, in a personal God, a God who really takes an interest in human affairs; a God, we might say, who is taken for granted.

3 See H. Cazelles, IB, I, pp. 348-80. This study has influenced our treatment of the traditions.

4 See B. W. Anderson, *Understanding the Old Testament* (Englewood Cliffs, N.J.: Prentice-Hall, 1957), p. 313.

5 See Cazelles, *op. cit.*, 370.

6 See H. Cazelles, *Le Deutéronome* (BJ), p. 17.

7 This truth is, of course, complex, and includes a number of facts such as the special creation of man; still these can be fairly considered as the component parts of one inclusive fact.

8 See W. Harrington, *Genesis and Evolution* (New York: Paulist Press, 1963), pp. 13-20; 24-26.

9 See Roland de Vaux, BJ, pp. 7 f.

10 See W. O hUrdail (Harrington), "Dlagacht na Luath-Staire—Gn. 1-11," *Irisleabhar Muighe Nuadhat* (Maynooth, 1964), 52-59.

11 In Gn. 1-11 the priestly material is distributed as follows: 1:1–2:4a; 5:1-32; 6:9-22; 7:6-11, 13-16a, 18-21, 24; 8:1-2a, 3b-5, 13a, 14-19; 9:1-17, 28; 10:1-32; 11:10-32.

12 See Roland de Vaux, *La Genèse* (BJ), pp. 53 f.

13 In Gn. 1-11 the Yahwistic material is distributed as follows: 2:4b–4:26; 6:1-8; 7:1-5, 7-10, 12, 16b, 17, 22b; 8:2b-3a, 6-12, 13b, 20-22; 9:18-27; 11:1-9.

14 See G. von Rad, *Genesis,* trans. J. Marks (Philadelphia: Westminster Press, 1961), p. 104. The presentation of the theology of these chapters owes much to Professor von Rad.

15 It is clear that originally the narrative spoke of Shem, Japheth, and Canaan. A redactor, wishing to restore the familiar triad, Shem, Ham, and Japheth, introduced Ham and described him as "the father of" Canaan. The inconsistency is evident in verse 24 where Canaan is Noah's "youngest son."

16 See M.-E. Boismard, *Vocabulaire de Théologie Biblique* (Paris: Cerf, 1961), pp. 342 f. Henceforth references to this work will be abbreviated VTB.

17 D.M.G. Stalker, *Peake's Commentary on the Bible,* M. Black and H. H. Rowley, editors (London: Nelson, 1962), n. 175 a. Henceforth references to this work will be abbreviated PCB.

[18] Von Rad, *op. cit.,* p. 130.

[19] See G. E. Mendenhall, "Law and Covenant in Israel and the Ancient Near East," *The Biblical Archaeologist,* 17 (1954), 26-76.

[20] See J. Giblet and P. Grelot, VTB, p. 21.

[21] See *ibid.,* pp. 22 f.

[22] See ANET, pp. 163-80.

[23] See P. Grelot, VTB, pp. 544-46.

TWO

THE DEUTERONOMICAL HISTORY

The reader who has, for the first time, patiently, or perhaps doggedly, worked through the Book of Kings will understandably feel more than a little confused by it all. He may have accepted the view that the religion of the Old Testament, just like that of the New Testament, is essentially historical. But surely *this* kind of history has no obvious religious bearing? If he has read further afield he may be excused for failing to find any real link between Joshua-Judges (with 1 Samuel thrown in for good measure) and Kings. Yet the link is there, and the whole has a religious significance; but one must be able to discern this.[1]

It is a vital matter for us to see the Bible through the eyes of the men who wrote it because, word of God though it is, it has come to us in human dress. This proper focusing is necessary, not only for the purpose of reading Scripture intelligently, but for the much more important reason—though it comes to the same thing in the end—that it is the only way in which we can understand the intentions of the divine Author. When we read biblical history in this light we quickly realize that it is not a hopeless muddle of

unrelated events or a mere procession of petty kings and
their tiresome squabbles. To the eyes of the biblical historian these details fit, each in its place, into the unified
plan of a great mosaic.

Thus we find that the apparently isolated books of the
Old Testament are in fact grouped to form larger units.
The books Joshua-Kings are closely bound together and
1,2 Chronicles, Ezra, and Nehemiah are so many chapters
of one work. Even 1 and 2 Maccabees are parallel accounts
of the same events. Biblical history is not aimless and,
despite the tragedies with which it deals, it is always ultimately hopeful. It could scarcely be otherwise since the
biblical historian is at all times keenly aware that God
holds the reins of history in a firm grasp. God is active in
history, above all in the history of his own people.

In the present chapter we shall consider the first of these
biblical histories, Joshua-Kings, together with the introduction which gives meaning to the work: Deuteronomy.
When we have grasped the background of the deuteronomical history and have reflected on the epoch in which it
took shape, we shall realize what a treasure has been be-
queathed to us. These varied pages straightway take on a
new significance as we see them now shot through with
the unshakable faith of men who could look long and
candidly on centuries of national infidelity and then turn
to Yahweh their God with greater trust and confidence
than ever. The sad story of failure is lighted up by hope,
by the conviction that the Lord who once led his people
out of Egypt, "with a mighty hand and an outstretched
arm," can set them up once more on the ruins of the past,
or can lead them back again from another captivity. Unfaithfulness was the cause of all the evils that had been
showered upon them, whereas trust in Yahweh and fidelity
to his Law are the gage of divine blessings, the blessings
that can yet be theirs if they will but turn to their God in
sincerity and truth. This confidence was the cornerstone
of postexilic Judaism, that cradle of the New Testament
and of a greater hope.

1. THE CONSCIENCE OF A NATION

The king of Assyria invaded all the land and came to
Samaria, and for three years he besieged it. In the
ninth year of Hoshea the king of Assyria took Samaria
and deported the Israelites to Assyria. . . . And this
happened because the Israelites had sinned against the
Lord their God who had taken them up out of the
land of Egypt, from the power of Pharaoh, king of
Egypt, and had adored other gods. . . . They built
for themselves high places wherever they dwelt . . .
they did wicked things, provoking the Lord to anger,
and they served idols. . . . They despised his laws and
the Covenant which he had made with their fathers
and the warnings which he gave them. . . . And they
rejected all the commandments of the Lord their God.
. . . Therefore the Lord was very angry with Israel,
and removed them out of his sight. The tribe of Judah
alone was left (2 Kgs. 17:5-7,9-11,15 f.,18).

The Lord did not turn from the fierceness of his
great anger which was kindled against Judah. . . .
And the Lord said: "I will remove Judah also out of
my sight, as I have removed Israel, and the Temple
of which I said: My Name shall be there" (2 Kgs.
23:26 f.).

Judgments such as these are understandable only when we
see in proper perspective the events that evoked them; the
main lines, at least, of Israel's history, up to the end of the
monarchy, must be recalled.

When in chapter twelve of Genesis Abraham is introduced, we enter a new era; we stand at a decisive moment
in religious history, and at the emergence of a Chosen
People. Abraham received a divine command to leave his
country and kindred and his father's house and to go into
a land which the Lord would show him; and at the same
time he was promised that he would be the ancestor of a
great nation. He heard and obeyed and came into the land
of Canaan. There he grew old with Sarah his wife; the
promise had not yet been fulfilled and still he put his trust

in Yahweh, the lifegiver. He had faith in God and in the word of God and found salvation:

" 'Look at the heavens and, if you can, count the stars.' And he said to him: 'So shall your posterity be.' Abraham believed the Lord, who credited the act to him as justice" (Gn. 15:5 f.). Abraham remains for all future ages the man of faith, the father of a great nation, the friend of God, recipient of the promise of God.

The promise was renewed to his descendants, Isaac and Jacob, and the brilliant career of Joseph seemed to herald its fulfillment. Then followed the hopeless years of slavery in Egypt. Where now was the glorious future promised to the sons of Abraham? Then an event occurred, a tremendous event, that was to echo through all the extent of Israel's history: Yahweh himself intervened.

> When the Egyptians maltreated us and oppressed us and imposed hard labors on us, we cried to the Lord the God of our fathers. The Lord heard our cry and saw our misery, our toil and our oppression, and the Lord brought us out of Egypt with a mighty hand and an outstretched arm, with great terror, with signs and wonders. He brought us into this place and gave us this land, a land flowing with milk and honey (Dt. 26:6-9).

Throughout the Old Testament we find that the Exodus is the central event in Israel's memory; the Exodus, though it is the work of Yahweh, immediately conjures up the dominant figure of Moses. He not only led the people from Egypt, but he it was who, afterwards, forged that motley crowd of refugees into a nation and set on foot a mighty religious movement and, further, gave the impetus to the great literary achievement that is the Pentateuch. "The religion of Moses has marked for all time the faith and practice of the people; the law of Moses has remained its rule of life."[2]

Moses indeed merited the glowing tribute paid to him in a later age: "Since then no prophet has arisen in Israel like Moses, whom the Lord knew face to face" (Dt. 34:10). Yet he had led the people only to the threshold of the Promised Land; it was for Joshua, his successor, to take the final step. But if Joshua was the man who led the people in to take possession of the land that Yahweh had given them, this was precisely because the mantle of Moses had fallen on him (cf. Dt. 34:9).

The Israelites were in the land, but they had not yet conquered the whole of it; the struggle went on for two centuries. Towards the close of that period the failure of Saul threatened the very existence of the nation, but David saved the situation and succeeded in establishing a kingdom and even a modest empire. By that fact, David took his place beside Abraham and Moses: these are the three great architects of the people of God. Once again there is a divine promise:

> The Lord declares to you that the Lord will make you a house. When your days are fulfilled and you lie down with your fathers, I will raise up your son after you, who shall come forth from your body, and I will establish his kingdom. . . . And your house and your kingdom shall be made sure forever in my presence; your throne shall be established forever (2 Sm. 7:11 f.,16).

This is the first of a long series of prophecies which pointed to a Messiah from the line of David. Culmination and fulfillment, both, are found in the opening words of St. Matthew: "The book of the genealogy of Jesus Christ, the son of David" (Mt. 1:1).

And yet the historical kingdom of David did not stand. Solomon was able to maintain, more or less intact, the conquests of his father, but on his death the kingdom, united by David, broke apart and Israel (or the Northern Kingdom) and Judah henceforth went their separate ways. A religious schism followed the political division and Judah alone remained true, not only to the Davidic dynasty, but also—in principle at least—to the orthodox faith. Israel fell to the Assyrians in 721 B.C. and disappeared from history. Judah alone was left. A century after the fall of Israel the Southern Kingdom seemed to be entering, with renewed vigor, into an era of promise; the young king, Josiah (640-

609 B.C.), asserted his independence and set on foot a religious reform. The future was full of hope, but these hopes were rudely dashed when the king fell in a disastrous battle and the kingdom of Judah moved quickly to destruction. In 587 B.C. Jerusalem fell to Nebuchadnezzar and its inhabitants were deported to Babylon. This must have seemed the end. The house built by Abraham and Moses and David had crashed in ruins and, worse still, the promises of Yahweh had failed.

For men of faith this was unthinkable. There must be a solution to the formidable problem, a problem that had faced them even before the fall of Jerusalem; for Judah had barely survived the Assyrian flood in which Israel had been swept away. History provided the answer: Yahweh had not failed, it was the people who failed their God. Such, at least, was the verdict of Deuteronomy.

The deuteronomical outlook was profoundly religious and striking in its singlemindedness: the nation stood or fell by its fidelity or unfaithfulness to Yahweh and to his Law. This outlook inspired men of faith and vision, who not only measured their history by that yardstick, but set about editing their traditions, giving, in the process, to that history, their own distinctive theological slant. We owe, then, to the deuteronomists not only the present form of the books Joshua-Kings, but also our awareness of the significance of their content. For us, no less than for them, it is the meaning of history that matters.

At the head of this section we have set out, as an indication of the spirit which animated their work, the deuteronomists' verdict on the fall of Israel and Judah. This work may be fittingly described as a national examination of conscience and they faced up to the task with pitiless candor. Like the prophets, they are witnesses to what is unique about the religion of Israel, not monotheism only, but ethical monotheism: the one God of Israel is a *just* God. It is because he is just that he punishes the sins of his own people more severely than the sins of those he has not chosen (cf. Am. 3:2). But all who turn to him will find only love and mercy: this is the final word of the deuteronomical history.

2. THE BOOK OF DEUTERONOMY

Quite like the other books of the Pentateuch, Deuteronomy has its roots firmly struck in the Mosaic tradition. The Law that Moses had given his people was destined to grow and develop and to be adapted to the changing circumstances of the history of the people. This Law was essentially religious, a precious heritage which had to be preserved intact and which could bear additions only in an authentic line of development—a task which fell to the Levites. At the sanctuaries, when the people came on pilgrimage, practical solutions were given in difficult cases and new regulations were formulated—but always in the spirit of the Mosaic legislation. In other words, the Law of Moses continued to be applied in new social and economic conditions; and some, at least, of these new solutions became fixed and were set down in writing (cf. Hos. 8:12). It was in this way that the legal material now found, not only in Deuteronomy but throughout the Pentateuch, took shape.

Before the final catastrophe of 721 B.C., when the kingdom of Israel came to an end, some of the Levites had sought refuge in Judah, taking with them their sacred traditions. Among these was the legislative part of Deuteronomy (the deuteronomical code, that is, Dt. 12-26). This brief document was to have a powerful and far-reaching effect—but not just yet. The great power which had destroyed Israel menaced Judah too, but the latter, thanks in large measure to the efforts of Isaiah, managed to survive. A century later Assyria, while still at its apogee, collapsed and disappeared with dramatic suddenness. In the short period that covered the decline of Assyria and the rise of the Neo-Babylonian Empire, Judah was granted a brief respite and the young and pious King Josiah was able to set on foot a religious reform. One of the first works to be undertaken was the restoration of the Temple, which had been sadly neglected during the long and disastrous reign of Manasseh. During the work of renovation the "Book of the Law" was discovered (2 Kgs. 22:8-10). This was the deuteronomical code which had been brought to

Jerusalem by the refugees from Israel one hundred years
before and which had been reverently deposited in the
Temple, only to be at first disregarded and ultimately forgotten. Now providentially coming to light again, it became
the charter of the reform and was published in the framework of a discourse of Moses; this first edition of the work
corresponds to chapters 5-28 of our Deuteronomy. Even
though the reform of Josiah failed, the book was now at
last known (Jeremiah gives evidence of his knowledge of
it).

The capture of Jerusalem by Nebuchadnezzar in 587
B.C. marked the end of the kingdom of Judah and the
beginning of the Babylonian Exile (587-538 B.C.). During
the Exile Deuteronomy was re-edited: the other discourses
of Moses were added. The first four chapters of the book,
which envisaged the conquest of the Promised Land, held
out to the exiles the prospect of return, a reconquest. And
at the close, the long canticle of chapter 32 will henceforth
stand as a witness against Israel and as a criterion of the
people's conduct.

A striking feature of Deuteronomy is that it looks back
to the time of the Exodus. Doubtless, the Northern origin
of the tradition explains a certain lack of concern with
David—though in Judaean surroundings this was speedily
redressed—but this "rediscovery of Moses" in the seventh
century B.C. is a significant development in Judah. There
was at that time a conscious effort to recapture both the
letter and the spirit of Mosaism. "Ask now of the days that
are past" is a characteristic appeal of Deuteronomy (cf.
Dt. 4:32). This nostalgic revival of interest in the past had
close parallels in the contemporary literature of neighboring peoples. The deuteronomic reaction was not merely
local, but was part of a general tendency which reached
to all the lands of the ancient Near East. "The sun of the
ancient Orient was beginning to set and its people could
not help but be obscurely and unhappily conscious of the
approaching darkness."[3] Divine Providence, however,
bends circumstances and trends to its purpose, and if the
eyes of the deuteronomists, in common with the people of
their time, were turned to the past, it is in very great meas-

ure thanks to the achievement inspired by this tendency
that the religion of Moses was able to come through the
dark days of the close of the monarchy and survive the
great trial of the Exile.

3. THE DEUTERONOMICAL HISTORY

The Book of Deuteronomy, or that part of it which was
brought to Jerusalem at the time of the destruction of
Samaria in 721 B.C., was destined to inspire a very important literary movement—though this was not until a
century later—during the reign of Josiah. In the fresh atmosphere of the young king's reform program the spirit
of the deuteronomical writing was contagious; but we
should not exaggerate its influence. The aftermath shows
that the majority of the people had given no more than
superficial assent to the new, radical policy, though it is
nonetheless clear that a certain element greeted the reform
with enthusiasm and pressed it forward wholeheartedly; to
these, the "Book of the Law" was a veritable source of
strength and consolation and life.

The history of the Chosen People obviously did not end
with Moses and the men of the seventh century B.C. would
have inherited a mass of traditions centered around Joshua,
the Judges, and the monarchy. In the latter period there
were also the royal archives. But these traditions were isolated; there was no obvious link between the various units
and, above all, there was no clear lesson to be drawn from
the whole of it. We owe it to the deuteronomists that they
not only collected and edited this material but that, in setting it out, they made manifest to all the one striking lesson
of their history. The books from Joshua to Kings bear the
stamp of the deuteronomists, even if, admittedly, in certain
parts the influence is not very marked, due to deliberate
policy, as we shall see.

Deuteronomy is the first volume of this great religious
history:[4] it justifies historically the doctrine of the choice
of Israel by Yahweh and outlines the theocratic constitution that is demanded by this divine election. Joshua presents the installation of the Chosen People in the Promised

Land and Judges traces the immediate aftermath, the succession of its apostasies and conversions. Samuel points out how the theocratic ideal was at last realized under David, after the initial failure of Saul. Kings describes the decline that set in even during the reign of Solomon, which eventually led to the fall and disappearance of the monarchy. Deuteronomy, which is the introduction to the whole, at a later date was detached from the work and was added on to the first four books of the Bible, for the obvious reason that it forms a fitting climax to the story of Moses.

But we must be careful how we understand the unity of the books Deuteronomy-Kings. On the one hand we speak of a deuteronomical *edition* of oral traditions and written documents which, generally speaking, had already been grouped in collections. Furthermore, this material was not everywhere retouched to the same extent, and whole books, or large sections within books, preserve their individuality. On the other hand, the books show traces of more than one edition in a deuteronomical context. There were at least two editions of Kings, for example, one during the reform of Josiah and the other after the Exile. It was during the Exile, in fact, that the final edition of the great history was made.

4. THE BOOK OF JOSHUA

The story of the conquest as presented to us in Joshua is complex—inevitably so, because it is really an amalgam of varied sources. There is enough evidence to show that, at the death of Joshua, the Promised Land was still far from being conquered; this is abundantly borne out by the Book of Judges apart from the many references in Joshua. The Israelites, for the most part, held only the hill regions and were quite unable to dislodge the better armed Canaanites from the plains. They must wait for two centuries before the whole land was theirs. The editorial additions, however, give a very different picture of the conquest. According to the deuteronomic view, Joshua, the leader of a united people, won mastery of the whole country in a few lightning campaigns. The "whole land" fell into the hands of Joshua "because the Lord, the God of Israel, fought for Israel" (Jos. 10:42; 11:23).

In general, we may say that the deuteronomists have carefully collected and presented the varied traditions and have done so with scrupulous honesty. But upon this material they have superimposed a simplified and idealized picture of the conquest, and have projected back to the time of Joshua the final realization achieved by David. This foreshortening of the historical perspective was justified in their eyes because the outcome was ultimately the work of God. For these editions "the taking of Canaan is not a profane event, it is a theological event."[5] The conquest is an episode in the history of salvation, an essential element of God's plan for his people. When the edition was being made the plan seemed in jeopardy: the Northern Kingdom had disappeared and Judah was in mortal danger. In this context the picture of the whole nation united under Joshua took on a prophetical significance, in harmony with the outlook of Jeremiah and Ezekiel: God himself will bring about the unity of his people.[6]

True to the spirit of Deuteronomy this ideal is set in the golden age of the Exodus. Joshua completed the work of Moses, the ideal of a people united under a leader who is entirely dedicated to the law of Yahweh; this alone could win the divine blessing. Where the prophets looked to the future the deuteronomists looked to the past, but the result was the same. The modest achievement of Joshua was already the seed of the ultimate triumph of God and that truth was expressed by attributing to him the success of later times. The ideal conquest of Joshua will be repeated on a grander scale when the people learn to observe the Law of Yahweh with all their heart and with all their soul and with all their might.

5. THE BOOK OF JUDGES

The Book of Judges bears the unmistakable print of the deuteronomic stamp and affords perhaps the best example, in this complex history, of the editorial method. The main part of the book (Jgs. 3:7–16:31) is a compilation of quite distinct traditions concerning various "Judges"—local charismatic heroes. These traditions are presented from a definite and clearly-expressed viewpoint, a point of view that is set out in the original introduction to the work (Jgs. 2:6–3:6); it is repeated further on (10:6-16) and is also indicated in the formulas which recur at the beginning of the story of each of the "greater" Judges. The viewpoint is this: The Israelites have been unfaithful to Yahweh; he has delivered them up to oppressors; the Israelites have repented and have called on Yahweh; he has sent them a savior, the Judge. This is a cycle of infidelity, punishment, repentance, and deliverance. But when the trials and the oppression have ceased, after a short period of tranquillity, the infidelities recommence and the cycle begins all over again.

The varied traditions describe conditions in Israel after the conquest and show the people in conflict with the nations round about. In Palestine itself these were first the Canaanites and later the Philistines. This situation is quite in agreement with the picture provided in Joshua, when one abstracts from the editorial presentation. The different traditions have not been worked over, but have been merely set in the general framework and thus given an appearance of homogeneity which they do not, in fact, possess, and the editors have achieved their purpose with the minimum of adaptation, if, indeed, with any at all. Once again the deuteronomists have made the point that everything depends on fidelity to Yahweh. This jealous God demands the undivided love of his people: he demands obedience to his Law. The Israelites of a later age can see in these stories of olden times the anticipation of their own graver problem, and the key to it. If they also repent and turn to Yahweh he will quickly take pity on them and raise up a deliverer.

6. THE BOOKS OF SAMUEL

The influence of Deuteronomy is less marked in the Books of Samuel. It is noticeable in some earlier chapters (1 Sm.

7 and 12) and in retouches to the Nathan prophecy (2 Sm. 7). On the other hand, we are given, more clearly than elsewhere, striking proof of the editors' respect for the ancient traditions. Though 2 Samuel 9-20 is a unit, the rest of the work (that is to say, 1 and 2 Samuel, which form one book) is composite. The very importance of the institution of the monarchy meant that it was variously judged in different circles. Similarly, the tragic figure of Saul was seen in both bad and good light. Above all, David, the people's king, was the subject of many traditions regarding his origin and his exploits. In the work of editing, the particular characteristics of the sources were preserved; we get juxtaposition rather than harmonization, with a consequent lack of logical sequence; on the whole, the various traditions are readily discernible.

This is especially obvious in the distinct presentations of the origin of the monarchy. The antimonarchist tradition (1 Sm. 8; 10:17-25; 12) can be clearly distinguished from the monarchist tradition (1 Sm. 9; 10:1-16; 11). Similarly, the lack of cohesion between the two traditions of David's entry into the service of Saul (1 Sm. 16:14—18:2) is even more obvious and, indeed, there are many such doublets in 2 Samuel. Though this method causes a somewhat disjointed narrative it increases our confidence in the deuteronomists. They did not take liberties with the material at their disposal, but treated it with such respect that they were prepared to sacrifice none of it, even for the sake of a more coherent presentation.

The Court History (2 Sm. 9-20) is certainly from the early days of Solomon and it is possible that the other collections were made in the first centuries of the monarchy: a primitive cycle of Samuel; two stories of Saul and David. These traditions, coming from the North and South, were joined together at a date much later than the events related in them (cf. 1 Sm. 27:6). This date would be after 721 B.C. The destruction of Samaria and the end of Israel provided an occasion for exalting the Dynasty of David and a means of completing the Southern traditions by those of the North.

The Northern bias of the original deuteronomical outlook was, naturally, modified in its Judaean development. Thus David, the ideal king, took his place beside Moses. And in 2 Sm. 7 the editors set in further relief the import of Nathan's prophecy, that first of a whole series of messianic prophecies. Samuel, as it now stands, is the story of the establishment of a kingdom of God on earth, and bears witness to the great difficulty of the task. The deuteronomists, writing with sad experience of the failure of the monarchy, looked back to David. They seized upon the prophecy of Nathan and dwelt on it, and found their messianic hope bolstered up by the divine promises made to the great king.

7. THE BOOKS OF KINGS

The hand of the deuteronomists is very evident in the Books of Kings. These books (in reality only one) continue the history outlined in Samuel; indeed, 1 Kgs. 1-2 is the conclusion of the family history of David, and describes the inauguration of Solomon as king. After this introduction, and apart from the lengthy insertions of the Elijah and Elisha cycles (1 Kgs. 17–2 Kgs. 13), the books are entirely taken up, first with the history of Solomon and then with the parallel histories of the kingdoms of Israel and Judah—until the fall of Israel when the story of Judah is carried on and brought to its conclusion. Three main sources are explicitly named: a History of Solomon; the Annals of the Kings of Israel; and the Annals of the Kings of Judah. Independent of these are the traditions underlying the cycles of Elijah and Elisha and the description of the Temple (1 Kgs. 6-7).

Where not interrupted by these other sources, the events of the history of the two kingdoms are fitted into a stereotyped framework. Each reign is treated individually and fully (in its religious aspect), and each is introduced and rounded off by formulas that are more or less constant. The essential part of these formulas is the judgment passed on each king. All the kings of Israel are condemned because of the "original sin" of Jeroboam I: the setting up of schismatic sanctuaries at Bethel and Dan.[7] Only eight

of the kings of Judah are praised for fidelity to the prescriptions of the Law of Yahweh; six of them, however,
with the qualification that they had failed to remove the
"high places." Hezekiah and Josiah alone merit unreserved
approval. This judgment is clearly inspired by the law of
Deuteronomy on the unity of the sanctuary, and that book
is undoubtedly the "Law of Moses" referred to in 1 Kgs.
2:3; 2 Kgs. 14:6; it is the "Book of the Law" found in the
Temple during the reign of Josiah (2 Kgs. 22:8). "One
God, one sanctuary" is a fundamental article of that Law,
a concrete way of demanding undivided loyalty to a "jealous God" and unwavering fidelity to his commands. But
the polemic against the "high places" also has in mind the
historical fact that the scattered local shrines—often on the
site of former Canaanite shrines—were open to the intrusion of Canaanite cultic elements and, in many cases, became centers of idolatrous worship.

The first edition of the Books of Kings was surely made
in the days, full of promise, of Josiah. The eulogy of the
king (2 Kgs. 23:25)—less the final words—would have been
the conclusion of this first work: "There was no king before him whom more than he had turned to the Lord with
all his heart and with all his soul and with all his strength,
in perfect faithfulness to the Law of Moses."

A second edition, also deuteronomical, was made during
the Exile; this may have been before 562 B.C. (date of the
release of Jehoiachin), because 2 Kgs. 25:21 has all the
appearance of a conclusion.[8] In this case, 2 Kgs. 25:22-30
forms an appendix.

Though the later editors must bear witness to the tragic
failure of Josiah's great effort and must record the dark
days leading to the catastrophe of 587 B.C., the book, in its
very last words, sounds a note of hope. It closes on the
favors granted to Jehoiachin (2 Kgs. 25:29 f.) who was,
in Jewish eyes, the last reigning successor of David. It is
the dawn of redemption.

8. CONCLUSION

The deuteronomical history closes with the Books of

Kings, but the influence of Deuteronomy does not end there. The idea, which it emphasizes so strongly, of a revealed and written Law, dominated postexilic Judaism. It inspired, to a notable extent, the great work of the Chronicler, and its echoes linger in Daniel and Maccabees. Its spirit served as a balance and as a corrective to an outlook that tended to be excessively legal, for it is essentially a law of love and not of minutiae. "Thou shalt love the Lord thy God with all thy heart and with all thy soul and with all thy strength" is singled out by Christ, and the love of the neighbor which completes this precept is also typical of the book.

But the real importance of Deuteronomy and the deuteronomical history is that it helped, in very great measure, to make postexilic Judaism possible. Its theology gave new hope, the hope of survival. By facing up courageously to the tragedy of Israel's history and in resolutely defending the fidelity of Yahweh it became a great treatise on grace; it is precisely because everything depends on God that there can be no room for despair. In the gloom of the Babylonian Exile the people hear the reassuring words: "In your distress, when all these things shall have come upon you, you shall finally return to the Lord your God and obey his voice, for the Lord your God is a merciful God who will not fail you or destroy you and who will not forget the covenant which, under oath, he made with your fathers" (Dt. 4:30 f.).

---

[1] See W. Harrington, "A Biblical View of History," *The Irish Theological Quarterly,* 29 (1962), 207-22. The article in question forms the basis of this chapter.

[2] Roland de Vaux, BJ, p. 5.

[3] W. F. Albright, *From the Stone Age to Christianity* (New York: Doubleday, 1957[2]), p. 316.

[4] See de Vaux, *op. cit.,* p. 215.

[5] Roland de Vaux, RB, 61 (1954), 261.

[6] Cf. J. Delorme, IB, pp. 399-401.

[7] See Roland de Vaux, *Les Livres des Rois* (BJ), pp. 14 f.

[8] See *loc. cit.*

THE PROPHETICAL BOOKS

Though in its earliest form prophetism in Israel was little different from the same phenomenon in Mesopotamia—and especially in Phoenicia and Canaan—it developed into something distinctive, into something unique in fact, becoming one of the most significant factors in the history of the Chosen People. Indeed the prophetic movement by itself goes far to answering a major problem:

Why did the Jewish nation survive at all, when so many of the smaller nations of antiquity sooner or later lost their identity in the melting-pot of the great empires of the Middle East? Few nations were to all appearances more effectively put down: exhausted by successive defeats in war, reduced to a mere remnant, deported to distant countries, subjected to the long-continued domination of alien and highly civilized Great Powers. And yet they survived, reconstructed their community, and handed down a continuous and developing tradition which exerted a creative influence upon the whole of subsequent history. Why was it? The only answer that explains the facts is that the great prophets worked out a particular interpretation of the course of history, and induced their people to accept it, at least in sufficient numbers to give a new direction to their history for the future.[1]

But the prophets did more than insure the survival of a people. They carried on a religious tradition which they had inherited, fostered its development between the eighth and fourth centuries B.C., and passed it on, immeasurably enriched, to Judaism. They were entirely faithful to the dogma fixed in the Mosaic age—ethical monotheism[2]— and exploited it to the full. They were guides, carefully chosen and specially raised, along a vital and precarious stage of the spiritual journey that led to Christ. We shall try to explain the meaning and significance of prophecy and to indicate the personal contribution of the prophets whose teaching has been preserved.

1. THE PROPHETICAL MOVEMENT

1) *The Name*

In Hebrew the current appellation of the prophet was *nābî'*. The origin of the word is uncertain; most likely it means "one who is called."

In the Septuagint (LXX) *nābî'* is always translated *prophētēs*. The etymology of the Greek word presents no difficulty, though the word has been misunderstood. The word is from the verb *phēmi*—"to say," "to speak," plus the prefix *pro*. This *pro* is not temporal (foretell) but sub-stitutive (to speak in the place of, in the name of, another). The prophet is a spokesman, a herald, who speaks in the name of God; he is one called by God to be his spokesman.

We must beware of understanding the terms "prophet" and "prophesy" according to their common usage in every-day English—a prophet being one who "predicts," and to prophesy meaning "to foretell." The biblical prophets were indeed predictors of the future, but to a limited extent; they were more concerned with the present and often just as much concerned with the past. In other words, "prophet" and "prophecy," in the Bible, have a technical sense that differs widely from current usage. This is not the end of the matter, however, for the term *nābî'* is bewildering in its range: it can designate a great figure like Jeremiah or a member of a group that seems little different from Muslim dervishes. The verb "to prophesy" can describe the sublime oracles of an Isaiah or the ravings of Saul before Samuel (1 Sm. 19:23 f.). We shall need to sort out the different meanings of the word as it occurs in different contexts.

2) *The Prophetical Groups*

THE EARLY PROPHETICAL GROUPS[3] In the eleventh and tenth centuries B.C. in Israel we meet with a certain prophetical movement and a form of prophecy known as ecstatic prophecy. It was a time of crisis. Guilds of prophets offered a resistance to the dangers that threatened to destroy the nation spiritually (1 Sm. 9-10). They lived in groups near the sanctuaries of Yahweh (1 Sm. 19:20); they may have had a cultic role, though this is by no means certain. They "prophesied" by working themselves into a state of frenzy; this state was induced by music and dancing and was contagious (1 Sm. 10:5 f.).

In many ways this institution resembled that of the Phoenician and Canaanite prophets of Baal, as we know it from profane documents and from biblical references (for example, 1 Kgs. 18). But the resemblance was external only. We may say that a Canaanite-type institution was transformed into a charismatic institution of Yahwism. The prophets were, in fact, the champions of anti-Canaanism. At a later date the great prophets acknowledged their humble predecessors (cf. Am. 2:10 f.; Jer. 7:25).

Yet, at first sight it does surprise us that Israelite prophecy should have had such a humble, and seemingly inauspicious, beginning. When we look at it more closely we find that it exemplifies the constant development within the Old Testament, and that it is not as singular as it appears. The following has been established:

The prophetic movement takes root in group-ecstaticism, that is, in dances or other physical motions repeated so often by the members of a group that they finally succumb to a kind of hypnotic suggestion, under the influence of which they remain unconscious for hours. In this state the subconsciousness may be abnormally active, and persons of a certain psychological type may have visions and mystical experiences which thereafter control, or at least affect, their entire life. This phenomenon is universal among mankind, being found among savages, in antiquity, and among the highest religions of today.[4]

God deals with men patiently, that is, according to their mentality, culture, and education.

THE "SONS OF THE PROPHETS"　In the ninth century B.C. we find confraternities of "the sons of the prophets"; the designation is a Semitic idiom meaning the members of prophetic groups. These were not quite the same as the earlier groups, though they also had their centers at the sanctuaries of Bethel, Jericho, and Gilgal (2 Kgs. 2; 4:38-41; 6:1-7); or if they were direct descendants of the others the ecstatic element in their "prophesying" was severely curtailed or had disappeared. They were spontaneous groupings of those who wished to defend Yahwism against the prevalent Baalism. Thus Elijah, the champion of Yahweh, made common cause with these prophets (1 Kgs. 18:22; 19:10,14), and Elisha associated with them and employed them in his mission (2 Kgs. 2:3,15; 4:38; 9:1-3). However, neither Elijah nor Elisha came from the number of these prophets.

INSTITUTIONAL OR PROFESSIONAL PROPHETS　During the monarchy, side-by-side with the classical prophets, there was another type of prophetism which may be called institutional or official. These prophets accompanied the king (1 Kgs. 22); they were an integral part of the nation (Jer. 18:18; 2 Kgs. 23:2); they spoke their oracles in the Temple enclosure (Jer. 28; Neh. 6:12). This prophetism was not in itself a bad or degraded thing, but the prophets were, by their position, constantly tempted to identify the cause of Yahweh with that of the king. In fact, the vocational prophets often opposed them (cf. Am. 7:14; Jer. 28), and Zech. 13:1-6 tells of their disappearance. The rules for the discernment of spirits given in Dt. 13:1-5; 18:21 f. clearly envisage these prophets—for there were indeed false prophets among them.

THE CLASSICAL   The classical prophets are not a group
PROPHETS   but individuals. They are, in short, those whom we commonly mean when we speak of "the prophets."

3) *The Vocational Prophets*

Vocational prophets are commonly divided into "preaching" prophets and "writing" prophets. This distinction is arbitrary and inaccurate for there were no "writing" prophets until the eighth century B.C. and always the message of the prophet was first delivered by word of mouth. Since, however, the best-preserved oracles of Amos, Hosea, and Isaiah are poetic addresses couched in perfect literary form, we may speak, from Amos onwards, of "literary" prophets. Hence a legitimate division would be: "preliterary" prophets and "literary" prophets. The latter group is our main concern throughout this chapter, and we shall be content to give a brief sketch of the prophetical movement from Samuel to Amos.

Samuel may be regarded as the first of the vocational or individual prophets. David had as advisers two representatives of the theocratic ideal, heirs of Samuel: Nathan (2 Sm. 7:1-17; 12:1-5; 1 Kgs. 1-2) and Gad (1 Sm. 22; 2 Sm. 24). Under Solomon, apparently there was a prophetical opposition, represented by Ahijah of Shiloh, who foretold the schism of 931 B.C. (1 Kgs. 11:29-39). In both reigns the intervention of these prophets was inspired by a common motive: they wanted to maintain the old values of equality and justice which were menaced by the royal policy, the peace which was threatened by division, and the ritual and cultic unity. Therefore Ahijah condemned the house of Jeroboam for its cultic schism (1 Kgs. 14:1-19). Shemaiah forbade Rehoboam to reconquer the North (1 Kgs. 12:21-24). Under Jeroboam an unnamed prophet cursed the altar of Bethel (1 Kgs. 13:11-32). Jehu ben Hanani foretold the end of the usurper Baasha (1 Kgs. 16:1-4, 7-13).

The dynasty of Omri marks a very important period in the history of the prophetical movement; it is the eve of the age of the great prophets. There were many interventions of religious and national bearing (1 Kgs. 20:13 f.,28, 35 f.; etc.). That of Micaiah ben Imla is significant because of his opposition to the professional prophets (1 Kgs. 22).

The vocation of Elijah was to affirm the exclusive and ethical Yahwism of his ancestors. He opposed the nature religion, whose influence was now accentuated by the introduction of the Tyrian Melcarth (Baal) by Jezebel, and was the herald of a religious revival whose spirit was that of the desert where he had relived the experience of Moses (1 Kgs. 19:1-18). From his fidelity to Yahweh flowed his proclamation of social justice (1 Kgs. 21), his political intervention against Ahab and Jezebel, and his warnings to the people. His work, both political and religious, was completed by his disciple Elisha who, through the instrumentality of Jehu, brought about the downfall of the Dynasty of Omri.

Practically no oracles of these two men have survived, perhaps because their sayings were few, since they were men of action rather than men of words. But we can know how they must have spoken by turning to those who were their spiritual heirs. "If we want to know how Elijah and Elisha reacted to the evils of the ninth century, we have only to read what Amos, Hosea, and Isaiah said in the eighth, though they may have expressed themselves differently."[5] The first of the literary prophets began to appear in the eighth century B.C. They continued throughout the following centuries until the prophetical movement came to an end with deutero-Zechariah in the fourth century B.C. We are concerned here with these prophets or, more precisely, with those among them whose message (or part of it) has been preserved for us in writing.

2. THE PROPHETICAL WRITINGS

1) *The Prophet and Prophecy*

PSYCHOLOGY OF
THE PROPHET[6]
The vocational prophet is a man who has received a divine call to be a messenger and an interpreter of the divine word; he is a man who has had a personal and extraordinary encounter with God. The word which has come to him compels him to speak: "The Lord has spoken, who can but prophesy?" asks Amos (Am. 3:8). Jeremiah, despondent because of his unchanging message of woe to the people he loved, would stifle the word: "If I say, 'I will not mention him, or speak any more in his name,' there is in my heart as it were a burning fire shut up in my bones, and I am weary with holding it in, and I cannot" (Jer. 20:9). Not only the words of the prophet, but his actions, even his life, is prophecy. The marriage of Hosea is a symbol (Hos. 1-3); Isaiah and his children are signs (Is. 8:18); Ezekiel multiplies the prophetic gestures (Ezek. 4:3; 12:6,11; 24:24).

What really matters is the relationship between the prophet and the word of God, for the prophet is a man who has had immediate experience of God and who feels himself constrained to speak what—he is convinced—is the divine word. In short, the prophet is a mystic, but a "constructive mystic." This perhaps helps to explain the true dimension of the phrase *kôh 'āmar Yahweh*—"thus says Yahweh"—which so often introduces or closes the prophetic oracle. It does not, each time it occurs, imply a direct revelation. Rather, one should see in this frequently-repeated formula the normal development of an initial vocation.[7] The prophet's vision of God has penetrated the whole manner of his thought, so that he sees things from God's point of view, and he is convinced that he so sees them.

[The prophets] were not philosophers, constructing a speculative theory from their observation of events. What they said was, "Thus saith the Lord." They firmly believed that God spoke to them (spoke to an inward ear, the spiritual sense). He spoke to them out of the events which they experienced. The interpretation of history which they offered was not invented by process of thought; it was the meaning which they experienced in the events, when their minds were opened to God as well as open to the impact of outward facts. Thus the prophetic interpretation of history, and the impetus and direction which that interpretation gave to subsequent history, were alike the Word of God to men.[8]

The immediate experience of God, the revelation of God's holiness and of his will, makes of the prophet one who "judges the present and sees the future in the light of God and who is sent by God to remind men of God's demands and to lead them along the road of obedience to God and love of him."[9] For the prophet's message is always primarily to his contemporaries; he is a preacher who speaks to the men of his own generation. He does so even when he predicts the future. This is an important observation because it implies that any interpretation of a prophetic text that would have no meaning for the prophet's contemporaries is certainly a misinterpretation.

CRITERION OF THE TRUE PROPHET   The prophet claimed to speak in the name of God; this claim is explicit in the formula *kôh 'āmar Yahweh*. But the phrase alone is not sufficient to authenticate the message, for those whom we call "false prophets" could—and did—declare: "Thus says Yahweh." Jer. 28 is illuminating on this score. Hananiah is called a *nābî'*; he spoke in the name of God (Jer. 28:2) and yet his words are not true. He may have been deluded (confusing his own mind with Yahweh's [Ezek. 13:2 f.]), though Jeremiah would seem to suggest that he deliberately deceived the people (Jer. 28:15). In either case, the hearers of Hananiah and Jeremiah could not discriminate between them merely from their words and formulas. Hence Jeremiah gives two criteria: (1) the fulfillment of his prediction (Jer. 28:9,16 f.); (2) the conformity of his teaching to the traditional doctrine (Jer. 28:7 f.)—what we might call the "analogy of faith."[10] Deuteronomy gives these criteria: one is the fulfillment of prophecy (Dt. 18:21 f.); the other and more important criterion is the doctrine and life of the prophet (Dt. 13:1-5), which should be in the line of pure Yahwism.

2) *The Prophetic Literature*

The prophets were primarily preachers who delivered their oracles and sermons by word of mouth, with the original oral character still stamped on the written record of their sayings. In exceptional cases the prophets did write (cf. Is. 8:1-4; 30:8; Ezek. 43:11 f.; Jer. 36:2,28). It may be that the work of Second Isaiah is a sustained literary composition; though even this is more likely to be a collection of oracles originally delivered orally, for despite a remarkable unity, there is a certain lack of sequence in the arrangement.[11] There can be little doubt that the last part (chapters 40-48) of the Book of Ezekiel is a literary composition. But these are the exceptions and, by and large, the prophets were certainly speakers rather than writers. This means that the units which make up the prophetic collections are short and many, and that the literary forms are varied. It is absolutely essential for an intelligent reading of the prophets that the limits of these units be determined and their literary forms identified.[12] While we list the most notable of these literary forms,[13] it should be kept in mind that the greater part of Old Testament prophecy is in poetic form.

COMPOSITION   It has become clear that the oracles and
OF THE BOOKS   sermons of the prophets were preserved by their disciples and eventually edited by them. These words must soon have been written down and we may visualize a primitive prophetical literature circulating in the form of short and separate writings. In the gradual work of collecting and editing, elements were added: earlier collections were sometimes broken up, and the material was finally arranged according to a plan—sometimes very vague —that must be determined (if possible) for each book. The

complex genesis of the prophetical books (or many of them) goes far to explain the disconcerting disarray that can confuse and exasperate the reader. The realization, for instance, that the Book of Isaiah bridges several centuries and really is an anthology of sermons and oracles, puts the reader on his guard and enables him to follow the work intelligently. Otherwise, his consternation must be that of one who would regard Palgrave's *Golden Treasury* as a single poem.

3) The Prophetical Books in Chronological Order

1. Prophets of the eighth century B.C.:
   Amos
   Hosea
   Isaiah 1-39
   Micah

2. Prophets of the seventh century B.C. and beginning of the sixth century B.C.:
   Zephaniah
   Nahum
   Habakkuk
   Jeremiah

3. Prophets of the Exile:
   Ezekiel
   Second Isaiah (40-55)

4. Prophets of the sixth century B.C.:
   Isaiah 56-66
   Haggai
   Zechariah 1-8

5. Prophets of the fifth century B.C.:
   Isaiah 34-35; 24-27
   Malachi
   Obadiah

6. Prophets of the fourth century B.C.:
   Joel
   Zechariah 9-14

3. PROPHETS OF THE EIGHTH CENTURY

1) *Amos*

THE
PROPHET
Amos is the earliest of the Old Testament prophets whose words have been preserved for us in book form. The heading of this book (Am. 1:1) tells us that Amos was a peasant of Tekoa (about six miles south of Bethlehem) and that he was active during the reign of the contemporary kings, Uzziah of Judah and Jeroboam II of Israel. Since his ministry was clearly set in the height of Israel's prosperity, it must have been well into the reign of Jeroboam II (783-743 B.C.), in other words, around the year 750 B.C.

The passage of Am. 7:10-15 gives a more detailed picture of Amos' background. He spent part of his time as a shepherd and part as a "dresser of sycamore trees"—this expression refers to the puncturing of the fig-like fruit so that the insects which form inside may be released.[14] The mission of a prophet of Judah in Israel is a striking indication that a common religious tradition bound the divided kingdoms. When Amaziah, the priest of Bethel, warned Amos that he should earn his living in Judah (by accepting fees like the professional prophets [cf. 1 Sm. 9-8; 1 Kgs. 14:3; 2 Kgs. 8:8]), Amos replied that he was not a *nābî'* of that kind, nor was he one of the "sons of the prophets": he had received a special vocation.

THE
BOOK
The Book of Amos is a compilation, made by his disciples or in prophetical circles, of oracles and sermons of the Prophet spoken in various situations. Though his message was primarily to Israel, as a Southerner he did not altogether neglect Judah (Am. 6:1; 8:14).

THE
MESSAGE
Amos is the great champion of justice. He took his stand on the essential justice of God and vindicated the moral order established by God and enshrined in the Covenant. Thus he mercilessly castigated the disorders that prevailed in an era of hectic prosperity. To his eyes the symptoms of social decay were glaring: wealth, concentrated in the hands of a few—the leaders

of the people—had corrupted its possessors; oppression of the poor was rife; the richly-endowed national religion, with its elaborate ceremonial, provided a comfortable atmosphere of self-righteousness. "The ordinary Israelite, we may be sure, felt that he had the privilege of belonging to an uncommonly religious nation, which was properly rewarded for its piety by this unwonted prosperity."[15] It is this dangerous complacency that the Prophet set out to shatter.

The series of oracles (Am. 1:2–2:16) shows how dramatically he could accomplish this. The people listened, doubtless with approval, to the threatened punishment of God on six neighboring nations: Damascus, Gaza, Tyre, Edom, Ammon, and Moab. Then comes the climax, the seventh oracle (the oracle against Judah—Am. 2:4 f.—is a later addition), and out of the blue the Prophet's thunderbolt strikes Israel! Yahweh is clearly shown to be master of all peoples (cf. Am. 9:7), but he has chosen one people: the whole family which he brought up out of Egypt (Am. 3:1). With the privilege of that choice goes a corresponding obligation: "You only have I known of all the families of the earth, therefore I will punish you for all your iniquities" (Am. 3:2). Israel has received more, and of her more will be required; divine justice demands it.

Amos saw that nothing short of a radical change of life could save Israel (Am. 5:4-6, 14 f.) and he feared that it would not come. He warned those who looked to the "Day of the Lord" as the time of the triumph of God's people over all her enemies that the Day would be darkness and not light (Am. 2:18). He saw that the slumbering Assyrian giant would soon waken and destroy Israel (Am. 3:9-11). There was only one way to avert that wrath to come: "Hate evil, and love good, and establish justice in the gate; it may be that the Lord, the God of hosts, will be gracious to the remnant of Joseph" (Am. 5:15).

2) Hosea

THE
PROPHET   Hosea was a younger contemporary of Amos who preached during the latter years of Jero-

boam II and during the turbulent years that preceded the fall of Samaria in 721 B.C. (though there is no evidence that he witnessed the final disaster). We may fit his ministry between 745 B.C. and 725 B.C. He was a Northerner and a man of higher social position than Amos. We have little information about Hosea; in fact we are provided just enough data to establish one of the thorniest problems in the Old Testament. This is the problem of the prophet's marriage.

The picture is unclear because Hosea was not primarily interested in giving biographical details, since it was the symbolism of the marriage that occupied his attention. The marriage is described in biographical style (Hos. 1) and in autobiographical style (Hos. 3). From this arrangement two questions emerge: Do chapters one and three represent successive stages of the Prophet's experience with one woman, Gomer? Is the woman of chapter three—she is unnamed—another woman and not Gomer? If the second alternative is correct, then chapter one describes the real marriage and chapter three is the description of a prophetic symbol: the purchase and seclusion of a cult-prostitute as a symbol of God's plan for his unfaithful people.

It is much more probable that both chapters recount Hosea's experience with Gomer, for if the woman of chapter three were another, we should expect more explicit mention of it. The analogy with Israel (Hos. 3:1b) suggests that the Prophet is to be reconciled with Gomer, just as Yahweh will take back to him the Israel he had rejected. "In chapter one the theme is the faithlessness of Israel; in chapter three it is the steadfastness of Yahweh's love in the face of infidelity. These themes are not based on one event of Hosea's life, but on a sequence of events in his relations with Gomer."[16]

Am. 1:2 is best regarded as an introduction to the chapter written in the full knowledge of the events. The woman whom Hosea married was not yet a harlot; only later did her true character appear. It is even more likely that his call to prophesy came through his personal experience, and had not preceded it. He came to see that his life mirrored the tragic relationship of Yahweh and Israel and he realized that what had happened to him was guided by a divine purpose. Then, too, the meaning of his broken marriage became clear: "for the land commits great harlotry in forsaking the Lord." As Isaiah will do (Is. 7:3; 8:3), Hosea gave meaningful names to his children, so that he and they become living signs of God's word to Israel. In chapter three we read that the Prophet took back his unfaithful wife. Gomer appears to have become one of the cult-prostitutes mentioned in Hos. 4:13 f. Hosea brought her back and kept her shut off from her lovers until she turned to him: it is thus that Yahweh will treat Israel—a reference to the Exile of Israel (721 B.C.).

The symbolism of the events is clear enough. The marriage with a prostitute signifies that Yahweh is the spouse of a people which worships the Baals—in prophetical language idolatry is "prostitution." The corrective seclusion of Gomer symbolizes the purification of the Exile; the names of woe given to the children point to the chastisement of Israel; the renewed marriage life of Hosea and Gomer promises the restoration of good relations between Yahweh and his people. Of course the whole story has not been told, but it is obvious that Hosea had suffered as husband and father. Out of his own personal experience he realized the aptness of the marriage image to describe the relations between Yahweh and his people.[17]

THE MESSAGE   Hosea was profoundly aware of the Mosaic past. He looked back with nostalgia to the beginning of Israel's tradition; to the desert, to the "days of her youth" (Hos. 2:17 [15]) and to the Covenant (Hos. 13:5). The baneful influence of a materialistic society had caused Israel to forget Yahweh (Hos. 13:6), so Yahweh will bring her back into the desert and speak to her heart (Hos. 2:16 [14]; 12:10). Here the decisive event in Israel's history—the Exodus—comes to the fore. The Prophet reminds the people of the divine intervention that called Israel into being and set it apart from all nations—Yahweh had called his *son* out of Egypt (Hos. 11:1).

Hosea was the first to represent the Covenant relation of Yahweh with his people as a marriage. It would, of course, have seemed natural enough that the Covenant, a treaty between God and Israel, might have been likened to the marriage contract between man and wife. The singular fact is that it is not the contract aspect that was exploited, but rather the love aspect, and especially the love of a husband for his wife. It is out of his own personal experience that the marriage image came to Hosea and that he realized its aptness in describing the relations between Yahweh and his people. He understood that the psychology of human love can wonderfully illustrate the mystery of God's relations with men, the reality and depth of his love. The divine Husband has been betrayed by his wife who has given herself to adultery and prostitution. Yet he seeks only to win her again to him, and if he chastises her it is with that sole end in view. As a last resort he determines to bring her back once more to the conditions of the Exodus, the honeymoon period of their love (Hos. 2:16 f.). In fact, he ultimately goes beyond this and promises to bring her into the harmony of a new garden of Eden (Hos. 2:18) where their love will be the crowning and fulfillment of the mutual love of the first human couple:

"I will betroth you to me forever,
I will betroth you to me in righteousness and in justice, in kindness and in love.
I will betroth you to me in faithfulness,
and you shall know the Lord" (Hos. 2:21 f.).

Hosea has to speak of judgment too; he warns of the approaching Assyrian danger (Hos. 13:15). It will come like a whirlwind (Hos. 8:7) and soon (Hos. 10:15), bringing destruction (Hos. 8:14; 12:12) and death (Hos. 14:1) in its wake. But his lead idea remains the divine goodness (*hesed*), which explains the origin of Israel (Hos. 11:1-9) and which will have the last word (Hos. 2:21 [19]). This divine *hesed* is demanding; what God asks is "steadfast love (*hesed*) and knowledge of God" (Hos. 6:6). True religion is a practical, loving acceptance of God, an affair of the heart.

3) Isaiah 1-39

THE
PROPHET   Isaiah seems to have been an aristocrat and, apparently, a native of Jerusalem. In 740 B.C., the year of the death of King Uzziah, he had his inaugural vision in the Temple. Yahweh appeared to him like an oriental monarch, surrounded by a corps of seraphim who proclaimed the holiness of God. The Prophet's first reaction was fear and trembling (Is. 6:5); but then, cleansed of his sins, he responded without hesitation to the divine call (Is. 6:8). His mission was to be difficult, for the people would refuse to listen to his preaching (Is. 6:9 f.). There was a ray of hope, however: a "Remnant" will remain faithful (Is. 6:13).

Judah had been prosperous under Uzziah and continued so under Jotham (740-736 B.C.). Like Amos before him, Isaiah attacked luxury and social abuses; this is the burden of many of the oracles of chapters 1-5. The Prophet's mission continued under Ahaz and to the end of the reign of Hezekiah. But he seems to have withdrawn from public life during most of the reign of Ahaz (from 734 B.C. onwards). Jewish legend has it that he was martyred under Manasseh. The historical background of Isaiah is given above in Chapter One.

Isaiah was one of the most gifted poets of Israel and a man of deep religious sensibility. A measure of his stature is the fact that more than any other prophet he inspired his disciples, so that an "Isaian school" carried on his ideas and produced oracles in his name until the fifth century B.C.

THE
BOOK   In the Book of Isaiah modern criticism has distinguished a number of different groupings or sections, and these date from different epochs. The three main parts are: Isaiah (chapters 1-39), Second Isaiah (chapters 40-55), and Isaiah 56-66. Though the book has been divided up, modern criticism also takes account of certain constant elements running through the whole. Thus throughout the book God is the "Holy One of Israel" and his transcendence is strongly emphasized. The whole is

pervaded by a messianic and eschatological atmosphere, which makes this book the classic of hope.

Isaiah 1-39 is very complex. It is, to a notable extent, an anthology of prophetical sermons and oracles, with selections even from the sixth and fifth centuries B.C. However, the great bulk of the material of these chapters is the work of the eighth-century Prophet. The genuine prophecies of Isaiah are: 1-11; 14:24—23:18; 28-32—though even here some short passages may be postexilic.

THE   On the one hand Isaiah reaffirms the promise
MESSAGE   made to David by Yahweh; on the other hand he recalls the moral obligations included in the covenant which made Israel a people (5:1-7). His inaugural vision shows to be at once conscious of the awesome holiness of Him who reigns in Zion, and of the grave sinfulness of the nation. Isaiah vehemently denounces this sin, but he has no illusions about the success of his preaching (6:9-13). Blind to the future, deaf to his warnings, the nation is dashing headlong to its ruin. Only a "Remnant" will remain (10:22 f.). And judgment will come very soon in the form of Assyrian domination. In 735, Ahaz, threatened by an anti-Assyrian coalition, appealed to Tiglath-pileser and Judah became a vassal of Assyria.

Isaiah insists on faith—the practical conviction that Yahweh alone matters; one must lean on God alone (8:13; 28:16; 30:15). He vainly sought, in Ahaz, the faith which would turn the king from human alliances and enable him to stand, unperturbed, in the face of threats and even in the presence of hostile armies. Bluntly, he warned him: "If you will not believe, surely you will not be established" (7:9). Ahaz would not listen and the prophet wrote down his words of warning to stand as witness against him. Later, when Hezekiah, counting on Egyptian help, toyed with the notion of revolt, Isaiah opposed him too, and for the same reason: Yahweh, and he alone, will save the nation. For, despite the weakness and faithlessness of its kings, Sion, in the prophet's eyes, remained inviolable: it was the dwelling place of the holy God (28:16; 37:33-35). Thus he could encourage Hezekiah when Sennacherib had overrun Judah and had shut up the king "like a bird in a cage."

The God of Isaiah is the "Holy One." This holiness, thrice proclaimed by the seraphim, indeed expresses the moral perfection of the divinity; above all, however, it indicates his transcendence and his majesty. Furthermore, for Isaiah, Yahweh is the "Holy One of Israel": this transcendent God is a God who acts in history on behalf of his Chosen People. The title itself expresses the mystery of an all-holy God who yet stoops down to frail and sinful man.

4) Micah

THE
PROPHET
The little information we have about Micah comes from two brief notes, one in his own book and the other in Jeremiah. In Mi. 1:1 we learn that Micah was a native of Moresheth (a town of the Shephelah near Gath [cf. Mi. 1:14]) and preached during the reigns of Jotham, Ahaz, and Hezekiah, that is, between 740 B.C. and 687 B.C.; this makes him a contemporary of Hosea and Isaiah. From Jeremiah we learn that the preaching of Micah under Hezekiah was efficacious and played its part in the religious reform of that king (Jer. 26:18-20; cf. Mi. 3:12). His mission, primarily to Judah, did not exclude Israel, whose end he witnessed. His blunt language is like that of Amos and he has that Prophet's approach to social injustice and the same insistence on the justice of God. He saw that the rot, condemned by Amos, had spread to Judah and he proclaimed, in uncompromising terms, the fearful judgment of Yahweh. The fate of Samaria added weight and urgency to his words.

THE
BOOK
Some scholars would argue that the genuine prophecies of Micah are found in chapters 1-3 only—but this is hypercritical. Many, however, would claim that chapters 4-5, at least, are later, for they are concerned with the salvation of God's people and the destruction of its enemies, themes that are largely postexilic. However, it may well be that these two chapters "date from the period of messianic enthusiasm that resulted from the rout

of Sennacherib's army, and therefore can be the work of Micah."[18] There are some later additions, but the bulk of the work is quite conceivable in the setting of the Prophet's own time.

THE MESSAGE Like Amos, Micah viewed social injustice as a crime that cried to heaven for vengeance (Mi. 2-31; 6:9-11), and he stresses the impending divine judgment on this and similar crimes. He does go beyond Amos by looking past the day of reckoning to the reign of Yahweh and the triumph of Sion (Mi. 4-5). In his most famous saying (Mi. 6:8) he presents his message as a synthesis of the preaching of his predecessor and contemporaries: "He has showed you, O man, what is good; and what does the Lord require of you but to do justice [Amos], and to love kindness [*hesed*—Hosea] and to walk humbly [Isaiah] with your God?"

4. PROPHETS OF THE SEVENTH CENTURY AND BEGINNING OF THE SIXTH CENTURY

1) Zephaniah

THE PROPHET The little we do know of Zephaniah is gleaned from his short writing. His genealogy (Zeph. 1:1) is traced back to a certain Hezekiah, who may be the king of that name. The object of the genealogy probably is to make clear that, despite the name of his father (Cushi means "the Ethiopian"), the Prophet was a Judaean. He prophesied under Josiah. The tone of his preaching indicates that his mission fell during the minority of that king and before the reform; most likely between 640 B.C. and 630 B.C., just prior to the ministry of Jeremiah. His oracles give us an idea of affairs in Judah on the eve of Josiah's great task: the cult of foreign deities (Zeph. 1:4 f.); foreign customs (Zeph. 1:8); false prophets (Zeph. 3:4); violence and social injustice (Zeph. 3:1-3; 1:11). His work must have prepared the ground for the coming reform.

THE   Today it is almost universally acknowledged that
BOOK   the whole of the writing—apart from two or three
small retouches—is authentic.

THE   Like Amos, Zephaniah warned his hearers of
MESSAGE the "Day of Yahweh," a universal catastrophe
that will sweep away Judah and the nations. The chastisement of the nations should be a warning to Judah (Zeph.
3:7), but the "shameless nation," defiled by pagan practices and proudly rebellious (Zeph. 3:1,11), will not take
heed. But a Remnant will be faithful, a people "humble
and lowly" (Zeph. 3:12 f.), the 'anāwîm—the "poor of
Yahweh" who will inherit the kingdom of God (Mt. 5:3).

2) *Nahum*

THE   We know nothing of Nahum, not even his place
PROPHET of origin, since Elkosh has not been identified.
It is clear that he prophesied not long before 612 B.C.
(date of the fall of Nineveh), and perhaps soon after 616
B.C. when the downfall of Assyria was imminent. Nahum
was a poet of unusual talent and his words ring with a
passionate patriotism. The fall of the great oppressor is
contemplated with uninhibited satisfaction; but Nahum believes that Nineveh's fall will mean the restoration of Israel
and Judah.

THE   The book opens with an alphabetic psalm (from
BOOK   *aleph* to *kaph* only) (Na. 1:2-9), which develops
the theme of the Wrath of God. In Nahum 1:9—2:3 short
oracles of weal for Judah (Na. 1:12 f.; 2:1,3) are mingled
with oracles of woe for Nineveh (Na. 1:9-11,14). The
poem Na. 2:4—3:19 has the power and movement of the
Song of Deborah (Jgs. 5).

THE   Behind the patriotic outburst at the doom of a
MESSAGE tyrannical foe we find the conviction that the
destruction of Nineveh is an expression of God's justice:
it is the punishment for accumulated crimes (Na. 3:1,4;
3:19). Besides, Nineveh had become the image of a world

that stood opposed to Yahweh; its downfall was his triumph and the triumph of his people.

3) Habakkuk

THE   Unlike the earlier prophetical books, the title
PROPHET   of Habakkuk does not indicate the date of the
Prophet's mission; the *haggadah* in Dn. 14:33-39 is no
help to us. In fact, we know nothing whatever about the
person of the Prophet. Some have argued that the oppressors of Judah are the Assyrians and that the date of the
book would be about 615 B.C. It is more reasonable to
maintain that the Chaldeans (Babylonians) named in Habakkuk 1:6 are in view throughout and that the oracles
fall between Nebuchadnezzar's victory at Carchemish (605
B.C.) and the first siege of Jerusalem (597 B.C.). This
would make Habakkuk a contemporary of Jeremiah.

THE   The Book of Habakkuk has all the appearance of
BOOK   having been carefully composed; and though the
unity of the work has been contested, a strong case can
be made in its favor.

THE   Habakkuk faces up to the scandal of God's ac-
MESSAGE   tion in history and of his treatment of Israel.
How can he, who hates sin, use the ruthless Babylonians,
"guilty men, whose own might is their god" (Hb. 1:11),
to chastise his own people who, though far from guiltless,
are at least "more righteous" than their oppressors (Hb.
1:13)? "It is the problem of evil on an international
plane and the scandal of Habakkuk is also the problem
of many men of our day. To him and to them the same
divine answer is given: by strange and paradoxical means
the all-powerful God prepares the way for the final victory of right, and 'the righteous man shall live by his
faith.' "[19] (Cf. Rom. 1:17; Gal. 3:11; Heb. 10:38.)
Among the scrolls found at Qumran (Cave I) was a *pesher*
(commentary) on Habakkuk 1-2. The book is interpreted
as though it were a prophecy of events in the history of
the Qumran Essenes.[20]

4) Jeremiah

THE **Jeremiah** is better known to us as an individual
PROPHET than any of the other prophets, for his book
contains many passages of personal confession and autobi-
ography, as well as lengthy sections of biography. He
stands out as a lonely, tragic figure whose mission seemed
to have failed utterly. Yet that "failure" was his triumph,
as later ages were to recognize.

Jeremiah came from Anathoth, a village four miles
north-east of Jerusalem. His father, Hilkiah, was a priest
(Jer. 1:1), and so Jeremiah may have been a descendant
of David's priest Abiathar, who was exiled to Anathoth by
Solomon (1 Kgs. 2:26). His prophetic call came in 626
(Jer. 1:2) while he was still quite a young man, and his
mission reached from Josiah (640-609) to Zedekiah (597-
587) and outlasted the reign of the latter; that is to say, he
lived through the days, full of promise, of the young re-
former king, Josiah, and through the aftermath, the tragic
years that led to the destruction of the nation.

There have been very different assessments of Jeremiah's attitude to the reform of Josiah, because we have
very little information about his early career. Some hold
that he was an enthusiastic supporter of it, while others
argue that he was hostile to it. It seems that he was initially
in sympathy with its aims but found himself disappointed
at its eventual outcome. There is no doubt that he thought
highly of the king and was convinced of his sincerity
(22:15 f.), but he quickly realized that "you cannot make
people good by act of parliament."

What he had demanded was sincere and heartfelt repentance, an inner change, and what he found was a more
elaborate liturgy which encouraged self-complacency and
invited hypocrisy (7:21-28; 5:26-31). It was his role to
try, in vain, to bring his people to a true change of heart,
and to hold out hope and lay a foundation for this change,
beyond the crucible of national disaster.

The Book of Jeremiah is a collection made by many
hands. This is typical of all the prophetical books. Indeed

one gets the impression that it is a collection of shorter "books," with some additional miscellaneous material, or that it is not merely an anthology of prophetical material but rather an anthology of anthologies.

THE   In Jeremiah 36 we read of a "scroll" which con-
BOOK   tained a selection or a digest of the prophet's words uttered between 627 and 605. It cannot have been very long since it was read three times in a single day (36:10,15,21) with notable intervals between. The scroll, destroyed by Jehoiakim, was subsequently rewritten and supplemented by Baruch to Jeremiah's dictation (36:32). Here we have the first step in the composition of Jeremiah, but it is idle to try to dig the original nucleus out of the existing book. What we may say, with confidence, is that this nucleus is contained in Jer. 1-25.

Chapters 46-51, which consist of oracles directed against foreign nations, make up another separate collection. While there is no reason to think that the bulk of this material is not genuine, there has been some amplification. The collection is a fairly late attempt to gather together a series of threatening oracles against as many as possible of the neighboring peoples. A third grouping includes chapters 30 and 31 and, perhaps, 32-33 as well; it is Jeremiah's message of hope and is called the Book of Consolation.

We find, then, three collections or "books," separated by a series of biographical narratives. But, since each of the "books" is itself a loose collection, our approach to the book of Jeremiah is not made much easier by their presence. We must accept the fact that, due to the long and complex process of composition, there is no consistent arrangement of the book of Jeremiah. The presence of various literary forms is a further complication. Although these can be described under three major types (poetic sayings, biographical prose, and prose discourses), their variety and distinctiveness make it more difficult to discern the process through which the book was formed.

THE   It is possible to trace the spiritual progress of
MESSAGE   Jeremiah and to see in him the purifying and strengthening effect of suffering, for the most impressive

message of the prophet is his own life. He was a man of rare sensitivity with an exceptional capacity for affection —and his mission was "to pluck up and to break down, to destroy and to overthrow" (1:10) and to cry out, without respite, "violence and destruction" against the people he loved (20:8). We find in him, to a marked degree, personal involvement (4:19), a feeling of solidarity with his people in their tribulation (8:19-23), and even with the land itself in its devastation (4:23-26). The *Confessions* are central for an understanding of Jeremiah (11:18– 12:6; 15:10-21; 17:12-18; 18:18-23; 20:7-18). They are a record of his communing with his God and were surely never meant for public proclamation. Not only are they fascinating because they permit us to gaze into the heart of a prophet; they are also encouraging because they let us see how very human the prophet is. Jeremiah had never really wanted to be a prophet (1:6; 17:16; 20:7-9) and he continued to discuss the trials of his office with Yahweh throughout his life. He was overwhelmed by the sheer burden, the humanly impossible demand of his task; his prayer is the prayer of Gethsemane.

Jeremiah has particular relevance for our day. His predecessors, as far as we know, accepted their prophetic mission with submissiveness—Isaiah indeed with eagerness (Is. 6:9). But Jeremiah had to question and to understand; there is in him even a certain rebellion against decrees of the divine will. And he was not at all satisfied to accept, uncritically, traditional theological positions. He struggled, as the author of Job was to do centuries later, with the problem of retribution (12:1) and asserted the principle of individual (as against collective) responsibility (31:29g). But, mostly, it was his own prophetic office that was his burden, and it was indeed a burden far heavier and more painful than that of any other prophet. He needed, all the more, the support of his God. His obedience was so much the greater because of his questioning, because he felt its yoke, because it led to a feeling of abandonment. It is God's secret why he asked the most faithful of his ambassadors to walk this dark road.

Baruch, the disciple of Jeremiah, has sketched for us the

outward circumstances of his *via dolorosa,* the story of what he had suffered through fidelity to his prophetic vocation between 608 and 587 (Jer. 19:2—20:6; 26; 36; 45; 28-29; 51:59-64; 34:8-22; 37-44). He has shown us the cause of all Jeremiah's suffering. It was the prophet's firm conviction that, at this time, by the instrumentality of Nebuchadnezzar, God was to bring about great changes in the international field, and he would punish Judah with the Babylonian rod of his anger (27:5-11). Consequently, he could hold out no hope of deliverance and asserted, with emphasis, that the capture of Jerusalem was certain (37:8,17; 38:3; 34:2); his advice was to surrender without delay (38:17). Not surprisingly, his preaching was not welcomed by the war party who had forced the hand of Zedekiah.

The sufferings of the prophet are described with a grim realism that recalls the description of the Passion. There are no miracles here, no legion of angels: Jeremiah is abandoned to his enemies and is powerless. And he makes no impression on them. It is not surprising that Christians have seen him as a type of Christ. Jeremiah's clashes with his own prophetical colleagues (those whom we would term the "false prophets") were probably among his hardest battles. We can gather this from his tract against the prophets (23:9-40) and from his dramatic encounter with Hananiah (ch. 28). His message was entirely different from that of his colleagues.

No doubt in part as a result of Jerusalem's remarkable deliverance from Sennacherib's army a century before, and on the basis of Isaiah's words, belief in the inviolability of Zion had hardened into a dogma by Jeremiah's time. The notion that the city could fall and the Davidic dynasty end was simply not entertained. The prophets against whom Jeremiah contended were imbued with this outlook (23:32; 28:3 f.,11). It is understandable that the people listened rather to their encouraging words than to his lonely cry of disaster. Indeed, it appears that he had earned the nickname of old *Magor Missabib* (20:10) from his own familiar warning: "Terror on every side" (6:25; 20:3; 46:5; 49:29).

His calm conviction that faithless Jerusalem would fall is found, among other places, in his letter to those exiled to Babylon in 598 (29:16-20). Yet, in the same context, he can frame a promise: "For I know the plans I have for you, says the Lord, plans for welfare and not for evil, to give you a future and a hope" (29:11). This hope is held out not to those left in Jerusalem, but to the exiles—a point of view more explicitly expressed in the vision of the two baskets of figs (24:5-7). Thus there is the remarkable factor that the same Jeremiah, who so pitilessly demolished false hope, put before his people a positive hope for the future. His efforts to bring his people to their senses had failed, but it is the greatness of the man, and the grandeur of his faith, that precisely during the most tragic moment of his life he spoke his optimistic oracles, notably those of chapters 30-33. He saw that the old covenant would be replaced by a new one (31:31-34) when God would act directly on the heart of man, when he would write his law on that heart, and when all men would know Yahweh.

What is new about the covenant is not the *torah* (the "instruction," "guide of life") which it enshrines. The revelation given at Sinai is not to be cancelled; a covenant given by Yahweh cannot be cancelled or taken back. The covenant itself was not inadequate—it was the people who had failed. What is new is that there is a change in the way in which the divine will is to be conveyed to men. Yahweh is to by-pass the process of speaking and listening, and put his will straight into Israel's heart, and Israel will hear and obey perfectly. Jeremiah's own experience is reflected here: he had preached to a hopelessly obdurate people; he is convinced that God must take a hand and change the heart of man (cf. 32:37-41). He glimpses the era of the Spirit as St. Paul will describe it—the "law of the spirit of life" (Rm. 8:2); he beholds the new man led by the Spirit, moved from within.

The greatest tribute to Jeremiah was paid by the one whose way he had prepared. On that night before the Lord went to his death, he brought the most solemn promise of the prophet to fulfillment: "This cup is the New

Covenant in my blood" (Lk. 22:20). God had set his seal on the life and message of his servant.

APPENDIX: LAMENTATIONS   The Hebrew Bible has this little book among the Writings (the third of its three-fold division of the Bible). The Greek Septuagint and Latin Vulgate place it after the book of Jeremiah, with a title which attributes it to him. The traditional attribution is based on 2 Chr. 35:25 and is supported by the content of the poems which fit the time of Jeremiah—at least, the last days of the prophet. Nevertheless, Jeremiah is not the author of Lamentations. He could not have stated that prophetic inspiration had ceased (Lam. 2:9), nor have praised Zedekiah (4:20), nor have hoped in Egyptian help (4:17); and his spontaneous poetic talent would not have been bound by the artificial form of these poems. Besides, the influence of Ezekiel is noticeable in chapters 2 and 4.

The poems are laments for a fallen Jerusalem and ruined temple, composed by some of those who had been left in Judah after 587. Undoubtedly, they were designed for a simple liturgical service in the ruins of the temple (cf. Jer. 41:5 f.; Zech. 7:3 ff.; 8:19 f.). Through all of them runs a sentiment of invincible confidence in God and an air of profound repentance. They are at home in our liturgy of Holy Week.

5. PROPHETS OF THE EXILE
1) Ezekiel

During the first part of his ministry, Ezekiel's message was very like that of Jeremiah. We might summarize it thus:

> The people of Judah are gravely culpable. God is just and is preparing to punish them. Very soon the siege of Jerusalem and the great deportation will show what an intervention of Yahweh means.

The prophet seeks to justify the action of Yahweh by insisting on the culpability of Israel. The account of Ezekiel's call (1:4—3:15) is not unlike that of Isaiah (Is. 6). Ezekiel too saw the "glory of Yahweh"—one seated on a throne. As an ambassador of the King, he received a scroll containing his instructions: "words of lamentation and mourning and woe." Like Isaiah, too, he is reminded of the difficulty and even the hopelessness of his position: he is to preach without avail, "because all the house of Israel are of a hard forehead and of a stubborn heart" (Ezek. 3:7).

Ezekiel's ministry falls into two periods: from 593 to the ending of Judah with the fall of Jerusalem in 587; and from the fall of the city to 571, the date of his last recorded prophecy (29:17-20). According to the present form of the book, the whole mission of Ezekiel was to the Jewish exiles in Babylon, although the oracles of the first part (chs. 1-24) were addressed to the inhabitants of Jerusalem, and Ezekiel gives the impression of being present in the city (cf. 11:13). However, he always distinguishes sufficiently between the exiles (to whom he speaks in the second person) and the people of Jerusalem (whom he threatens in the third person), and his schematic picture of the city is not that of an eye-witness. The great interest with which he followed the course of events in Jerusalem, with all of an exile's deep concern, sometimes gives the *impression* that he is living among the people in the homeland.

THE   Ezekiel was by temperament a visionary and four
BOOK   great visions dominate his book: The Chariot of Yahweh (1-3), the Sins of Jerusalem (8-11), The Dry Bones (37), and The New Jerusalem (40). The vivid imagination displayed in these descriptions is also evident in the allegories: The Sisters Oholah and Oholibah (23), The Shipwreck of Tyre (27), The Crocodile of the Nile (29 and 32), The Great Cedar (31), The Dwellers in Sheol (32). At the same time, simple everyday things could inspire him: a sentry mounting guard (3:17-21), a wall being built (13:10-16). His own personal experiences could move him: the death of his wife (24:15-24), a mysterious and prolonged illness (4:4-17). Ezekiel used the technique of prophetic gesture more often and more elaborately than any other—for example, the symbols of Jerusalem under

siege (4:1-3,7), of years of exile (4:4-8), of exile and siege (12:1-20), of the union of Judah and Israel (37:15-28). Paradoxically, his powerful imagination and his elaborate allegories find expression in a style which is generally stiff and dry.

At first sight the book of Ezekiel seems to display a remarkable unity of plan, but on closer examination the impression of striking unity is dissipated. It follows that Ezekiel is no different from Isaiah 1-39 and Jeremiah—a compilation made by the disciples of the prophet. We find in the book a series of oracles and symbolic actions, all precisely dated, though they do not stand in correct chronological order. More specifically, these fall into two series of dates: (i) passages which concern Jerusalem and Israel; (ii) oracles against foreign nations.

THE MESSAGE   In one respect Ezekiel differs notably from Isaiah and Jeremiah: when he speaks of sin, he has in mind less transgressions of the social and moral commandments than liturgical offences. For him, the cause of Israel's approaching fall lay in a failure in the sphere of the holy. She had defiled the sanctuary (5:11), turned aside to other cults (8:7-18), and taken idols into her heart (14:3-11); in a word, she had "rendered herself unclean" in the sight of Yahweh. The great allegories of chapters 16 and 23 and the historical retrospect of chapter 20 are emphatic on this score. There can be no mistaking the priestly point of view. Though truly a prophet, Ezekiel's roots are in the tradition of the priesthood; and so, the standards by which he measures Israel's conduct are the "ordinances" and the "judgments" which Yahweh gave to his people (5:6; 18:5-9; 33:25). The priestly tradition colored his preaching, and his great vision of the future (40-48) is aptly called the Torah of Ezekiel.

The three historical reviews (chs. 16; 20; 23) hold not only liturgical interest; they occupy a special place in Israel's conception of her history. True, the allegories are lengthy and repetitious, and the language is consciously crude. Ezekiel seems to wish to say all that can be said about Israel's unfaithfulness, her indifference to the love of

God, and her utter failure to obey. The picture he paints could scarcely be blacker than it is. But we need to keep in mind that he is justifying the divine judgment which is to come about in the near future: even the divine patience has at last run out. We also need to observe that the prophet points to God's saving will—now more than ever seen to be free and unmerited (cf. 16:60-63; 20:40-44). In this sense, the three somber chapters are the prelude to the glory of Yahweh's saving act, for it is evident that his salvation cannot be based on any good in Israel herself.

Ezekiel is concerned not only with the nation but with the individual too. At this time the old conception of a man's guilt being incurred by his whole family, especially by his children who had to answer for it, was proving inadequate (cf. Jer. 31:29; Ezek. 18:2). The celebrated vision of the sins of Jerusalem (Ezek. 8-11) provided Ezekiel with the elements of the solution; he developed these and proclaimed the moral principles in chapter 18 (cf. ch. 35). From these principles a fundamental religious truth, belief in retribution after death, will one day be deduced—but that day is centuries later. In the meantime, the prophet showed himself the great champion of individual responsibility. True, this idea was not absent from Yahwism before his time; it was present, vaguely at least, from the beginning, but now it receives powerful expression:

> The soul that sins shall die. The son shall not be responsible for the iniquity of the father, neither shall the father be responsible for the iniquity of the son; the righteousness of the righteous shall be his alone, and the wickedness of the wicked shall be his alone (18:20).

Ezekiel was called to be a "watcher" for the house of Israel, a pastor of his people (33:1-9). He had not only to deliver the divine "word" of prophecy; he was also like a sentinel on the city wall who would warn the people of approaching danger, who would give Israel a chance to "turn," to repent. He saw his pastoral office as not just an extension of his prophetic calling; rather, it became his duty to live for other people, to seek them out and to place himself at their disposal. His words were designed to give comfort and hope to the individual and to demonstrate that Yahweh desires only repentance and obedience. When the heaviness of divine judgment brings his exiled people to the verge of despair, he faces the problem squarely. He faces the alternatives of life and death: man lives by righteousness, he dies through sin. Man is free to choose between the two and the open door to the choice is repentance (33:10-20). The exiles are to live by Yahweh's word—he will perform his promised works (12:24 f.). It is Ezekiel's pastoral concern to help his people to see themselves as they really are and to know their God as he truly is. Then right relations will be restored and he will be their God in earnest, and they will be his people indeed.

Ezekiel had a sublime vision of the majesty of God, one notably influenced by the priestly tradition to which the prophet is heir. Yahweh is exalted above all creation, enthroned in majesty above his universe; no words can describe him. He is the holy one, transcendent, rather remote; hence the prophet's insistence on a worthy liturgy. Yet, at the same time, he sees this God as the redeemer. In a moving chapter (34) Yahweh is portrayed as the good shepherd who cares for his sheep, who performs the functions of the righteous ruler, who searches for the lost in dark ravines, and who finds for them fresh pasture. That is why Ezekiel's call for a sincere conversion to Yahweh, for a new heart and a new spirit, points to a personal God, a God who is intensely present. His insistence on the need of interior religion indicates a personal relationship to God which, if not as movingly expressed as it is by Jeremiah, is nonetheless very real.

To the exiles, suffering from a sense of the distance of Yahweh and a despair over the destruction of Jerusalem, Ezekiel offers words of hope and comfort in two great visions:

(a) The vision of the Chariot of Yahweh (ch. 1)— whatever its date—is meant to prove to the prophet and to his hearers that Yahweh is not attached to Palestine, nor even to the Temple, that he is essentially mobile, that he can follow (indeed has followed) his exiled people in order to dwell with them.

(b) The vision of the Dry Bones (37:1-10) with its commentary (37:11-14) teaches that the chastisement is not final, that God can raise up what appears to be dead, and that he promises a triumphal return to Palestine.

The messianism of Ezekiel is distant and rather obscure, but it is nonetheless real. He has an unshakable faith in a future salvation (5:3; 20:40-44). In chapter 34 Yahweh's care for his people is contrasted with the neglect of the kings. Yahweh himself will bring about the restoration of his people, and then the Messiah will appear (34:23 f.). His portrait of the faithful shepherd, the new David, who tends his sheep with justice and love, is not only the inspiration of the shepherd image in John 10; it also expresses the ideal embodied in the very man who uses this image—Jesus himself.

In the promise of a new heart and a new spirit (Ezek. 36:23-28) the prophet echoes Jer. 31:31-34. Here, too, the purpose of God's saving activity is the re-creation of a people capable of obeying the commandment perfectly. "A new heart I will give you, and a new spirit I will put within you; and I will take out of your flesh the heart of stone and give you a heart of flesh" (Ezek. 36:26). Thus equipped with a new heart and the bestowal of the spirit, Israel will be able to walk in the path of the divine ordinances. The promise of salvation is prefaced by the words: "It is not for your sake, O house of Israel, that I am about to act, but for the sake of my holy name" (36:22). This is a recurring thought: that by gathering Israel and bringing her back to her own land, Yahweh manifests his holiness in the sight of the nations (20:41; 28:25; 36:23). Israel, by her infidelity, had profaned the name of her God before the nations; now God owes it to his honor that the covenant should be re-established. But there is more to it than that. Many of the predictions of coming events conclude with the words: "that they may know that I am Yahweh." The final goal of divine activity is that Yahweh should be recognized and worshiped by those who have never known him, or who do not know him as he is.

In the last nine chapters of his book (40-48) Ezekiel describes exactly the New Temple and its rites; and the division of the country among the sanctuary, the prince, and the twelve tribes. These chapters, from our modern viewpoint neither very intelligible nor very interesting, have really had a greater influence than the rest, for they give expression to a religious and political ideal that, in large measure, set the pattern for the restoration of Israel.

Ezekiel is often named the father of Judaism. Sometimes the title is a reproach, as if he were responsible for the imperfections of decadent Judaism. It is true, of course, that by a certain ideal of aloofness and of ritual holiness, he contributed to aspects of postexilic Judaism which found exaggerated form in pharisaism. But he was certainly not a legalist. Indeed, with him the conception of the office of the prophet receives a new development (3:16-21; 33:1-9): if he fails to warn the wicked man, the prophet can incur his guilt. And, in reproaching the false prophets, he points to what, in his eyes, was the heart of prophetic service: they "had not gone up into the breaches, or built a wall for the house of Israel" (13:5). A prophet must not hold back but must fight in the vanguard; he must lay down his life for his people. A legalist would be more circumspect in language, more prudent in conduct, and would not lay his own life on the line!

2) *Second Isaiah*

AUTHORSHIP AND DATE Since the end of the eighteenth century, and especially from the late nineteenth century, scholars have come to separate Is. 1-39 (which, in the main, goes back to the Prophet of the eighth century B.C.) from the remainder of the book. In this second part, chapters 56-66 are regarded as postexilic, while, for the rest, "the general opinion of scholars is that Isaiah 40-55 forms a unit, coming from the period just before and just after Cyrus' victory over Nabonidus of Babylon (539 B.C.)." The author of these chapters, an anonymous

prophet of the Exile, is, for convenience, named Second
Isaiah (or Deutero-Isaiah). We have no inkling of the
identity of this man, one of the foremost poets and theologians of Israel. All we do know is that he certainly be-
longed to the "Isaian school" and found his inspiration in
the work of his eighth-century master.

Between Isaiah and Second Isaiah there are many re-
semblances and constant links. It is significant that Is.
1-39 contains a notable proportion of later material, some
of it much later than Second Isaiah. This is why we can
speak of an Isaian school of thought and see in Second
Isaiah the outstanding exponent of that school.

THE   Second Isaiah knows that Yahweh is Lord and
MESSAGE   that his word lasts forever. His control of present world events is manifest, as is the fact that he was
master of "the former things." Like Hosea, this prophet
goes back to the origins of Israel's history, back to the
desert, the starting point of new faith in God. Its transformation in 40:3-5; 41:17-20 proclaims the glory of the
Lord and is at the same time (43:16-21; 49:11) part of
his provident care for his people. The past was a kernel
holding the germ of future growth but the New Exodus
is what they must think about now (43:18 f.).

The new deliverance will lead to a new Sion; most of
49-55 speaks of this. Thus, Yahweh again consoles his
people (49:15). Has he given Jerusalem a bill of divorce?,
he asks (50:1 ff.). Sion, the barren woman, is to rejoice, to
make room for innumerable children (54:1 ff.; 49:19 ff.),
and all the years of exile are summed up in one phrase
(54:6-8).

Whatever Israel's doubts may have been, Second Isaiah
had no doubt about the immediacy of Yahweh's intervention. A vivid, primitive portrayal of the warrior God
(42:10-17) underlines the urgency of his coming and recalls the ancient victory song of Deborah in Jgs. 5. Yahweh, victorious in battle, the Lord of hosts—this was one
of Israel's earliest ideas of him. Another image going back
to early times was that of the *go'el*, the redeemer or
avenger. This title designated the man who would uphold

and protect the rights of members of the clan. He would buy back one sold into slavery, redeem property, avenge murder. Yahweh is Israel's protector, her *go'el*.

Another title began to take on significance in the 6th century B.C., that of Creator. Up to the time of the captivity in Babylon the problem of creation does not seem to have merited much consideration, although other peoples had elaborated mythologies to explain it. From these Israel adopted some terminology, but the contrast between her understanding and theirs at this time makes a striking impression. It is to the author of Gn. 1, another 6th century writer, that we owe a profound and systematic meditation on the beginning of things. Second Isaiah, too, was with the "New Theology." He repeatedly declares that Yahweh creates. The words he uses show what he means. These are three: "to form," "to make," and the verb never predicated of anyone but God, *bara*. While God's creative act is comparable to that of man, it is at the same time unique. In this, too, he is God—"and there is no other"; and he creates not only things past but also present beginnings, "new things," created now.[21]

Second Isaiah cast Israel in the role of witness and mediator. It stands at the center of world history as a witness to monotheism (Is. 40:18,25; 43:11; 45:5 f., 18-22; 46:5-9). Israel is a mediator too because it will be the means of the conversion of all nations (Is. 40:5; 42:10; 45:14; 52:10; 54:5); the universalist outlook is strikingly expressed in Isaiah 45:22-24; 44:5. The Israel entrusted with this responsible role is a qualitative Israel: the "Remnant" (Is. 41:14; 46:3), the "poor of Yahweh" (Is. 49:13), the servants of the Lord (Is. 44:1; 54:17).

The Assyrians and Babylonians had been the scourges of God in the punishment of his people; now appears one who is a deliverer. Isaiah 41:2 f.,25 present in veiled terms the conqueror, who is expressly named in Isaiah 44:28—45:13—Cyrus, Yahweh's "messiah" (Is. 45:1), his shepherd (Is. 44:28), his loved one (Is. 48:14). This is the man, raised by God, who will set the exiles free (Is. 45:13) and rebuild Jerusalem and its Temple (Is. 44:28;

45:13). The anti-Babylonian oracles of Isaiah 13-14, looking to the capture of Babylon by Cyrus, belong to this
same epoch.

The triumphal advance of the liberator opened up a
perspective of return. Israel, led by Yahweh (Is. 52:11 f.),
will journey in solemn pilgrimage along a *Via Sacra,* a
processional way, across the Syrian desert (Is. 40:3 f.).
At that passage the desert will be transformed (Is. 40:3-5;
41:17-19; 43:19 f.) and Yahweh will reign in Sion (Is.
52:7). The return is a new Exodus, another decisive intervention of Israel's God. This is not all poetic imagery,
for the restoration is a sign of salvation; it is a redemption, a new Creation.

3) *The Suffering Servant of Yahweh*

Frequently throughout Second Isaiah Israel is named the
"Servant of Yahweh." Yet there are four passages (Is.
42:1-7; 49:1-6; 50:4-9; 52:13—53:12) where the title has
a distinctive meaning and can no longer be said to designate Israel in the same manner as elsewhere. We have
no intention of going into the vexed question of the relationship of these poems among themselves and to their
context, nor do we intend to give a survey of the immense
field of interpretation. All we shall do, when we have
pointed out some characteristics of the Servant figure, is
to outline two main lines of interpretation.

The Servant of the canticles stands in contrast to the
Israel-Servant found elsewhere in Second Isaiah. Israel is
deaf and blind (Is. 42:19 f.); the Servant hears (Is.
50:4 f.) and enlightens (Is. 49:6). Israel is sinful (Is.
42:18-25; 43:22-28); the Servant is just (Is. 53:9-11).
Israel has need of consolation (Is. 41:9 f.); the Servant
has a courageous faith (Is. 42:4). The Servant must restore Israel (Is. 49:5 f.).

The Servant is a mysterious figure who has been chosen
by Yahweh and filled by his Spirit (Is. 42:1) and who
plays a role at once national and universalist. On the one
hand, though he seems inseparable from the Israel whose
name he bears, from the Remnant "in whom God will

be glorified" (Is. 49:3), he must lead back Jacob (Is. 42:6) and reassemble (Is. 49:5 f.) and teach (Is. 50:4-9) Israel. On the other hand he must be the light of nations. Patient (Is. 50:6) and humble (Is. 53:7) he will, by his sufferings and death, accomplish the plan of Yahweh: the justification of sinners of all nations (Is. 53:8,11 f.).

While the identification of the Suffering Servant is, and doubtless will remain, a widely-discussed problem, almost all scholars would agree that he is a messianic figure. No one who acknowledges the unity of the two Testaments and accepts the messianic role of Jesus can doubt this for a moment.

6. PROPHETS OF THE SIXTH CENTURY[22]

1) *Isaiah 56-66*

AUTHORSHIP According to the generally-accepted view, Isaiah 56-66 is the work of a postexilic prophet, or prophets, of the Isaian school, and was produced in Palestine shortly after the return from the Exile (538 B.C.). Several reasons indicate that these chapters are distinct from Is. 40-55. The subject matter is no longer deliverance and restoration; in many passages the people are regarded as already settled in Palestine and social injustice has had time to make itself felt (Is. 58:3-6; 59:3 f.; 56:10-12). In Is. 40-55 the Prophet's attention is fixed on the immediate future—the fall of Babylon and the deliverance, but this is no longer the perspective of Isaiah 56-66. It is also generally held that these chapters are the work of different writers.

THE Isaiah 56-66 is influenced both by Second MESSAGE[23] Isaiah and by Ezekiel. From the latter these chapters take the notion of a city sanctified by its Temple, and their insistence on fasting and the sabbath observance. To Second Isaiah they owe their interest in the Gentiles and their preoccupation with interior religion, and the idea of the glory of Sion. From both of these prophets comes the idea of a new and purified Jerusalem. Here, for the last time in the prophetical books, idolatry is denounced.

2) *Haggai*

THE   The first return from Babylon in 538 B.C., un-
PROPHET   der Sheshbazzar, was on a very small scale and
the returned exiles soon became disillusioned. A later
group under Zerubbabel and the priest Joshua gave new
hope, and the task of rebuilding the Temple was warmly
urged and supported by the Prophets Haggai and Zechariah who seem to have come with Zerubbabel. We have
no information concerning Haggai beyond that of his book
and the brief references of Ez. 5:1; 6:14. His recorded
prophecies are dated from August to December, 520 B.C.
(Hag. 1:1,15; 2:1,10,20); the construction of the Second
Temple was begun in August of that year, and the immediate concern of these prophecies is the rebuilding of
the Temple.

THE   The Prophet addresses Zerubbabel the gover-
MESSAGE   nor and Joshua the high priest and all the "people of the land" (Hag. 2:4)—the "Remnant" (Hag.
1:12-14; 2:2) in the prophetical sense. He exhorts them
to rebuild the Temple, for this will mark the beginning of
the messianic era. Thus messianic hope takes flesh again
around the sanctuary and around Zerubbabel, the Davidic
prince, the Lord's "signet ring" (Hag. 2:23).

3) *Zechariah 1-8*

Scholars are agreed that chapters 9-14 of Zechariah are
not authentic; indeed they are much later than the time of
the Prophet.

THE   Zechariah was a contemporary of Haggai, and
PROPHET   apart from the references in Ez. 5:1 and 6:14
we have no independent information concerning him. Obviously he was greatly influenced by Ezekiel and was probably a priest-prophet. His oracles are dated from Novem-
ber, 520 B.C., to December, 518 B.C. Zechariah, like Haggai, was preoccupied with the rebuilding of the Temple,

and also, and more emphatically, with national restoration and the demands of ritual purity and morality.

THE   Zechariah is concerned with the rebuilding of
MESSAGE the Temple, but he regards this event as the
prelude to the messianic age that is his principal concern.
He sees Zerubbabel as the Davidic Messiah (Zech. 3:8-10;
6:12 f.) but, true to the spirit of Ezekiel, he also exalts the
high priest Joshua (Zech. 3:1-7). Indeed, the two
"anointed ones" (Zech. 4:14) will rule together in perfect accord (Zech. 6:13). This is not to say that these are
two Messiahs—as two Messiahs were later expected at
Qumran—but Zechariah resurrected the idea of royal messianism and linked it with the priestly perspective of
Ezekiel.

7. PROPHETS OF THE FIFTH CENTURY
1) Isaiah 34-35; 24-27

ISAIAH 34-35: THE   It is not strictly accurate to de-
"LITTLE APOCALYPSE" scribe these chapters (and the
same is true of Is. 24-27) as apocalypse—though some
features of the apocalyptic form are present (for example,
universal judgment, the triumph of God's people).

1. *Authorship and Date.* The two chapters, which form
a unit, are inspired by Is. 40-66 (cf. Is. 34:6-8 and
63:1-6; 35:10 and 51:11). Chapter 35 is written throughout in the style of Second Isaiah: Yahweh's final salvation is depicted as a New Exodus. The chapters are
patently a product of the Isaian school, and though it is
not possible to fix a precise date, the early fifth century
B.C. seems probable.

2. *Ideas.* "The two chapters, probably by the same
hand, constitute a sort of diptych: an Inferno followed
by a Paradiso."[24] Chapter 34 describes the Day of Yahweh, the final judgment of God—for Edom is a type of the
enemies of God's people. Chapter 35 is the redemption of
Israel. Prominent are the transformation of nature and the
Holy Way along which God leads his people home. A vast
return of the Diaspora is presented as a solemn pilgrimage
to Sion.

ISAIAH 24-27: THE   1. *Authorship and Date*. These
"GREAT APOCALYPSE"   chapters are a collection of originally independent eschatological prophecies and hymns
brought together to form a unified composition. In view
of this arrangement it is not easy to posit unity of authorship for the various pericopes. In thought, style, and language the section is postexilic, but it is impossible to fix a
precise date. A fourth-century B.C. date is not impossible,
but it seems better to settle for the fifth century B.C. At
any rate, Isaiah 24-27 is the last product of that prolific
Isaian school which had so long kept alive the spirit of the
great eighth-century B.C. Prophet.

2. *Ideas*. Hymns and oracles differ in outlook. The
theme of the hymns is the ultimate triumph of the City of
God. The apocalyptic oracles have in view all humanity
and the whole universe: God will chastise the host of
heaven and the kings of earth (Is. 24:21), and he will
destroy Leviathan, symbol of the forces of evil (Is. 27:1).
Then all nations will be invited to the great messianic feast
(Is. 25:6-8) and the dispersed of Israel will be gathered
together (Is. 27:12 f.).

2) *Malachi*

AUTHORSHIP   The Book of Malachi is really an anony-
AND DATE   mous writing, because the name "Malachi"
comes from Malachi 3:1 where the word is a common
noun meaning "my messenger." The title of the writing
(Mal. 1:1) corresponds to Zech. 9:1 and 12:1; it is likely
that originally these were three anonymous collections.
Malachi is later than 516 B.C., the date of the renewal of
cult in the Second Temple (cf. Mal. 1:13) and seems to
be earlier than the interdiction of mixed marriages by
Nehemiah in 445 B.C. (cf. Mal. 2:10-12). A date shortly
before 445 B.C. is likely.

THE   The Book of Malachi is strongly influenced by
MESSAGE   Deuteronomy (cf. Mal. 1:2; Dt. 7:8; Mal. 1:9;
Dt. 10:17; Mal. 2:1,4,33; Dt. 18:1; Mal. 2:6; Dt. 33:10;
Mal. 4:4; Dt. 4:10), and is preoccupied with the cultic

faults of priests (Mal. 1:6—2:9) and people (Mal. 3:6-12). The Day of Yahweh is presented in a cultic setting and the world to come will see the perfect cult (Mal. 3:4). By his criticism of mixed marriages (Mal. 2:10-16) the Prophet hits at current abuses and anticipates the reforms of Nehemiah and Ezra. The contribution of the writing to messianic doctrine is restrained but significant: the "pure offering" of Malachi 1:11 is the perfect Sacrifice of the messianic era, and the forerunner of the Messiah is indicated in Malachi 3:1,23 f.—the Gospels tell us that this new Elijah was John the Baptist (Lk. 1:17; Mt. 11:10-14; 17:12).

3) Obadiah

AUTHORSHIP AND DATE We know nothing of Obadiah apart from the fact that he was a man of intense nationalistic outlook. This prophecy, the shortest Old Testament writing, falls into two parts: 1) 1-14 + 15b: a curse on Edom because of her treatment of Judah after 587 B.C.; 2) 15a + 16-21: the destruction of Edom is the presage of the judgment of Yahweh on all the enemies of God's people, and of the final restoration of Jerusalem.

THE MESSAGE An appreciation of the situation in Judah from 587 B.C. to the mission of Nehemiah will help to explain the bitter resentment of Obadiah. Here is no trace of the universalism of Second Isaiah; instead we find that narrow nationalistic outlook so brilliantly satirized in Jonah—indeed the author of Jonah might have modeled his prophet on somebody like Obadiah! This writing must be seen as a footnote to the great volume of prophetic literature—while we should not overlook the fact that it exalts the power and justice of Yahweh.

8. PROPHETS OF THE FOURTH CENTURY
1) Joel

AUTHORSHIP AND DATE Joel is mentioned nowhere else; all we learn of him from his book is that he was a postexilic prophet of Judah. As in the case of Obadiah, the two parts of the book (chapters 1-2 and 3-4) might indicate dual authorship, but the date of the work is not affected by this possibility since both parts are closely associated. The book is, in all probability, a product of the early fourth century B.C. This date is indicated by borrowings from late writings (for example, Jl. 2:11 and Mal. 32; Jl. 3:4 and Mal. 3:23), and by the particularist and cultic mentality of the writing. The apocalyptic style of chapters 3-4 is also in favor of a late date. On the other hand, the changed perspective of these chapters does not demand another author: the description of a calamitous plague of locusts could easily lead to a picture of the final plague of God, his judgment on sinners. While we cannot be certain, it is reasonable to regard the book as the work of one author.

THE   Joel marks a transition from prophecy to apoc-
MESSAGE   alyptic, but it is essentially a prophetical book. The Prophet not only, in typical prophetic fashion, interpreted a terrible plague as a punishment of sin, but also saw it as a symbol of the Day of Yahweh. "Joel is the prophet of Pentecost (cf. Jl. 3:1 f.). He is also the prophet of penance, and his invitation to fasting and to prayer, borrowed from the ceremonies of the Temple or modeled on them, fit quite naturally in the Christian liturgy of Lent."[25]

2) *Zechariah 9-14*

AUTHORSHIP The second part of the Book of Zechariah
AND DATE   consists of two groups of material (chapters 9-11 and 12-14) introduced by the term *massa* ("burden" —oracle of woe). In the traditional order of prophetical books Mal.—which has the same heading (Mal. 1:1)— comes last, immediately after Zechariah; it appears that Zechariah 9-11; 12-14, and Mal. were three collections of prophetic material which were placed at the end of the

prophetical writings, by way of appendix. Later, the third of these collections was regarded as a separate book (Mal.) and the other two were attached to Zechariah 1-8; this obtained the significant number of twelve Minor Prophets.

The center of interest of Zechariah 9-14 is certainly not that of the first part of the book: there is no mention of Zerubbabel or of Joshua, nor any word on the rebuilding of the Temple. Assyria and Egypt appear only as symbols of all oppressors and, on the other hand, the Greeks are mentioned in Zechariah 9:13. The conquest alluded to in the oracle of Zechariah 9:1-8 would seem to be the action taken by Alexander the Great to safeguard his flank after the battle of Issus (333 B.C.). It would seem that Zechariah 9-14—an anonymous compilation—was given final shape at the close of the fourth century.

THE Zechariah 9-14 is important for its messianic MESSAGE doctrine. The oracle of Zechariah 12:1—13:6 speaks of the re-establishment of the house of David. This restoration is linked with the death of a mysterious personage: ". . . he whom they have pierced" (Zech. 12:10); doubtless we should look to the Suffering Servant of Is. 53. The Messiah is presented as a royal figure, but he is not clothed in worldly pomp (Zech. 9:9 f.). In the messianic age all things in the land of Israel will be sacred to the Lord (cf. Ezek. 40-48). Quotations from, or allusions to, Zechariah 9-14 are frequent in the New Testament (for example, Mt. 21:4 f.; 27:9; 26:31; Jn. 19:37).

9. MESSIANISM

Any study of the Old Testament would be sadly incomplete without a treatment of messianism. While the theme is not exclusively prophetical, it was so notably developed in prophetical writings that we can fittingly deal with it at the close of this chapter. However, we shall have scope for little more than a sketch of that distinctive feature of Israel's religious heritage.

1) *Development of the Messianic Idea*[26]

Israel had broken with the prevalent cyclic conception of
time: in the biblical view history was meaningful; it had a
beginning and, tending towards a God-given goal, it will
have an end. It is a view that was particularly applicable
to the history of Israel, dominated by the idea of covenant
and presented in the Bible as *Heilsgeschichte*. This original
conception of history is the basis of messianic hope. Messianism, in the widest sense of the word, is Israel's expectation of a glorious destiny. More precisely, it is the expectation of an ultimate era of salvation that involves the
manifest inauguration of the kingdom of God. This reign
of God will first be established over Israel and then,
through Israel, it will extend to all mankind.

It is to be noted that messianism consists essentially in
confident expectation of the establishment of God's reign;
there was, at first, no mention of a Messiah. And even
when, with the passage of time, the figure of a Messiah did
emerge, he was always regarded as God's instrument in
the bringing in of his kingdom—an event that called for a
special intervention of God in person. The Messiah was
never the object of Israel's messianic expectation; he was
the one through whom that expectation was to be fulfilled.
Instinctively we think first of the Messiah who has come
and we measure all the past by him. But Israel looked to a
future that was vague even to the prophets who were
granted a glimpse into it, and to eyes not fully enlightened
the Messiah of the future did not stand out as a sharply-
defined figure.

Messianic expectation ran through the whole of Israel's
history; the essential feature of that hope was there from
the beginning, but the centuries and events brought clari-
fication and refinement. While hope remained constant
there was a steady growth in the appreciation of the election of Israel and her true destiny. The figure of the Messiah emerged and began to assume an increasingly important role in the nation's hope. We may trace three

clearly-defined stages in the development of messianic doctrine.

1. GENERAL MESSIANIC EXPECTATION Messianic expectation has its roots in the historical beginning of the people of Israel. The call of Abraham—the first moment in the election of a people—already explicitly looked to the destiny of that people and to its universal mission (Gn. 12:1-3). The succeeding patriarchs heard the same promise and were links in a line that reached into the future. Israel's hope was confirmed by the events of the Exodus and by the Sinai Covenant; the seed of Abraham had at last grown into a people, and the Promised Land was in sight. Possession of that land marked another step forward, but the slow and painful conquest brought home to the people that fulfillment would come only through sweat and tears—history would prove how high the cost was to be. In the meantime Israel, precariously established in Canaan, did not lose hope when, under Philistine pressure, the plan of God seemed in jeopardy. As it turned out, the weathering of that crisis carried the messianic expectation on to a new level.

2. DYNASTIC MESSIANISM The first attempt at kingship under Saul had failed, but his successor, David, brought Israel to the most powerful political position she was to achieve. It was a moment of high hope and great expectation. God was patently with the king, and the oracle of Nathan (2 Sm. 7:8-16) linked the destiny of Israel to the family of David, and the people continued to look hopefully and steadfastly to the dynasty. This faith explains the different outlook on royal succession in the Northern Kingdom and in Judah. In the North there was nothing sacrosanct about any royal family; indeed usurpation was the order of the day. In Judah, however, though assassination was not unknown, the principle of Davidic succession was rigidly adhered to: none but a son of David might sit on the throne of David.

The Davidic king had become the representative of the people, and the father-son relationship that had been es-

tablished between Yahweh and Israel on the basis of the
Sinai Covenant (Ex. 4:22) now existed, in a more personal way, between Yahweh and the king (2 Sm. 7:14).
But the divine promise had been made to the dynasty as a
whole and the individual king owed his privileged position
to his membership of that dynasty. Individuals might fail,
but the divine plan would not be thwarted for it was guar-
anteed by an unconditional divine promise. Yet, as it
turned out, not only did individual kings prove wanting,
but the dynasty itself ended in disaster.

It is not clear when the prophets had grown disillusioned
with the historical Davidic kings: it seems that Jeremiah
was the first (though he may have been anticipated by
Isaiah) who looked to the future and realized that the
special intervention of God which would usher in the messianic age called for one, specially raised up, standing in
contrast to the historical kings. At any rate, the disaster
of 587 B.C. and the end of the monarchy in Judah forced
men to take stock of the situation. From the conflict of
two discordant facts—an irrevocable divine promise of per-
petuity to the house of David, and the actual failure of the
monarchy—a new refinement of messianic fault emerged,
and the third stage of development was reached.

3. PERSONAL   When the ultimate failure of the monarchy
MESSIANISM   was evident, and when it did in fact come
to an end, Israel's prophets and theologians looked again
at the facts. The one constant element was the unconditional promise to the Davidic dynasty—that could not fail.
But since the monarchy was no more, the only possibility
now was that God would, in the future, raise up a son
of David and through him bring about his reign over Israel
and over mankind. Messianic expectation was no longer
centered on a dynasty but on a person. True, this man was
still a son of David, but he was not just one of a line: he
was an extraordinary personage of the future. This Messiah was seen as a king, but he was presented too as a
prophet—the Suffering Servant of Yahweh—and as the
glorious Son of Man of the end time. And while Jesus was
greeted by the people as son of David, he preferred to

present himself as one who, through suffering, would enter into his glory.

MESSIANISM WITHOUT A MESSIAH We should not forget that messianic expectation looked to the coming of the kingdom of God. This was the essence of it, and the role of the Messiah in the establishment of the reign of Yahweh could, in practice, slip into the background. Particularly in postexilic times, when the monarchy had ceased, men could look again straight at Yahweh, the King of Israel, and celebrate his kingship; they came to live in vivid expectation of the future kingdom of God. The idea of the kingship of Yahweh is presented with great clarity in Second Isaiah (for example, Is. 41:21; 43:15; 52:7) and is exclusively the theme of the Kingship of Yahweh psalms. Here we cannot do more than draw attention to this important aspect of messianism, but it is well to recall that what Jesus proclaimed was not primarily the coming of the Messiah, but the presence of the kingdom of God.

2) Messiah

It may seem a singular procedure to have treated, however briefly, of the development of the messianic idea before turning to an explanation of the term "messiah." However, it was important to make the point that messianic expectation predated the expectation of a messiah and could exist without direct reference to a messiah. We believe that our procedure is justified when it is seen against the background of historical messianism.

The noun "messiah" (*mashiah*) comes from a verb meaning "to anoint," "to rub with oil," a verb that in the Old Testament is reserved almost exclusively for sacred anointing, consecration by oil. The derived substantive (messiah) designates the subject of anointing and is applied only to persons.[27]

1. In ancient Israel there is frequent mention of royal anointing (Jgs. 9:8; 1 Sm. 9:16; 10:1; 15:1; 16:3,15 f.; 2 Sm. 2:4; 12:7; 1 Kgs. 1:34 f.; 5:1; 2 Kgs. 9:3-12; 11:12;

23:30). It is certain that, before the Exile, the king was the Anointed One *par excellence*. From the moment that the oracle of Nathan (2 Sm. 7:12-16) had fixed the hope of Israel on the Dynasty of David, each king of that line became in his turn the actual "messiah" through whom God would accomplish his purpose in regard to his people. And the accession of each new king brought renewed hope and the expectation of peace and justice and prosperity—the blessings of the messianic age—and eventual rule over the whole world.

2. No text prior to the Exile speaks of the anointing of priests. After the Exile the priesthood grew in prestige: now that there was no king the high priest became the leader of the community. The high priest had become the Anointed Priest (Lv. 4:3,5,16—these are postexilic additions—[2 Mc. 1:10]); therefore an actual "messiah" as the king had formerly been.[28]

3. The prophets were not anointed. The apparent exception in 1 Kgs. 19:16, which has reference to the anointing of Elisha, is explained by 2 Kgs. 2:9 where Elisha is to receive "a double share of the spirit" of Elijah. This metaphorical anointing by the Spirit is expressly indicated in Is. 61:1.

After the Exile the high priest had inherited the royal anointing and had become the focus of messianic expectation. True enough the oracles of Zech. 4:8 and 6:12 give Zerubbabel the title of "Branch" (cf. Is. 4:2; Jer. 23:5; 33:15), but it is already significant that Joshua and Zerubbabel are associated in Zech. 4:11-14 and are called the two "sons of oil," that is, anointed ones. A clear development in the same line is the substitution of Joshua for Zerubbabel in the symbolic coronation (Zech. 6:9-14). In Dn. 9:25 f. the "anointed one" is the high priest Onias III. The failure of the later Hasmonaeans—who had assumed the office of high priest—brought about a return to the old Davidic hope. The Psalms of Solomon (apocryphal), especially Ps. 17, are a witness to this trend.[29]

Jewish eschatology gave an important place to the expectation of a messiah: a royal messiah everywhere; a priestly messiah in certain milieux. The agent of salvation appeared also as the Servant of Yahweh and the Son of Man, while the promises always looked to the inauguration of the kingdom of God. It was not easy to coordinate all the data; the coming of Jesus alone shed full light on the prophecies and reconciled apparent contradictions.[30]

---

[1] C. H. Dodd, *The Bible Today* (New York: Cambridge University Press, 1960[2]), pp. 50 f.

[2] Ethical monotheism: belief in one God who imposes a moral order; the one God of Israel is a just God who demands of his people obedience to his righteous law.

[3] See A. Gelin, IB, pp. 469-76. This whole chapter owes much to Gelin's fine treatment of the prophets (IB, pp. 467-82).

[4] Albright, *op. cit.*, pp. 301 f.

[5] *Ibid.*, p. 306.

[6] See W. J. Harrington, *Record of Revelation: The Bible* (Chicago: The Priory Press, 1965), pp. 29-34.

[7] See Gelin, *op. cit.*, p. 478.

[8] Dodd, *op. cit.*, p. 51.

[9] Roland de Vaux, BJ, p. 973.

[10] See Harrington, *op. cit.*, p. 114.

[11] See D. R. Jones, PCB, n. 447 c.

[12] This is one of the many notable features of the *Bible de Jérusalem.*

[13] See Gelin, *op. cit.*, pp. 479-82; J. Muilenburg, PCB, n. 413.

[14] See B. W. Anderson, *Understanding the Old Testament* (Englewood Cliffs, N.J.: Prentice-Hall, 1957), p. 228.

[15] Dodd, *op. cit.*, p. 39.

[16] Anderson, *op. cit.*, p. 242.

[17] See Gelin, *op. cit.*, pp. 395 f.

[18] Vawter, *op. cit.*, p. 131.

[19] Roland de Vaux, BJ, p. 986.

[20] See Harrington, *op. cit.*, p. 78.

[21] E. Dorgan, *New Hope for a Conquered People* (Dublin: The Catholic Communications Institute, 1971), 15-17.

[22] While Ezekiel and Second Isaiah obviously lived in the sixth century B.C., they stand apart from the other, later, sixth-century prophets because their mission was to the exiles in Babylon.

[23] See Gelin, *op. cit.*, p. 569.

[24] J. Bright, PCB, n. 445 a.

[25] Roland de Vaux, BJ, p. 988.

[26] See A. Gelin, "Messianisme," *Dictionnaire de la Bible* (Supplement) (Paris: Letouzey et Ané, 1961), V, cols. 1165-1212 (further references to this work will be abbreviated DBS); J. L. McKenzie, *Myths and Realities* (Milwaukee:

Bruce, 1963), pp. 203-50; P. F. Ellis, *The Men and the Message of the Old Testament* (Collegeville, Minn.: The Liturgical Press, 1963), pp. 312-42; J. Obersteiner, "Messianismus," *Bibeltheologisches Wörterbuch*, J. B. Bauer, editor (Graz-Wien-Köln: Verlag Styria, 1962²), I, pp. 848-69 (further references to this work will be abbreviated BW); Bonnard-Grelot, "Messie," VTB, pp. 608-14.

[27] See C. Larcher, *L'Actualité Chrétienne de l'Ancien Testament* (Paris: Cerf, 1962), pp. 93-96.

[28] See Bonnard-Grelot, *art. cit.*, 610 f.

[29] See Larcher, *op. cit.*, p. 94.

[30] See Bonnard-Grelot, *art. cit.*, 611.

FOUR

THE WISDOM LITERATURE

THE WISDOM OF THE EAST
THE WISDOM OF ISRAEL
THE BOOK OF PROVERBS
THE BOOK OF JOB
QOHELETH
SIRACH
THE BOOK OF WISDOM
THE DIVINE WISDOM
THE SONG OF SONGS

As we read through the Old Testament we must notice that the theme of the Exodus keeps on recurring, often unexpectedly. Indeed, we cannot miss the resonance of that mighty intervention of God which marks the emergence of Israel as a nation; and we cannot fail to realize that this is unquestionably the central event in Israel's memory. But the Exodus is not only a great religious moment, it was essentially a historical experience. Henceforth Yahweh is the God of Israel, and Israel is the people of Yahweh. The literature of the Old Testament bears striking witness to Israel's keen awareness of its unique history. It is all the more surprising, then, to find that in one important and extensive group of writings within this literature the historical sense is almost entirely lacking—only the latest of the wisdom books regard the special destiny of the people of God. This is perhaps the main reason why the wisdom literature stands apart from the rest of the Old Testament writings, though the subject matter and the style also mark its distinctiveness. Nevertheless it is an authentic part of the peerless literary and religious legacy of Israel.

In this chapter we shall first examine briefly the wider

setting as well as the peculiar national genius of the Israelite wisdom movement. Then we shall range rather hur-
riedly through the five wisdom books,[1] and close with a
consideration of the developed concept of divine wisdom.
It is hoped that the treatment will give a hint of the immense worth of these writings, and a further appreciation
of the literary as well as of the religious achievement of the
Chosen People.[2]

1. THE WISDOM OF THE EAST

In this matter of wisdom, as in most other respects, Israel
was not unique (under certain aspects at least), but fitted
into the common pattern of the ancient Middle East. The
Bible has many allusions to the wise men of other peoples
(cf. 1 Kgs. 5:10 f.; Jer. 49:7; Obad. 8). Archaeology has
brought to light extensive remains of a widely-diffused wisdom literature. Nearly all of it is older, and most of it much
older, than anything in the Bible. It is also evident that the
movement was international, for wisdom writings circulated widely and had an influence far beyond the country
of their origin. The sage, as such, was not circumscribed
by age or culture; though he was, inevitably, a man of his
own epoch and milieu, the problems with which he dealt
were human problems, and these, fundamentally, are much
the same wherever men dwell.

The Eastern sages are met with especially among the
ruling classes or, more precisely, among the court officials:
ministers and counsellors, scribes and annalists. They
formed an educated and cultured class who readily became
teachers: passing on to others the results of their experience, inculcating the principles which should guide conduct, and pointing out the path to success in an administrative career. Thus they composed wisdom writings: sayings and instructions in Egypt; fables and allegories in
Babylon; maxims and picturesque parables in Canaan and
Phoenicia. Such writings were intended for those who
would follow in the footsteps of the sages or, as we might
put it, for the formation of aspiring civil servants. We
must not imagine, however, that the wisdom movement

did not look beyond such a utilitarian horizon. The sages, we have remarked, were very much concerned with human problems; ultimately this meant the problems of the individual. Looming largely in their field of interest was man's anguished search for the meaning of life; and it is not surprising that this quest should have inspired some of the most notable products of the movement, works like the Egyptian *Dispute over Suicide,* the Babylonian *Dialogue on Human Misery,* and the *Book of Job.*

2. THE WISDOM OF ISRAEL

1) *The Origin of Wisdom in Israel*

Just as the Pentateuch was attributed to Moses and the Psalms to David, so also the bulk of Israel's wisdom literature was attributed to Solomon. He is traditionally the author of Proverbs, Qoheleth, Wisdom, and the Canticle of Canticles—and his influence is not reckoned to end with these. While, apart from Proverbs (or certain sections of it), the attribution of these writings to Solomon is consciously pseudepigraphical, a valid basis for the procedure lies in the king's undoubted interest in wisdom. His own reputation for wisdom is illustrated by the popular story of his decision in the case of the two women who claimed the same baby (1 Kgs. 3:16-18). Elsewhere we read that "Solomon's wisdom surpassed the wisdom of all the people of the East and all the wisdom of Egypt," and that people from all other lands came to hear him for "he was wiser than all other men" (1 Kgs. 4:30,31).

Indeed, the Book of Kings goes so far as to claim that Solomon uttered three thousand proverbs and a thousand and five songs (1 Kgs. 4:32); an assured reputation must underlie such a manifest exaggeration. At any rate, he undoubtedly must have played an important part in the development of a wisdom movement in Israel, though his own personal contribution to the wisdom literature or, at least, to the extant literature, is modest. We have no reason to doubt that some of the maxims in the oldest sections of Proverbs are his, but the rest of the sapiential books are much later than the age of the wise king. What is more important is that it was Solomon who first provided the atmosphere in which wisdom could flourish. His own outlook was cosmopolitan and he welcomed foreign currents of thought; his close relations with Egypt and Phoenicia were not, and could not have been, exclusively commercial. Besides, in order to handle his complicated administration, Solomon had to organize a civil service, and in this, the cultured milieu of the day, wisdom thrived. A striking example of Egyptian influence about this time is the literary dependence of Prv. 22:17–24:14 on the *Instructions of Amen-em-opet*. Of course, such dependence is to be expected: coming, as she did, late to the field, Israel had to learn from her neighbors. But soon her sages developed a typically Israelite literature; before long, not only in terms of a higher morality, but also on literary grounds, she had far outstripped her masters.

2) *The Nature and Forms of Wisdom in Israel*

The court origin of a large element of Hebrew wisdom is manifest. Much of Proverbs and a great deal of Qoheleth and Sirach have to do with conduct in society and, as a rule, the "thing to do" comes in for careful consideration. The scribe should be a man of taste and elegance, a man possessing prudent reserve, one who shuns ostentation—in short, the perfect gentleman. Since the very purpose of the instructions was to form a cultured civil service, their whole tenor could not have been any different. Significantly, respect for constituted authority is repeatedly inculcated.

We must not forget, however, that this is not the whole of it: many wisdom writers searched the deeps of man's heart and weighed his yearnings and his fears. Quite apart from this, nevertheless, the Israelite sages were well aware that true wisdom comes from God only. It is emphasized that the celebrated wisdom of Solomon was a gift which the king had obtained in answer to his prayer (1 Kgs. 3:6-14). It is God alone who gives to man "an understanding mind to discern between good and evil" (1 Kgs.

3:9). The biblical writers are conscious that the first sin was a revolt against this truth and that ever since, the same wily Serpent has held out to man the same false wisdom (Gn. 3:5 f.,13; Wis. 2:24). This is the wisdom of men who judge all things from the human viewpoint, like the scribes who make the law of Yahweh into a lie or like the royal counsellors who follow their own way (Jer. 8:8; Is. 29:15 ff.). But the true human wisdom has a divine source; God can and does communicate wisdom to whom he pleases. This is why the wisdom writers are pleased to contemplate the divine Wisdom: they realize that their own has flowed from it.

In the Old Testament the chief term for the basic literary unit in the wisdom literature is *māshāl*. The simplest type of *māshāl* is a proverb in couplet form, with the lines of the couplet almost always in parallelism. In the oldest sections of Proverbs this form prevails almost exclusively. But the *māshāl* is not exhausted by this simple literary unit—its range is bewildering. The noun meaning "comparison," "parable" is derived from a verb meaning "to become like," "to be comparable to." It is applied not only to proverbs but also to long poems or hymns (Jb. 27:1; 29:1; Pss. 49 [48]:5; 78 [77]:2), and it can designate a "taunt song" (Is. 14:4 ff.; Mi. 2:4 f.; Heb. 2:6 ff.) or a "byword" (Dt. 28:37; Pss. 44 [43]:15; 69 [68]:12 f.; Ezek. 14:8). In view of this complex usage we can best render *māshāl* as "saying," with all the vagueness of that term. It is noteworthy that in the Gospels, *parabolē* is a rendering of the Hebrew word (or of its Aramaic equivalent) and has the same elasticity of meaning.

3. THE BOOK OF PROVERBS

It is clear that the Book of Proverbs, as we know it, is the result of a long process of growth. The cultural and literary activity which produced the work began in the era of Solomon and the book seems to have received its final form in the fifth century B.C. (or perhaps as late as the fourth century B.C.). Thus Proverbs is representative of some five centuries in the life of Israel's wisdom movement; it is, in a true sense, an anthology of wisdom.

PRV. 1:1-7	TITLE	
1:8—9:18	*Prologue.* Complex literary form. —Invitation to acquire Wisdom; the fruits of Wisdom and its praise.	Anonymous
10:1—22:16	Couplets in antithetical (10-15) or synonymous (16-22) parallelism. —Rules of conduct.	"Solomon"
22:17—24:34	Quatrains in synonymous parallelism. —Duties to neighbor; temperance; laziness.	"The Sages"
25-29	Couplets and quatrains. —Various maxims.	"Solomon"
30:1-14	Quatrains in synonymous parallelism. —Divine Wisdom; pettiness of men.	"Agur"
30:15-33	Numerical sayings in synonymous and progressive parallelism. —Varied.	Anonymous
31:1-9	Quatrains in synonymous parallelism. —Instruction for kings.	"Lemuel"
31:10-31	Alphabetic poem in progressive parallelism. —Praise of the Virtuous Wife.	Anonymous

1) The Structure of Proverbs

On grounds of internal criticism (attribution to different authors; variety of matters treated; diversity of literary forms) eight sections may be discerned in the Book of Proverbs.

The last editor of Proverbs added, by way of conclusion, the alphabetical poem in praise of the Virtuous Wife (Prv. 31:10-31), and provided the long Prologue (chapters 1-9). (The consequent late date is to be kept in mind when assessing the doctrine of the prologue.)

2) *The Message*

Proverbs conceives a world divided into two distinct categories: the wise and the foolish. An intermediate category is that of the uncommitted, the simple or inexperienced who have yet to fall under the influence of one of the two groups and join one or other of them. The contrast "wise-foolish" (and not "wise-ignorant") is significant: even the highly-skilled, cultured man is a "fool" if he has not grasped the true meaning and purpose of life. The sages do not waste time addressing themselves to the foolish, but turn to the wise, and to the simple who may yet become wise.

In keeping with the accepted notion of wisdom, the maxims of Proverbs are concerned with right conduct. Self-discipline is urged: sobriety in food and drink; control of the tongue. Many of these counsels strike further into the moral order and regard honesty in business, faithfulness in marriage, impartiality in judgment, and the value of almsgiving. On a still deeper level it is recognized and stressed that religious faith is the necessary foundation of the moral life. Ultimately, the wise and the foolish are identified with the religious and the ungodly, for religion, or the "fear of the Lord," is the one basis of wisdom (Prv. 1:7). Thus it is that, if Proverbs does resemble the wider wisdom literature, especially that of Egypt, it has its own special characteristics. For Israel's wisdom, though much of it is mundane enough and trite enough, is never merely secular. Wisdom does not really come by observing human conduct or by reflecting on the teaching of the sages. It is a fact of course that attentive observation and balanced reflection do play their part in the education of the wise man, but he can attain true wisdom only when he is guided by a reverential fear of God (Prv. 15:33).

In this, wisdom joins hands with the prophetic and priestly traditions and Israel's sages would give unhesitating approval to the declaration of Jeremiah: "Let not the wise man glory in his wisdom . . . but let him who glories glory in this, that he understands and knows me, that I am the

Lord who practice kindness, justice, and righteousness in
the earth" (Jer. 9:23 f.). The Torah also plays its part;
in particular, the deuteronomic doctrine of reward and
punishment is now applied to the individual. Where the
historians had shown the principle at work in Israel's history, the sages contended that the happiness and misery
of every man depended on his fidelity to or disregard of
Yahweh's law. But the principle had to be applied within
the narrow limits of this life; after a while the logic of the
facts troubled men and impelled them, in sweat and tears,
to prepare the ground for a new seed, the revelation of an
afterlife, with reward and punishment beyond the grave.

4. THE BOOK OF JOB

The Book of Job belongs to the stage when the idea of
individual retribution in this life palpably ran up against
insoluble practical difficulties. For an understanding not
only of this book but of the great bulk of the wisdom literature, it is important to have in mind that the Hebrews had
a very vague notion of the afterlife. At death a man did
not quite disappear, he continued to exist in some dim,
undefined way in Sheol; but in that dismal abode of the
dead all, rich and poor, good and bad, were equal. Given
this situation, it is inevitable that, throughout most of the
Old Testament, retribution of good or evil was seen in an
exclusively earthly perspective and was concerned with
temporal sanctions only. It was not until the first half of
the second century B.C.—a good two centuries later than
the Book of Job—that the doctrine of retribution after
death made its appearance (cf. Dn. 12:2). Progress, divinely guided, was made by troubled souls (cf. Ezek. 18:2;
Jer. 31:29; Mal. 2:17) searching for a solution that was
truly the measure of reality. The Book of Job marks the
longest stride in that progress.

Job has become a figure of proverbial patience, but anyone who has troubled to read the Book of Job may well be
at a loss to understand how he came to win such a reputation. After all, he curses the day of his birth in no uncertain terms, and more than once he practically serves

God an ultimatum. But what if there are two Jobs! This, indeed, is more or less the case. The author of the book found his inspiration in a story about a legendary Edomite sheik who, when tried by the Satan—not yet the evil spirit of later biblical tradition—proved unshakably faithful. On the basis of this story, Israel's greatest poet built his masterpiece.

1) Division

It is clear that in Job we have a carefully-planned literary scheme. The central poetic part is made up of three cycles of discussion (Jb. 3-31), followed by Yahweh's answer from the whirlwind (chapters 38-41). The third cycle (chapters 22-27), however, has been thrown out of order, either through scribal confusion at an early stage or, and this is more likely, through the efforts of an editor who wished to tone down Job's utterances. The poem on wisdom (chapter 28) has been interpolated by later editors (perhaps by the original author). The speeches of Elihu (chapters 32-37) are also an intrusion into the literary scheme. Elihu is not mentioned as one of Job's friends in either the prologue or epilogue. He has nothing to say during the three rounds of discussion, and his advice comes as an afterthought, following the statement that "the words of Job are ended" (Jb. 31:40). It is generally held that the Elihu speeches were added by a later Jewish writer who sought to uphold the traditional doctrine more rigorously than the three friends. (Many scholars tend to regard Jb. 39:13-18 and 40:15—51:26 as later additions to the speeches of Yahweh.)

1. The prose Prologue (Jb. 1:1—2:13).
2. Three cycles of discussion.
   a) Job's lament (3).
   b) First cycle:
   Eliphaz (4-5).
      Job's answer (6-7).
   Bildad (8).
      Job's answer (9-10).

       Zophar (11).
          Job's answer (12-14).
  c) Second cycle:
       Eliphaz (15).
          Job's answer (16-17).
       Bildad (18).
          Job's answer (19).
       Zophar (20).
          Job's answer (21).
  d) Third cycle:
       Eliphaz (22).
          Job's answer (23:1—24:17,25).
       Bildad (25:1-6; 26:5-14).
          Job's answer (26:1-4; 27:1-12).
       Zophar (27:13-23; 24:18-24).
          Poem on Wisdom (28).
          Job's final defense (29-31).
          Speeches of Elihu (32-37).
3. Yahweh's answer from the whirlwind.
  a) The first speech (38-39).
          Job's submission (40:1-5).
  b) The second speech (40:6—41:34).
          Job's repentance (42:1-6).
4. The prose Epilogue (42:7-17).

The Book of Job has an undeniable unity but, in its present form, it is equally certain that the literary equilibrium has been disturbed. The relationship between the prose sections and the poetic part is easy to divine. The author had come across a popular writing (*Volksbuch*) which suggested the idea of his work and which served to preface and round off his poem. Into the first part of the traditional story he introduced the three friends of Job (Jb. 2:11-13), and, in the epilogue, he also inserted a reference to the interlocutors (Jb. 42:7-9). Then he composed the poetic dialogue and the discourses of Yahweh. Later, the same author—or, more likely, another—going over the work, introduced the person of Elihu (chapters 32-37) and the praise of Wisdom (chapter 28). (The speeches of Yahweh may likewise have received additions

[Jb. 39:13-18; 40:15—41:26]). The book thus has an organic unity. The original work (prose booklet, dialogue, theophany) has *grown* into its present form by the additions of new elements which have been skilfully fitted into the original plan.

2) *Authorship and Date*

The date and authorship of Job are difficult to determine because the writer gives us no hint of the historical circumstances of his time. The hero of the book is an Edomite sheik and the scene of the drama is in Edom, but there is no doubt that the writer was a Jew. "The time—patriarchal age—and the place—Edom—are part of the imaginative setting; the thoughts expressed are those of a Palestinian Jew of the postexilic period."[3]

While modern scholars are agreed that the book belongs to the postexilic period, they may differ as to the precise date within that period. A postexilic date is indicated by the language of the book and by the fact that, in general, the wisdom literature is a product of the postexilic age. The end of the fifth century B.C. would seem to be the most likely date.

The prose narrative is earlier than the poetic composition. Ezekiel mentions Job together with Noah and Daniel (a Phoenician sage) as legendary righteous men (Ezek. 14:14,20); the story of Job (that is, the prose narrative) must have circulated orally for many years before it was written down as we now have it.

3) *The Problem of Job*

In the dialogues Job wrestles with a tormenting problem: he is suffering, yet knows himself to be innocent. The inadequacy of the traditional position[4] has become apparent, but men can close their eyes to a disturbing new truth. Here the three friends are the champions of "orthodoxy"; they have accepted the classic teaching without question and quite refuse to admit that it will not fit the facts of the present case. Their position is very simple: suffering is punishment for sin; if a man suffers it is because he is a sinner—the facts must be made to fit the traditional viewpoint! Hence they proceed to comfort the sufferer by pointing out that he must be a sinner—and a great sinner at that judging by his sufferings—and they grow more and more insistent as he protests his innocence.

For Job does protest. He *knows* that he is innocent; at least he is certain that he has done nothing to deserve such trials. His world has broken in pieces about him, for he too had subscribed to the traditional doctrine. Now he sees that it does not meet his case—but he has no other solution. He struggles manfully with his problem, but there is no outlet; his sufferings are now utterly meaningless and he is tempted to question the justice of God. This Job is not the improbable hero of the older tale, but a man of flesh and blood, striving to find a glimmer of meaning in the inscrutable ways of God, a man groping in thick darkness —but it is the darkness of faith. The grandeur of Job is that he can "defy the sufferings which overwhelm him to rob him of his faith in a hidden God."[5] In his agony he may have criticized God and his ways, but this is balanced by his cry for God and his yearning to meet him. And, fittingly, in the climax, God does speak to Job. Then, overwhelmed by the marvels of God's works, he makes his final profession of faith and his submission:

"I had heard of thee by the hearing of the ear,
    but now my eyes see thee;
Therefore I despise myself,
    and repent in dust and ashes" (Jb. 42:5 f.).

Yet, though he speaks of having seen God, the mystery remains, for Job has no knowledge of retribution beyond the grave. God's ways towards him are still inscrutable. But if, theoretically, the problem looms as largely as ever, he has solved it as a practical issue: he has come to accept God as he is and he no longer questions the divine purposes. Hence, though we may have shattered the stained-glass Job—the inhumanly patient man—we have raised instead the real Job, the man of faith. And from him we can learn that faith in a God whose ways we cannot know does lead to patience, and to peace.

5. QOHELETH

The Book of Qoheleth (Ecclesiastes) comes after Job and marks a further development in biblical thought. Once again the problem of personal retribution is taken up, and again the traditional doctrine is criticized. This is not to say that the position of Job is just restated in more emphatic terms—it is not at all a parallel treatment of the matter. Job was able to show that suffering does not presuppose sin in the sufferer and can be quite independent of guilt; but what about the reward of the virtuous man? It is precisely this other side of the picture, the view that the just man must be happy, that Qoheleth questions. He observes that when a man, even a just man, has all he wants, he is not content. Now, at last, the inadequacy of the accepted position has been well and truly challenged, but the time is not yet ripe for the revelation that will enable theologians to come forward with the final, satisfactory solution. In the meantime, even so gifted a sage as ben Sirach will still take the "orthodox" view for granted. Conservatism can often be a very effective soporific.

Qoheleth is of a very different cast: he refuses to take a mechanical view of Providence. For him God is no accountant keeping a rigid balance sheet and doling out life and death, happiness and misery in strict proportion to man's virtue or guilt; God is in no way answerable to man. In contrast to the naïve optimism of some of the sages, he denies that the human mind can ever understand the ways of God: "I saw all the work of God, that man cannot find out the work that is done under the sun. However much man may toil in seeking he will not find it out; even though a wise man claims to know, he cannot find it out" (Qoh. 8:17). This is very much the final position of Job, but Qoheleth takes the further step of opposing the view that would regard earthly happiness as the goal of life. Life cannot be a mere seeking after pleasure. Happiness is never man's due; his duty is to accept whatever comes from the hands of God: "In the day of prosperity be joyful, and in the day of adversity consider; God has made the one as well as the other" (Qoh. 7:14). Qoheleth does not solve the problem, but he has cleared the way by contesting illusory solutions and by forcing men to face up to the veritable state of affairs. His is a providential role. "Qoheleth did not reach the threshold of the gospel. But it is true to say that before one could understand: 'Blessed are the poor' it was first of all necessary to have recognized that: 'Blessed are the rich' is not true."[6]

1) *Authorship and Date*

"Ecclesiastes," the name by which the book is usually known, derives by way of the Vulgate from the Greek *Ekklēsiastēs* of the Septuagint (LXX), and is a rendering of the Hebrew *Qōheleth*, a feminine singular participial form, peculiar to Qoheleth which is connected with the noun *qāhāl*—"assembly." Apparently the Hebrew word refers to "one who speaks to an assembly," that is, a speaker or preacher. Thus Qoheleth (Ecclesiastes) is not a proper name but a description of a function.

The title (Qoh. 1:1) identifies Qoheleth with Solomon (cf. Qoh. 1:12,16; 2:4-10), but this is no more than a literary convention, since many of the wisdom books are similarly attributed to the king. Most scholars agree that Qoheleth comes, chronologically, between Job and Sir. The language of the book is late Hebrew, with many Aramaisms; on the other hand we may not descend too low—fragments of two manuscripts of Qoheleth have been found at Qumran and the oldest of these (4QQoh[a]) has been dated about 150 B.C. Sometime in the second half of the third century B.C. would seem the most likely date of composition.

Qoheleth is influenced by Greek culture, but not in any fundamental way. Its era is that of Ptolemaic dominance, and hence of close contact with Egypt—not the Egypt of the ancient sages but an Egypt very much Hellenized. The atmosphere of Hellenism was all around; hence the author could not escape it. But the most we may legitimately say is that Qoheleth, while remaining essentially Israelitic in outlook, does mark a step towards Greek thought.

The fourth of the five festal *megilloth* (rolls), Qoheleth was read (and still is read) in the synagogue on the third day of the Feast of Tabernacles. It adds a serious note to the festivities by reminding the congregation that the joys of life are transient.[7]

2) The Outlook of Qoheleth

Qoheleth is a complex character. He has been differently evaluated according as one or other aspect of his thought has been seized upon and emphasized to the exclusion of other elements. He has been branded a pessimist—an existentialist *avant la lettre*—or again an epicurean, even a hedonist. Most commonly, perhaps, he is regarded as a thoroughgoing sceptic. Each of these views can find some support in his book, but all of them are far wide of the mark. He is not a sceptic, but a religious man who has faith in a just God and who professes, with conviction, his belief in the reality of Providence (Qoh. 3:11,14 f.; 8:17; 11:5). Nor is he an epicurean. Understandably he is no Christian ascetic, but he counts the pleasures of this life as gifts of God (Qoh. 2:24; 3:13; 5:18; 9:7) and condemns the abuse of them (Qoh. 2:1 f.; 11:8,10). He is not really a pessimist either (although he is a thinker who has written of pessimism), for he rejoices in creation (Qoh. 11:7) and has confidence in the foreknowledge of God, he who is man's last end (Qoh. 6:10; 12:7). In other words, he is a realist. And, in the ultimate analysis, he is something more. He has plunged more deeply yet into the dark labyrinth uncovered by Job, and he too, despite his vain searchings for an outlet, clings desperately to his faith in God.

6. SIRACH

The problems which were of such concern to the author of Job and to Qoheleth did not trouble other sages; ben Sirach for one (writing about 180 B.C.) does not consider them at all. He raises no doubt regarding temporal reward and punishment; rather he expounds the traditional doctrine in calm and concrete fashion (Sir. 1:12 f.; 9:11 f. [16 f.]; 11:14-26; etc.). His is the practical aim of teaching piety and morality and his book is an important witness to the moral outlook and to the doctrine of Judaism shortly before the Maccabaean age. (Sirach must have helped to form those Jews who opposed the advance of Hellenism.) The spirituality of the book is grounded on faith in the God of the Covenant, a faith which shows itself in works of cult and in the practice of justice and mercy towards one's neighbor. Thus ben Sirach exhorts men to humility, kindness to the poor, and almsgiving. He denounces pride, sins of the tongue, adultery, covetousness, and sloth. In general, man must flee sin of every kind. Prudence is highly recommended in one's attitude to women—like most of the sages he is something of a misogynist—and in various social contacts. He repeatedly gives advice on family duties. All this moral instruction is inspired by religion, the service of God, and the book abounds in religious counsels that are entirely practicable.

1) Authorship and Date

The Greek text of the book has the title, *The Wisdom of Jesus, Son of Sirach*, or, *The Wisdom of Sirach*. In Sirach 50:27 the author is named: "Jesus, the son of Sirach, son of Eleazar, of Jerusalem." The Hebrew text of the same verse reads: "Simeon, son of Yashuah, son of Eleazar, son of Sira," but textual critics omit "Simeon." The title *Ecclesiasticus* has come to us via the Old Latin; it indicates that the book, though not everywhere accepted as canonical, was at least "ecclesiastical," that is, it might be read in church. It was, in fact, used as a handbook for the training of catechumens. As a deuterocanonical book Sirach was rejected at the Synod of Jamnia about the year 90 A.D., and though, as part of the Greek Bible it was accepted from the beginning by the Christian Church, it was not regarded as canonical in certain quarters.

The author, named "Jesus" in the Prologue, names himself Sirach in 50:27 (29); what we know about him is gathered from his book and from his grandson's prologue to the Greek translation.

2) Text and Versions

Sirach was certainly written in Hebrew, but by the eleventh century A.D. the Hebrew text had disappeared, due no doubt to the fact that the book had been excluded from the Hebrew canon. Then in 1896 and the following years a substantial part of the Hebrew text, amounting to about three-fifths of the original, was found in the *geniza*[8] of an old synagogue in Cairo. When we compare the extant Hebrew text with the Greek, Syriac and Latin versions, it becomes clear that there are two forms of Sirach, one notably longer than the other; these are referred to, respectively, as the Primary and Secondary Texts. A rough idea of the differences between the Primary and Secondary Texts can be had by comparing the *Revised Standard Version* (substantially Primary) with the *Douay Version* (substantially Secondary). The additions of the expanded text are not the work of ben Sirach; indeed they are appreciably later than his time, and not all Catholic scholars accept them as inspired. In general, they supplement the rudimentary eschatology of the Primary Text by stressing the ideas of judgment at or after death, of conscious survival in the next world, of the moral aspects of human immortality, of lasting punishment and reward beyond the grave (e.g. 6:23; 15:8; 16:22; 17:25; 18:22; 20:4; 24:46).

3) Composition and Plan[9]

The literary form of the book would suggest that it has no regular and logical plan. Many commentators are content to distinguish two parts: a collection of proverbs (Sir. 2:1–42:14); the praise of God and of the ancestors (Sir. 42:15–50:29). It must be admitted, indeed, that the various themes follow one another without apparent order and that some of them are treated two or three times without any notable development. It is not likely that ben Sirach would have composed such a work all at once. Most of the material would have grown up over the years as he carried on his work of teacher, and the final phase would have consisted largely in the editing of that composite material. It is along these lines that we may explain the many repetitions of the book and also the clear mark of one hand on the whole of it.

It seems possible, however, to distinguish five parts in the book. Each of these parts is composed in an identical manner: a doctrinal introduction exalting wisdom (Sir. 1:1-30; 24:1-34; 32:14—33:19) or God the Creator (Sir. 16:24—18:14; 42:15—43:33), followed by practical teaching in no particular order. A comparison of the five introductions brings to light a parallel structure: they begin with God, or the divine Wisdom, and lead to the idea of wisdom communicated to man. The author concludes with a bit of practical advice which may take the shape of an exhortation to himself to write or of an invitation to fidelity or to thanksgiving. On the other hand, they exhibit a notable development. Wisdom is first envisaged in its widest acceptation, universal, destined for "all flesh," for "men" in general (Sir. 1:10,25). The second introduction (Sir. 16:24 ff.) represents the doctrine of God the Creator. In chapter 24 (third introduction) Wisdom is communicated to Israel, to Sion. The fourth introduction (Sir. 32:14 ff.) insists on the cult of the Law of Moses. Finally the treatment of the wisdom and power of the Creator God (Sir. 42:15 ff.) introduces the eulogy of the ancestors of Israel. In other words, the book, at first universalist in its outlook, tends to concentrate more and more on the Chosen People, regarded as the true depositary of the divine Wisdom on earth. Ben Sirach shows a particularly profound knowledge of the Pentateuch. It is significant that the development of his book is analogous to that of Genesis which begins with the Creation of the world and ends with the twelve patriarchs—and thus with the twelve tribes of Israel (Gn. 49:28)—after having successively eliminated all other races. If the body of the work does not show the same development, we may suppose that ben Sirach wrote the introductions when he came to publish his book, in this way putting some order into his earlier scattered writings.

4) *Doctrine*

The doctrine of Sirach is traditional. The wisdom which the book propounds comes from the Lord; it forms the young and insures the happiness of all who will receive it. The author believes in retribution, but takes his stand on the accepted teaching, and he is unperturbed by the practical difficulties of this view. Here there is no advance, but ben Sirach does break new ground when he identifies wisdom with the Law (Sir. 24:23 f.; cf. 15:1; 19:20). He differs more notably from the earlier sages in his concern with the history of Israel (Sir. 44:1—49:16). But even he is not interested in this history as such; rather he presents the saints of his people as men who were in love with wisdom and who were led along the road of sanctity by her. In his procession of great men the priesthood is conspicuously represented: Aaron and Phinehas have places of honor, and he closes with a eulogy of a contemporary, the high priest Simon.

Ben Sirach was evidently conservative in his views, but his book was ultimately to receive substantial additions which brought it into line with new ideas, especially those on the afterlife. The additions of the secondary or expanded text are largely concerned to supplement the eschatology of the primary text in the light of the new doctrine of retribution beyond the grave. The main point stressed is that there is to be a final, divine judgment of each one: for the wicked that will be a day of wrath and vengeance and unending punishment; for the just it will mean eternal reward in the world to come. At last, then, the problem of Job and Qoheleth has been solved; and Sirach, in its longer form, joins hands more firmly with the last great work of the wisdom movement.

7. THE BOOK OF WISDOM

In Alexandria, the most important center of the Diaspora, Jews were in close and constant touch with Hellenism. Some of the better educated among them sought to present their religion to the pagans. Naturally they strove to show it in the most favorable light possible, and they searched out points of contact between Greek culture and the traditions of Israel. It was in this milieu that the Book of Wisdom appeared. Written in Greek in such an atmosphere, it shows the influence of Greek thought, though the measure of this influence must not be exaggerated. For if the author displays some acquaintance with the various philosophies, this is no more than one would expect from the average cultured Alexandrian; he makes no attempt to syncretize Jewish and Greek ideas as Philo was to do. He is completely loyal to the faith of Israel, but borrows from the Greek thought of his environment whatever can serve him in the expression of his message.

1) Authorship and Date

In the Greek manuscripts (and in Syriac) Wisdom is entitled *The Wisdom of Solomon.* In the Vg. it is called *Liber Sapientiae.* The attribution of the book to Solomon is a literary fiction, common in wisdom writings (cf. Prv. 1:1; Qoh. 1:1; Ct. 1:1). Wisdom was written in Greek and is a deuterocanonical book.[10] The unknown author —who wrote Greek with ease—composed his work almost certainly in Alexandria. The place of origin is indicated by the spirit and outlook of the work as well as by the emphasis the author lays on the Egyptian phase of the Exodus and by his sustained criticism of animal worship (a feature of Egyptian religion).

We can be reasonably sure of the date of Wisdom. It is certain that the author has used the Septuagint, and since this version could scarcely have been completed before the beginning of the third century B.C., Wisdom cannot be earlier than that. The doctrine of the writing would suggest that it is considerably later. On the other hand the author shows no knowledge of the ideas of the Jewish philosopher Philo (20 B.C.-54 A.D.)—or of the prephilonian movement: his book would scarcely be later than 50 B.C. A date in the first half of the first century B.C. cannot be far off the mark. Wisdom is thus the last writing of the Old Testament.

2) *Plan*[11]

After an invitation to acquire wisdom (Wis. 1:1-15), the author goes on to show its unique importance in human

INTRODUCTION: TO SEEK JUSTICE, WISDOM, AND LIFE (WIS. 1:1-15)	
WISDOM AND HUMAN DESTINY (WIS. 1:16–5:23)	
1) Life according to the impious	1:16-2:20
2) Error of the impious	2:21-24
3) The lot of the just and of the impious	3:1–5:23
ORIGIN, NATURE, ACTION, AND ACQUISITION OF WISDOM (WIS. 6-9)	
1) Exhortation to kings	6:1-21
2) Solomon, Doctor of Wisdom	6:22–8:1
3) The Wisdom granted to Solomon	8:2–9:19
THE WISDOM OF GOD IN HISTORY (WIS. 10-19)	
1) The role of Wisdom from Adam to the Exodus	10:1–11:3
a) 1st antithesis: water, chastisement for Egyptians, salvation for the Israelites	11:5-14
Digression I: Mercy of God	11:15 (16)–12:27
Digression II: Folly and malice of the cult of idols	13-15
2) Marvelous action of Wisdom in the Exodus	16:1–19:17 (16)
b) 2nd antithesis: Egyptians tormented by animals / Israelites nourished by quails	16:1-4
c) 3rd antithesis: locusts and flies destroy Egyptians / bronze serpent heals Israelites	16:5-14
d) 4th antithesis: the elements strike the Egyptians / the elements help the Israelites	16:15-29
e) 5th antithesis: horrible darkness afflicts Egyptians / blessed light granted to Israelites	17:1–18:4
f) 6th antithesis: Egyptians lose the first born / Israelites are spared	18:5-25
g) 7th antithesis: Red Sea swallows the Egyptians / Red Sea opens to the Israelites	19:1-9
ISRAEL AND EGYPT (WIS. 19:10-21)	
CONCLUSION (WIS. 19:22 [20c])	

destiny (Wis. 1:16—5:23). Then he describes its origin, nature, and action, indicating the means of acquiring it (chapters 6-9), and represents it at work in the history of Israel (Wis. 10:1—11:3). From Wisdom 11:4 wisdom gives place to God, to his breath, spirit, word, hand, and arm; Wisdom 19:22 is the conclusion.

Thus the work has three parts: the way of wisdom, opposed to the way of the impious (chapters 1-5); wisdom itself (chapters 6-9); the works of wisdom in the unfolding of Israel's history (chapters 10-19). The first chapters (1-5) depend largely on the prophets, whose style is notably Hebraic; chapters 6-9 use Prv. and some Greek philosophical ideas; but the style is less biblical; the last chapters (10-19) are in a style unlike that of the rest of the Old Testament.

3) *Literary Form*

Wisdom, unlike Prv. and Sir. is a carefully-planned work; in general, however, it keeps close to the style of these writings. Nevertheless, from chapter 10—and more particularly from chapter 16—onwards, where the author points to the role of wisdom in the history of Israel, he introduces another literary form. For he is not content to reproduce the facts of that history but, according to the principles of *midrash,* he strives to discover the deeper meaning of them. In the first place he embroiders the traditional narratives with features borrowed from Jewish legends or suggested by himself. Some of these are merely descriptive and serve the interests of style (Wis. 17:17-20; 18:1 f.,15 f.; 19:9). Others are meant to render a particular event more impressive, more dramatic, and more meaningful (Wis. 17:3-6,9; 18:12; 11:11-13; 17:8,18,20; 18:17-19; 16:27-29). On the other hand, he has suppressed or modified whatever might reflect on God's goodness or on the reputation of the Chosen People, such as God's hardening of Pharaoh and the murmuring of the people in the desert.

Elsewhere the author takes the biblical narrative just as it is but, in order to fit it into his plan, he gives it a new interpretation. For instance, according to Exodus (23:28-30), God drove the Canaanites out of the land little by little lest the land should become a desert; the action is intended to benefit the Chosen People. Wisdom, however, regards it as an act of mercy towards the pagans: despite their culpability and their malice, God wished to give them a chance to repent (Wis. 12:3-6, 10 f.). It is a fine thought and a deeply-spiritual rendering of the old text, but it certainly falls outside the viewpoint of Exodus. This freedom of interpretation is best seen in the long parallel treatment of the respective fates of Egyptians and Israelites (Wis. 11:5-14; 16:1—19:9). In a series of seven antitheses the author boldly presents pairings which nothing in the Exodus narrative would suggest (for example: manna and hail; brazen serpent and locusts) and dramatizes the facts in order to heighten the contrast. In all this procedure he is guided by clear-cut ideas: God is essentially merciful and punishes only when he is constrained to do so; all the while he shows special solicitude for his own people. Underlying the method is the belief that the facts recorded in the Bible have a moral and religious value; it is the purpose of *midrash* to bring these to the surface.

Midrash.[12] In modern biblical studies, the word *midrash* may mean a rabbinic method of exegesis, or a special literary form. Rabbinic midrash, as a literary form, is a literature concerned with the Bible; it is "a literature about a literature." It is rewarding to look to the etymology of the word and the antecedents of the form.

1. *In the Old Testament*. The word *midrash* occurs twice only: 2 Chronicles 13:22; 24:27, and designates noncanonical sources used by the author; Sir. 51:23 has the expression *beth ha-midrash*. On the other hand, the verb *darash* ("to search," "to examine") occurs very frequently. Most often it is used in a religious sense: it means to frequent a place of cult, to seek God, to seek the response of God in the cult and in personal prayer (Am. 5:5; 2 Chr. 1:5; Dt. 12:5; Pss. 34 [33]:5; 69 [68]:33; 105 [104]:4, etc.). But, above all, one searches the Scrip-

tures. This last meaning is current in the postexilic age: one turns to Scripture to find the responses of God. *Darash*, therefore, signifies the study of the Torah (in the wide sense of all divine revelation considered as a norm of life): Ps. 119 [118]:45,94,155; 1 Chr. 28:8; or of the great interventions of God in the history of Israel: Ps. 111 [110]:2—"Great are the words of the Lord, studied (*derushim*) by all who have pleasure in them." Is. 34:16 (a postexilic text) is significant in this respect: it is an invitation to seek in "the book of the Lord" the prophecies concerning Edom (Is. 13:20-22) in order to show their realization.

Since the meaning of *darash* is fixed in the postexilic period, we have little doubt about the meaning of *midrash* in the Scripture passages mentioned above. Admittedly the nature of the writings which have served as the Chronicler's sources remains uncertain but, since the meaning of the verb *darash* is clear, it is probable that, when the Chronicler employs the term *midrash* he refers to works which gloss and amplify the Scriptures for the purpose of instruction and edification. As for the *beth ha-midrash* of which ben Sirach speaks, it is doubtless a place where Scripture was studied and interpreted.

2. *In rabbinical literature.* Here *midrash* has the general sense of "search" or "research," with the double nuance of study and explanation. More specifically, *midrash* designates a writing whose object is the interpretation of Scripture, normally on a homiletic level, like the *midrash rabbah* which is a commentary on the Pentateuch. In short, in the rabbinical literature, *midrash* has acquired a technical sense: it is always used in relation to Scripture, and means to search out, to strive to understand the content of a scriptural text—to explain and to expound the sense of Scripture.

THE FORMS OF MIDRASH. Though extremely varied in form, *midrash* may be reduced to two main types:

1. The form of midrash which is most limited in scope is the *halakah*. It is based on the legal texts of the Torah

and its purpose is to find in them rules of conduct and of action that fit later times and circumstances. While halakic midrash could find a place in synagogal sermons, it is understandable that its privileged *Sitz im Leben* was the discussions of the rabbinical schools.

2. The most widely occurring and elastic form of midrash is the *haggadah*. This is an interpretation of the non-legal texts of the Torah, and of the rest of Scripture. The viewpoint was varied (moral exhortation or doctrinal commentary) and the methods diverse (varying from a simple explanation of a text to a free narrative built on a text). Haggadic midrash is notably homiletic and the origin of much of it may be found in the liturgical assemblies. It is the commentary on, and an interpretation of, the text read in synagogue worship. However, the *pesharim* of Qumran, commentaries on prophetical texts which applied these texts to the history of the sect, also fit into this category. In the Old Testament itself, Dn. 9 is a characteristic example of *pesher midrash*.

From the viewpoint of literary structure, midrash may be exegetical (verse by verse exposition of the text), homiletical (traditional interpretation of texts presented in the form of homilies), or narrative (a completely rewritten biblical narrative embellished with legends and non-biblical traditions). But always the starting point of midrash is a text of Scripture. Its aim is to actualize a biblical text in face of new situations, to learn what the text has to say to us here and now, to draw out from it all the lessons it contains. An excellent biblical example of haggadic midrash is found in the homily of Wis. 11-19.

4) Doctrine

The God of Wisdom is the God of Israelite tradition: omnipotent Creator; sovereign Master of the destinies of the universe. But the author emphasizes certain of his attributes. God is infinitely wise (Wis. 11:20); he handles all things with justice and always "makes the punishment fit the crime" (Wis. 12:15-18). He is sovereignly good, the friend of men and desirous of their welfare; he loves all his creatures. He has pity on all men (Wis. 11:23) and goes to great lengths to win the conversion of sinners (Wis. 12:20).

The divine attribute on which the author insists above any other is unquestionably the divine *wisdom*. This wisdom is manifestly the same as that of Prv. 8:1—9:6 and Sir. 24, yet here there is a distinct development. Its origin and nature are expressed in more philosophical terms (Wis. 7:25 f.); its relations with God are more intimate (Wis. 8:3 f.; 9:4); its creative activity is more marked (Wis. 7:21; 8:5 f.; 9:2,9) and the same is true of its omnipresence (Wis. 7:23 f.), its omniscience (Wis. 7:23; 8:4), its universal providence (Wis. 8:1), its sanctifying role (Wis. 7:27), its beneficial role in the history of Israel (Wis. 10:1—11:3), its love for men (Wis. 1:6; 7:23), its care for them (Wis. 6:12-16), and its importance in the acquisition of virtue (Wis. 8:7). He attributes to it all the encyclopedic knowledge of the Greek world of the time (Wis. 7:17-21; 8:8).

The teaching of Wisdom serves as a prelude to that on grace in the New Testament. Wisdom dwells in holy souls (Wis. 1:4; 7:27) and it is set on a level with the spirit of God (Wis. 1:4-7; 9:17). It is a treasure which procures the friendship of God (Wis. 7:14,28). Furthermore, since it is God who grants it, one must ask him for it (Wis. 7:7; 9). Even if a man has all other good qualities, without wisdom he is nothing before God (Wis. 9:6). Wisdom assures the observance of God's law and leads to blessed immortality (Wis. 6:17-20; 8:17).[13]

More important than anything else is the new teaching, the new hope, which Wisdom brings: "God created man for immortality" (Wis. 2:23). After death the faithful soul lives on—not in the shadowy existence of Sheol, but in a life of unending happiness before God (Wis. 3:9). This doctrine appears abruptly and briefly in Daniel (12:2); it is treated more fully in the additions of Sir.; but here it is put forward with complete assurance. The bankruptcy of the traditional doctrine of retribution had long been evident to the discerning, for material well-being is no more a sign of God's favor than misery is a sign of reprobation. Now, at last, it is seen that what happens in this life is a preparation for the life beyond, and the sufferings of a just man serve to purify him and win for him a greater recompense. One thing alone matters: to do God's will and to live in his love, for this is the way to eternal life. Paul and John did not disdain to listen to the nameless author of the last Old Testament writing.

8. THE DIVINE WISDOM[14]

1) *The Source of Wisdom*

From the very first the Israelite sages acknowledged that true human wisdom has a divine source: God communicates wisdom to whom he pleases, and he can do so because he is himself the Sage *par excellence*. Wisdom is a divine reality; she has been from eternity and will endure forever (Prv. 8:22-26; Sir. 24:9). She has come forth from the mouth of the Most High (Sir. 24:3) like his spoken word; she is a "breath of the power of God and a pure emanation of the glory of the Almighty . . . a reflection of eternal light, a spotless mirror of the working of God, and an image of his goodness" (Wis. 7:25 f.). She dwells in heaven seated by the throne of God and lives in closest association with him (Wis. 24:4; 9:4; 8:2).

Wisdom is tireless. She was with God when he created heaven and earth (Prv. 8:27-31), and has remained the ruler of the universe (Wis. 8:1). She resides familiarly with men (Prv. 8:31) and was bidden to make her home in Israel (Sir. 24:8-12). As the providence that guides history (Wis. 10:1—11:4) and the bringer of salvation to men (Wis. 9:18) she has time and again gone forth on divine missions to men. She expresses her absorbing interest in men's welfare by warning them of judgment (Prv. 1:10-33) and by inviting all who will to share her goods and to sit at her table (Prv. 8:1-21, 32-36; 9:4 f.; Sir. 24:19-22). She it is who distributes the gifts of God to men (Prv. 8:21; Wis. 7:11) and, greatest service of all, it is she who makes men friends of God (Wis. 7:27 f.). In short, this presentation of divine wisdom is a prelude to the New Testament doctrine of grace and it is in the light of this doctrine that the Old Testament idea becomes more readily understandable for us.

2) *The Personification of Wisdom*

This striking presentation of wisdom gives rise to a problem of its own. The question is whether the texts indicated in the previous paragraph, and many similar passages, are to be taken in a strict sense, or whether they do not go beyond literary personification. Perhaps we should no longer describe it as a problem, since Scripture scholars agree that it is no more than a figure of speech, and the special interest of the matter now is the realization that a proper understanding of the biblical context points unerringly to the true interpretation; it was the intrusion of later theological ideas which led to confusion. Throughout the sapiential literature, wisdom is consistently practical. The wisdom authors were moralists who couched their teaching in poetic language, not philosophers speculating on the nature of God. If we are not to falsify their thought we must keep in mind the general context and the essentially practical purpose of their writings as well as the poetic quality of their style which abounds in imagery and picturesque touches. Here as elsewhere we may not impose on the Bible the categories of scholastic speculation —or do so at the peril of missing the import of what *God* says in his Scripture.

3) *Jesus and Wisdom*

The manner of teaching employed by our Lord resembled that of Israel's sages: he used the same forms as they (sayings and parables—the *māshāl* in all its range), and like them he laid down rules of life (cf. Mt. 5-7). The people were astonished at his wisdom (Mk. 6:2), and he could say of himself: "The queen of the South came from the ends of the earth to hear the wisdom of Solomon, and behold, something greater than Solomon is here" (Mt.

12:42). For it is in his own name that he promised to his followers the gift of wisdom (Lk. 21:15).

The New Testament writers understood that, if Jesus communicates wisdom to men, it is because he himself is the Wisdom of God (1 Cor. 1:24,30). Naturally, then, they apply to him the same terms used by the Old Testament sages: he is the first born of all creation (Col. 1:15-20; cf. Prv. 8:22-31); he is the reflection of the glory of God and bears the very stamp of his nature (Heb. 1:3; cf. Wis. 7:25 f.); he is the Incarnate Word of God (Jn. 1:1-18; cf. Sir. 24:3). The personal wisdom of God is fully revealed in Jesus Christ who has come forth from the Father to dwell with men and to win them salvation. In him all the wisdom of the wise men finds its term and its true significance.

9. THE SONG OF SONGS

The Song of Songs is traditionally classed with Jb., Prv., Qoh., Sir., and Wis. to form the "Books of Wisdom"; we shall see that there is a sound basis for this classification. However, the Song is distinctive and it is best taken by itself at the close of this chapter on the wisdom literature.

1) *The Book*

The Song of Songs finds its place in the Hebrew Bible among the Writings, at the head of the festal *megilloth* ("rolls") and was appointed to be read at the Pasch. The title, "Song of Songs," like "Holy of Holies" and "King of Kings," is a Hebrew form of the superlative and means the loveliest song. Jewish regard for the Song was expressed by the Rabbi Aqiba (second cent. A.D.): "All the writings are holy, but the Song of Songs is the Holy of Holies." The book met with some opposition at the Jewish Council of Jamnia (c. 90 A.D.), but was accepted as part of the Jewish canon. Since it is found both in the Hebrew and in the Septuagint (LXX), it passed without question into the Christian canon.

The Song is a love poem (or a collection of love poems). Its language of love, and if that language seems daring, perhaps at times even shocking, in its realism, this is because it is the product of another culture. It has undeniable contacts with earlier Egyptian love songs. A notable parallel is the use of the terms "sister" (Ct. 4:10,12; 5:1; cf. Tb. 5:21; 8:4,7,21) and "brother" (Ct. 8:1)—recognized terms in Egyptian love poems; common also are the themes of lovesickness and the absence of the beloved (Ct. 2:5; 3:1 f.; 5:6-8). A single example brings out the correspondence: "Seven days to yesterday I have not seen the sister. And a sickness has invaded me . . . more beneficial to me is the sister than any remedies . . . when I embrace her she drives evil away from me—but she has gone forth from me for seven days."[15] Parallels have been noted between the Song and the *wasfs* (songs sung in praise of bride and groom during rural weddings in Syria); such *wasfs* undoubtedly have a long history. But neither ancient Egyptian nor modern Syrian parallels are surprising or really significant, for in the nature of the case we should expect to find similarities of expression. Love is a fundamental human emotion and the language of love sounds much the same in all lands.

2) *Authorship and Date*

The Song of Songs is traditionally attributed to Solomon (Ct. 1:1), but he is no more the author of it than he is of Qoh.; the attribution is based on his reputation as a poet (1 Kgs. 4:32). The language of the Song is many centuries later than the time of Solomon; it shows the influence of Aramaic and has Hebraized Persian words (Ct. 1:12; 4:13,18; 6:11) and one Greek word ("palanquin" [Ct. 3:9]). Though some of the basic material may be older, the finished work is certainly postexilic. A date in the first half of the fourth century—a period of religious and political tranquillity following the reforms of Ezra and Nehemiah—seems indicated. The book was edited by wisdom writers about the same time.[16]

3) *Interpretation*

In the course of the centuries the Song has been interpreted in many ways, but no explanation has won universal acceptance. The two dominant approaches are diametrically opposed. These are:

1. *The allegorical interpretation.* The work is an allegory, immediately signifying the union of Yahweh with Israel.
2. *The literal interpretation.* The Song is in praise of human love as God willed it and created it.

The allegorical interpretation has been dominant among Jews and Christians; in recent years it has been warmly and competently presented by eminent scholars.[17] Both as a traditional view and on the basis of scholarship it merits serious attention, and yet, on both grounds, it is vulnerable. For one thing, it seems that the earliest evidence we have in support of the allegorical interpretation is a second-century A.D. Jewish tradition.[18] The Song was accepted as part of the Jewish canon in 90 A.D., not because it was regarded as an allegory but because of its popularity. On the other hand, this interpretation demands that too much should be read into the text. For instance, the historical and topographical significance attributed to descriptive details is forced and seems arbitrary.[19]

Perhaps the most serious difficulty is that nothing in the poems suggests that they are allegories. Elsewhere (as in Hos., Jer., Ezek.), where nuptial language is used to describe the relationship between Yahweh and his people, the allegorical nature of the language is always made clear. It is noteworthy too that, when the biblical writers have spoken of Yahweh and his people in marital terms, they have displayed an obvious restraint and have set definite limits to the imagery; the boldness of the Song's language would surely strike the earlier writers as out of place in this context. Besides, the marriage image is a prophetical theme, whereas the Song is lyric poetry and—as it is presented by its editors—belongs to the wisdom literature.

Another line of argument in favor of the allegorical in-

terpretation is that the author of the Song has employed
the "anthological" method, that is, that he has systemati-
cally used the words and expressions of earlier biblical
writings.[20] Here again the arguments are ingenious, but
the "anthological" method has been shown to be a double-
edged weapon.[21] All in all, despite its long tradition and
its eminent champions, the allegorical interpretation of the
Song is difficult to maintain. We turn, by choice, to the
literal interpretation.

The literal interpretation takes the Song at its face value,
regarding it as a love poem or a collection of love poems
celebrating the love of a man and a woman. It has been
urged in the past—and the prejudice still lingers—that the
theme of human love is unworthy of Scripture; or, at least,
that it is unlikely, unseemly even, that a biblical book
should have been wholly dedicated to it. This outlook
would appear to miss the true significance of Scripture.
The Bible is the word of God, certainly, but (we may ask)
to whom is that word addressed? God has not written this
work for his own pleasure; he has destined it for the human beings whom he had created; it is his gift to them. It
is he who made them men and women; it is he who has
implanted in them, deep in their nature, the mutual attraction that is meant to culminate in marriage. Like all
the gifts of God this may be abused but, in the divine
intention, the love which so strongly draws young people,
which inspires each of them to dedicate his and her life to
the other, and which later enables them, together, to support inevitable cares and troubles, is a good thing—it is
part of the work God himself has called very good (Gn.
1:31). It is eminently worthy of special treatment in the
Bible, that word of God *to men*.

4) The Message[22]

The Song of Songs takes its place in the Bible as the exalta-
tion of human love. Whether it is a collection of songs or
whether it is one elaborate poem, it is certainly lyrical. As
such it does not "teach," it has no "doctrine" to propound:

it is the expression of a state of mind and heart. It is concerned with the mutual love of two young people who, quite obviously, contemplate marriage; if, indeed, they are not already married. Its language is the language of love; if it seems daring to our Western ears, it is surely relevant to note that throughout the Old Testament, the same Hebrew verb and noun are used for human and divine love, but when we turn to the New Testament we find that Christian authors, writing in Greek,[23] could not use the ordinary word for love in their religious vocabulary, because its association had made it unfit for such usage. (The same is very nearly the case today when "love" is so often a synonym of "lust.")

The epilogue of Songs (or an editorial addition) would indicate that the author (and editors) understood the writing in its straightforward literal sense:

> "For love is strong as death,
>   jealousy is cruel as Sheol.
> Its flashes are flashes of fire,
>   a very flame of Yahweh.
> Many waters cannot quench love,
>   nor can floods drown it.
> If a man should offer all the wealth of his house
>   as a price for love,
>   he would be utterly scorned" (Ct. 8:6b-7).[24]

Such language is reminiscent of Prv. or Sir., and orientates the Song in the traditional direction of wisdom literature:[25] the writing was reinterpreted in terms of the mutual love of Yahweh and Israel only after the book had taken its place in the canon. The growing tendency among Catholic scholars to read Song according to its obvious sense is due to the realization that the theme of human love is no more out of place in the wisdom literature than is the theme of human wisdom of Prv.

A feature of the Song that often occasions surprise is the absence of the divine name; what should really surprise us is the absence of any allusion to a god or goddess of love. Israel did indeed feel the strong attraction of *Ashtaroth* (the Canaanite goddesses of fertility) even personified love. The explanation of this fact, which is truly remarkable when we view it in historical perspective, is to be found in the second chapter of Genesis. There is no essential difference between the admiration that attracted the first man to the first woman (Gn. 2:23) and the mutual wonder of the young couple of the Song. There is little difference between the comment of the editor of Genesis: "That is why a man leaves father and mother and cleaves to his wife, and they become one flesh" (2:24), and the reflection of the poet (or editor) of the Song: "For love is strong as death. . . . If a man should offer all the wealth of his house as a price for love, it would be utterly scorned" (8:6 f.). Both texts bear witness to the same attitude in face of the same human experience. Marital love belongs to the order of things created by God from the beginning, it is one of the wonders of God which should evoke admiration and gratitude.[26]

It is arguable that the Song was originally a collection of espousal songs or songs of the wedding feast; at the very least it has been inspired and colored by such songs. This explains its atmosphere, the springtime joy, the companions, and the young couple immersed in each other. The whole is, admittedly, on a natural plane, but is there anything reprehensible in that? Love is normally awakened by physical beauty, by very human qualities, and God made man's body as well as man's soul. It would be unrealistic, to say the least, to seek to ignore this; logically it ought to lead to a denial of the role of sex in marriage. Besides, and this is more to the point, such an attitude is entirely unbiblical.

There is yet another point that is well worth noting. By attracting attention to the personal element in marriage the Song has not merely provided a more balanced view, but has enriched the concept of marriage: Love brings out the unique value of the person (cf. Ct. 2:2 f.; 5:10; 6:8 f.) and establishes a real equality between man and woman; it is significant that the latter's freedom of choice is here quite obviously taken for granted. Perhaps even more striking is the fact that, in the context, a monogamous and indissoluble union is manifestly in view.

But there is still more to it. The important fact that a biblical writing has extolled the tender love of a young couple not only restores the balance of marriage but has its place in the development of revelation. It plays its part in the transformation of the essentially communitary Covenant of Sinai into the new Covenant foretold by Jeremiah (Jer. 31:31-34), a Covenant in which the place and dignity of the individual are explicitly affirmed. For, when love had been acknowledged as a constitutive element in marriage, side-by-side with the founding of a family, the individual had ceased to be absorbed in the group. It is a decisive step towards the recognition of the personal dignity of every man and woman.

---

[1] The canonical wisdom writings are: Proverbs, Job, Qoheleth (Ecclesiastes), Sirach (Ecclesiasticus), and Wisdom; the Canticle of Canticles was edited by wisdom writers. The influence of wisdom is also clearly evident in many psalms and in Baruch, Tobit, and Judith.

[2] See W. Harrington, "The Wisdom of Israel," *Irish Theological Quarterly*, 30 (1963), 311-25. This article forms the basis of the present chapter.

[3] E. J. Kissane, *The Book of Job* (Dublin: Browne and Nolan, 1939), p. 1.

[4] The traditional doctrine of retribution, in its simplest form, is that the good are rewarded and the wicked are punished *in this life*.

[5] H. Wheeler Robinson, *The Cross in the Old Testament* (London: S.C.M. Press, 1960[2]), p. 32.

[6] R. Pautrel, *L'Ecclésiaste* (BJ), p. 13.

[7] See B. W. Anderson, *Understanding the Old Testament* (Englewood Cliffs, N.J.: Prentice-Hall, 1957), p. 478.

[8] A *geniza* was a storeroom or hiding place attached to synagogues in which discarded manuscripts were deposited.

[9] See C. Spicq, *L'Ecclésiastique* (Pirot-Clamer, VI) (Paris: Letouzey et Ané, 1951[2]), pp. 553 f.

[10] See Harrington, *op. cit.*, p. 64.

[11] See E. Osty, *Le Livre de la Sagesse* (BJ), pp. 7-10.

[12] See R. Block, "*Midrash*" in DBS, V, col. 1263-1281; A. G. Wright, "*The Literary Genre Midrash*," in CBQ 28 (1966), 105-138; 417-457.

[13] See Osty, *op. cit.*, pp. 15-22.

[14] See P. van Imschoot, *Théologie de l'Ancien Testament* (Tournai: Desclée, 1954), I, pp. 226-36; A. Barucq and P. Grelot, VTB, pp. 974-81.

[15] ANET, pp. 468 f.; cf. P. F. Ellis, *The Men and the Message of the Old Testament* (Collegeville, Minn.: The Liturgical Press, 1963), p. 384.

[16] See J. Winandy, *Le Cantique des Cantiques* (Paris: Ed. de Maredsous, 1960), p. 55.

[17] Read A. Robert, *Le Cantique des Cantiques* (BJ), 1958[2]; A. Feuillet, *Le Cantique des Cantiques* (Paris: Cerf, 1953); A. Robert et R. Tournay (avec le concours de A. Feuillet), *Le Cantique des Cantiques* (Études Bibliques) (Paris: Gabalda, 1963).

[18] See J.-P. Audet, "Le sens du Cantique des Cantiques," RB, 62 (1955), 200-3; "Love and Marriage in the Old Testament," *Scripture*, 10 (1958), 81.

[19] See, for example, A. Robert, BJ, pp. 857-67. The sustained interpretation is a brilliant *tour de force;* one is impressed but not convinced.

[20] See Feuillet, *Le Cantique des Cantiques, op. cit.,* pp. 193-244.

[21] See A.-M. Dubarle, "L'amour humain dans le Cantique des Cantiques," RB, 61 (1954), 75-81; P. Grelot, "Le sens du Cantique des Cantiques," RB, 71 (1964), 49-51.

[22] See W. Harrington, *The Bible on Marriage* (Dublin: Dominican Publications, 1963), pp. 27-31.

[23] See Herbert, *art. cit.,* 406.

[24] W. F. Albright comments: "Nowhere in the entire range of world-literature can we find an equal to the praise of the love of man for woman in Canticle 8:6 f." (*Archaeology and the Religion of Israel* [Baltimore: Johns Hopkins Press, 1946], p. 13).

[25] For the same theme as that of the Canticle see Prv. 5:15-19; 31:10-31; Sir. 25:13—26:18.

[26] See Audet, *art. cit.,* 219 f.

FIVE

THE PSALMS

The history of Psalms, like that of most of the Old Testament books, is complex. The collection of 150 psalms that we know was not made all at once and it is not the work of one author or of one age. The Canticle of Deborah (Jgs. 5) is proof of the early origin of religious poetry in Israel, while the apocryphal *Psalms of Solomon* and the Qumran *Hodayoth* (thanksgiving psalms), as well as the *Magnificat* and the *Benedictus* show that the tradition continued to the time of Christ. It is altogether likely that many older psalms have been lost, while others of different dates exist outside the collection of 150 psalms (for example, 1 Sm. 2:1-10; Is. 38:10-20; 44:23-28; Jer. 15:15-25; Lam. 3:5; Dn. 2:20-23; 3:26-45, 52-90; Jon. 2:2-9; Tb. 13). However, the great bulk of extant Hebrew psalms is to be found in the Psalter.

The Classification of Psalms

A particular family of psalms may be discovered by the application of three criteria: (1) an identical concrete situation; (2) a common ground of concepts and sentiments; (3) a similar literary form, with the same style and the same structure. These three factors must be present together; one of them will not suffice to determine a literary form—this is particularly important in psalms of similar content. For example, psalms which develop a historical theme do not necessarily belong to the same family. The exegete, then, must examine not only the content of a psalm but also the concrete situation in which it was formed, and its literary form. In fact, it is the recognition of the *Sitz im Leben* and of the literary form that will enable him to be sure of the content and sense of the psalm.[1]

Of course, not all the psalms owe their existence to the cult; not all have a liturgical origin. This is true especially of the individual supplications which were born of a personal need or danger of the psalmist. But such psalms also became part of liturgical worship, after the Exile, for the Book of Psalms really came into its own in the second Temple where, as one psalmist puts it, Yahweh was "enthroned on the praises of Israel" (Ps. 21:3).

1. PSALMS OF SUPPLICATION

1) Psalms of Individual Supplication

With the psalms of individual supplication we associate the psalms of confidence, which do not form a distinct class; in them the motive of confidence in God, present in all the supplication psalms, is predominant.

THE SITZ　　The psalms of individual supplication did not
IM LEBEN　　originate in the liturgy, but were motivated by individual distress.[2]

1. *Imminent danger of death.* The Israelite feared nothing so much as premature death; his ideal was long life (Ps. 101:25; cf. 90:15 f.). The canticle of Hezekiah is a good example of this (Is. 38:10,12). Premature death was regarded as punishment for sin (Ps. 54:24). The reason for this attitude is that the Old Testament (before the second half of the second century B.C.) had an imprecise and incomplete idea of an afterlife. Sheol, the abode of the dead, is located beneath the earth (Pss. 21:29; 68:15 f.)

and is sometimes referred to as the "Pit." It is thought of
as a place of silence (Ps. 114:17), of darkness and forget-
fulness (Ps. 87:12). There the dead, ghostly replicas of
men lived a dreary existence, deprived of everything that
made life desirable, and cut off from fellowship with God
(Ps. 87:5). There is no praise of God (Pss. 6:6; 87:10-13).
The psalmist, in describing the danger of death, often has
recourse to hyperbole: he is about to enter Sheol; he is
already there (Pss. 68:15; 87:4). His thanksgiving for deliverance celebrates a return from the dead (cf. 1 Sm.
2:6).

Here we must forget our distinction between soul and
body. For a Semite, *soul* is a synonym of life or, often, the
equivalent of the personal pronoun: "my soul" = "me."
"My soul goes down to Sheol" = "I go down to Sheol"
(Ps. 85:13; cf. 15:10; 29:4; 48:16; 88:49). It is not *a part*
of man—what we call the soul—that survived after death,
but a shadow of the *whole man*. It was only in the Hellenistic era, due to the influence of Greek philosophy, that
the dichotomy soul/body was introduced into biblical
thought; the principal witnesses of this evolution are 2 Mc.
and Wis.

2. *Sickness.* The psalms have given us an excellent idea
of the mentality of Old Testament man in face of sickness.
It is Yahweh who has sent it and it is he who must cure it
—secondary causes remain in the background (Pss. 37:3;
68:27; 101:11; Is. 38:12; 29:3). The psalms often mention the reasons why God sent the sickness: it is most
often a punishment for sins (Ps. 37:4; 40:5). The prayer
frequently includes a highly-colored description of the illness (Ps. 37:101; Is. 38:14). The sickness also gave the
enemies of the stricken one an occasion of asserting themselves (Pss. 34:13-15; 40:6,9). Three kinds of enemies are
distinguished:

a) Friends and relatives who regard the illness as the
chastisement of a hidden fault (Ps. 37:12; Jb.; cf. Jn.
9:2): his friends have become his enemies.

b) The impious and blasphemers. The sufferer's virtue is ridiculed (Ps. 68:11-13). These men are really opposed to Yahweh and his providence.

c) Former enemies who take advantage of the stricken one's helplessness; besides, their previous charges against him are now vindicated: Yahweh has punished him (Pss. 30:12-14; 34:15 f.; 68:27; 108:22-25).

3. *False accusation.* Litigation was very common in Israel, while at the same time there was widespread corruption in the administration of justice. Here the distinction between rich and poor was glaring; too often the poor were oppressed by the ruling class (cf. 2 Sm. 12; 1 Kgs. 20; Dn. 13; Is. 1:23; 5:7; 11:3 f.; Am. 5:12; Jer. 5:26; 22:3). The situation was no better at the time of our Lord (cf. Lk. 18:2-5). The legislation of Israel had to take measures against false testimony and unjust sentences (Ex. 20:16; 23). The *lex talionis* was invoked (Dt. 19:18-20; cf. Ex. 21:23-25). Cases were generally tried before the gate of a town so that the phrase "before the gate" is often a synonym of "before the tribunal." A process could also take place in the royal palace (cf. Ps. 121:5). Before sentence the witnesses of both parties were heard: for acquittal a majority vote was necessary (cf. Ps. 126:5). Yahweh was often the best witness (Ps. 106:31). In default of witnesses a man might take an oath (Ps. 7:4-6). False witnesses and accusers are often indicated by metaphors: hunters (Pss. 7:16; 34:7; 56:7; 63:6; 139:6); robbers (Pss. 16:9-12; 55:7); lions (Pss. 7:3; 16:12; 56:5); dogs (Ps. 58:15 f.); snakes (cf. Ps. 57:5 f.).

In order to understand the background of the supplication psalms it is necessary to grasp the significance of anthropomorphisms in the Bible. For the Israelite, Yahweh was a living and personal God, never a first unmoved mover far apart from man and creation. The faith of Israel was not founded on philosophical reflection on the spirituality of Yahweh, but on the concrete experience of his active personality and of his nearness. This is why he is so easily represented anthropomorphically. He is approached as one approaches a man, with a surprising familiarity. We have only to read how men of God conversed with Yahweh: for example, Moses (Nm. 11:11-14); Joshua (Jos. 7:7-9); Elijah (1 Kgs. 17:20); Jeremiah (Jer. 15:17 f.; 20:7). But this does not mean that his transcendence was lost sight of; the prohibition to make any image of him is proof of that. It is, however, these anthropomorphisms that bring out the specific element in the Israelite concept of God: they emphasize the truth that the Holy One of Israel is near and living. Thus we find that, in these psalms, Yahweh is called upon with insistence, for the appeal is addressed not to some distant divinity but to a living and personal God. This is why the pleading is at once so human and so poignant. It is especially in extreme need that one discovers in Yahweh a Person who is all-powerful and close at hand and ready to help.

2) Psalms of Communal Supplication

These have the same structure as the individual supplications but they are the prayer of the whole nation. Here there is greater emphasis on the Covenant and the divine interventions of the past. Days of prayer and penance in Israel from the *Sitz im Leben* of these psalms. Such days of prayer were decreed on the occasion of national calamities, like war, a defeat in battle, a drought, a bad harvest, a pestilence, or an invasion of locusts. On the appointed day the people would assemble in the Temple (cf. 1 Kgs. 8:33-40; 2 Chr. 30:9; 1 Mc. 4:37), not to celebrate a feast but to do penance in sackcloth and ashes (1 Sm. 7:6; 1 Mc. 3:47; Jdt. 4:8-15). Joel has described a ceremony of this kind (Jl. 1:13 f.; 2:15-17).

The public supplication of the leaders of the people is to be seen in the same ritual context: Moses (Dt. 9:25-29); Joshua (Jos. 7:7-9); Jehoshaphat (2 Chr. 20:6-12); Ezra (Ez. 9:6-15; Neh. 9:6-37); Nehemiah (Neh. 11:5-11); similarly, the prayer of the people in 1 Mc. 3:50-53.

In these psalms one motive is stressed beyond others: Yahweh, this is your people—this is therefore your affair (Pss. 43:13; 73:2; 78:1; 79:16).

2. PSALMS OF THANKSGIVING[3]

1) Psalms of Individual Thanksgiving

THE SITZ   Like the rest of the Psalter, these psalms have
IM LEBEN   their place in the worship of Israel, but what
is of particular interest is that most of the thanksgiving
psalms came into being precisely as a liturgy. This is their
Sitz im Leben, the concrete, historical situation in which
they took shape. Clear traces of this origin are visible in
many of them. There is, surely, a liturgical nuance in the
following passages: Psalms 9:15; 91:1-4; 115:14-19; 117;
137:1 f. Regularly, the psalmist addresses the bystanders
(we may infer that he is thinking of worshipers in the
Temple): Psalms 9:12; 29:5; 31:11; 33:4; 106:1-3;
117:1-4. Some psalms speak of a liturgical reunion in the
Temple: Psalms 39:10 f.; 106:32; 115:18 f. The Temple
is indicated by references to sacrifices in fulfillment of
vows: Psalms 106:22; 115:17.

Admittedly, these psalms are very nearly the only evidence we have for the existence in Israel of a liturgical
ceremony of thanksgiving, but this evidence is compelling;
the passages indicated do not exhaust the relevant texts.
We may go further and assert that a close study of the
thanksgiving psalms will enable us to reconstruct the ceremony, at least in its broad outlines. It would have been
something like this: An Israelite, who had come safely
through a great danger, went up to the Temple, often
accompanied by his family and friends, there to be met by
a priest or priests. He brought a victim for sacrifice, usually
in fulfillment of a vow. He gathered about him a group of
worshipers and recounted what Yahweh had done for him.
Here we have all the essentials of the thanksgiving psalm.
The whole was concluded by the offering of sacrifice. Psalm
117 has preserved a remarkable description of such a
thanksgiving liturgy.

It seems clear that an individual's act of thanksgiving, at
least when it was performed in the Temple, was not regarded as a private devotion. Moreover, the ceremony was
not always carried through by, or on behalf of, just one

man. In this regard Psalm 106 is illuminating because it shows us a communal thanksgiving ceremony which is obviously a carefully-organized liturgy. It is natural that many Israelites chose one or other of the great feasts—doubtless the joyous Feast of Tabernacles was especially favored—as an occasion when they could most fittingly give thanks to God. Hence it would happen that many would wish to perform the ceremony on the same day and then the priests would arrange them in groups according to the favors they had received; Psalm 106 distinguishes four such groups: travelers (vv. 4-9); prisoners (vv. 10-16); the sick (vv. 17-22); and sailors (vv. 23-32). The psalm opens with a liturgical invitation to those present, those who have come from many lands, urging them to give thanks to the merciful Lord (vv. 1-3). Then, corresponding to the four groups, come the four main sections of the psalm, all built on an identical plan. First, the particular predicament is described, after which we are told:

"Then they cried to the Lord in their need
    and he rescued them from their distress" (6, 13, 19, 28).

Next the deliverance is outlined and each group is exhorted:

"Let them thank the Lord for his love,
    for the wonders he does for men" (8, 15, 21, 31).

The ceremony concludes with a general recalling of God's benefits to men (vv. 33 f.).

Thus it appears that the thanksgiving psalm was originally the product, or rather the accompaniment, of such a religious ceremony, a ceremony that could have involved an individual or which may have been communal. But soon a distinct literary form emerged and psalms may have been composed without reference to the Temple or to any special ceremony. It follows that not *all* the thanksgiving psalms necessarily grew in the manner we have described; some of them may well be the spontaneous and personal outpourings of a grateful spirit. But, once gathered into the Psalter, they became community prayers, and that too is the role they play in the liturgy of the Christian Church.

2) Psalms of National Thanksgiving

Thus far we have considered individual thanksgiving: hymns of gratitude for favors granted to individual Israelites, even though these benefits were regularly celebrated by a liturgical ceremony which could have taken a marked communal form. Now we may glance briefly at a smaller class of psalms: psalms of national thanksgiving. The *Sitz im Leben* of these psalms is to be sought in feasts of a national character, whether these are annual and recurring or whether they were extraordinary celebrations. Some of the psalms of this type have been occasioned by a victory or, more probably, by deliverance from imminent danger on a national scale (cf. Pss. 65; 123; 128). Others, like Psalm 64 and Psalm 66, thank God for a bounteous year of healthy stock and abundant harvest:

> "The hills are girded with joy,/the meadows covered with flocks, the valleys are decked with wheat./They shout for joy, yes, they sing" (Ps. 64:14).

Thus the nation, no less than the individual Israelite, acknowledged the great goodness of its God. Surely these psalms must blend, with conspicuous ease, into the Christian cult, the thanksgiving and praise of the whole new Israel.

3. HYMNS OF PRAISE[4]

The hymn of praise has its roots in the beginning of Israel's history. The song of Miriam (Ex. 15:21)—which is the source of the earlier canticle of Moses (Ex. 15:1-18)—was a spontaneous celebration of the saving power of God manifested in the crossing of the Red Sea. The introduction to the ancient song of Deborah (Jgs. 5:3) also has a hymnal form, again in praise of a divine intervention. In short, each time that Yahweh shows himself in a terrifying theophany or in an event of history a hymn must follow (cf. Jdt. 16:1 f.,13). These canticles of praise, springing

spontaneously from the recognition of a liberating intervention of Yahweh, receive a new value, one might say a
"sacramental" quality, in that encounter of Yahweh with
his people which is the liturgy. For it is in the liturgy that
the *qahal*, the "church," relived the high deeds which God
had wrought for the former generations; it is there that
the old traditions of the Exodus and of Sinai were celebrated. It is there too that Israel became more conscious
of being the people of the Covenant.

It is, therefore, in the framework of the feasts of Israel
that we must generally set the origin of the psalms of
praise. Hence we find that Elkanah went each year to
Shiloh to offer sacrifice and "to worship the Lord of Hosts"
(1 Sm. 1:3). The Prophet Amos, in condemning religious
hypocrisy, mentions disdainfully "the noise of your songs
. . . the melody of your harps" (Am. 5:23). Song was
a constant factor in the feasts of Israel. For example, we
find evidence of choral chants in the psalms: 135; 117:2-4;
134:19 f. Psalm 150 reminds us of a conductor of an
orchestra inviting each instrument in turn to join in.

The active participation of the people took the form of
rhythmical handclapping (Pss. 46:2; 97:8) and cries and
exclamations of joy (1 Kgs. 1:39 f.; 2 Chr. 23:11-13;
29:30). The principal exclamation was the divine name
"Yahweh," generally in its shortened form "Yah." (*Allelu-
Yah* = "Praise Yahweh.") Another exclamation of joy was
"Amen" (cf. 1 Chr. 16; 36; Jdt. 15:10; Pss. 40:14; 17:19;
88:53; 105:48). The phrase, "for his love has no end,"
occurs not only in the psalms but in several other places
(for example, 2 Chr. 5:13; 7:3,6; 20; 21; Jer. 33:11). The
participation of the people expressed itself also in certain
rites and gestures: lifting up of hands (Pss. 27:2; 76:3;
133:2; 140:2); bowing low (Pss. 94:6; 95:9); kneeling
(Ps. 94:6); prostrations (Pss. 5:8; 94:6). Other examples
are: 2 Chr. 6:12–7:3; 29:28 f.; Ez. 3:11; 1 Mc. 4:54-59.

4. ROYAL PSALMS

A number of psalms are concerned with the king of Israel.
There is no question of any new literary form; these are

hymns, thanksgiving psalms, supplications, but the place which the king occupies in them gives them a special character. For the king of Israel had a privileged role in the religion of Israel: he is not the profane leader of a people called to a supernatural destiny; rather, he is himself the instrument of the divine plan; he participates in the promises and in the supernatural character of the history which he helps to shape. He is at once the representative of God who leads the people, and the people's spokesman before God. But, above all, the king is the representative of a dynasty which is the object of divine favor and the recipient of the divine promise (2 Sm. 7). The royal psalms, or most of them, are messianic.

The setting of these psalms is to be sought in the court of the kings of Israel. It must be kept in mind that the king of Israel was the prince of a theocratic nation and not an autonomous sovereign. Yahweh was the true King of the nation and his earthly representative was his "anointed"— "chosen to sit upon the throne of the kingdom of the Lord over Israel" (1 Chr. 28:5). He must walk before Yahweh as David did (1 Kgs. 9:4; 2 Chr. 7:17). When the day of his accession, or its anniversary, was celebrated, when a royal marriage was solemnized or when an exultant procession went to meet his triumphal return after a victory, when prayers were offered for the success of a campaign— it was never forgotten that he was the Lord's anointed. On such occasions the royal canticles were sung in the palace or Temple.

The royal psalms are ancient poems dating from the monarchic age and reflect the court language and ceremonial. In their original composition they speak of a contemporary king and they visualize directly a king seated on the throne of David. But the king of the Chosen People is an "anointed one," a "messiah," and the promises made by God to the Dynasty of David envisaged a privileged descendant in whom God will be well-pleased and whom he will employ to bring his saving plan to fulfillment. These psalms are messianic from the beginning.

5. PSALMS OF SION

When David had captured the Jebusite stronghold of Jerusalem he first of all made it his capital and then, by trans-
porting the Ark there, established it as a religious shrine.
With the building of the Temple of Solomon, Sion became
very definitely the religious center of the kingdom, the
place which Yahweh had chosen (Pss. 77:68 f.; 67:17).
Later, when Jerusalem alone had withstood the assaults of
Sennacherib, belief in the inviolability of Sion assumed the
nature of a dogma, and Jeremiah, in vain, tried to break
down that presumptuous confidence (cf. Jer. 7:4-7). Nebuchadnezzar proved that the Prophet's threats were not
empty words. During the Exile, ruined Sion became the
center of messianic hopes (Is. 60; 66; Zech. 8). Though
the Second Temple was not built according to the ideal
specifications of Ezekiel (chapters 40-43), it was raised in
the atmosphere of his teaching and looked to the future,
to the new Jerusalem, the spiritual capital of all men. It is
to be expected that there are psalms, both before the Exile
and after the restoration, which sing of the city and its
Temple.

These psalms of Sion are particularly in place on the
lips of pilgrims to the holy city. If not all of them were
composed precisely for this purpose, at least the pilgrimage
must speedily have become their natural liturgical setting.
The Law prescribed three annual pilgrimages—Pasch,
Pentecost, and Tabernacles—which all adult Israelite men
were bound to attend (Ex. 23:17; 34:23; Dt. 16:16); in
practice, those who lived at any distance from Jerusalem
chose one or other of the feasts. Jews of the Diaspora made
a valiant effort to visit the holy city at least once in a life-
time. It is clear that pilgrimages to Sion were frequent and
were accompanied by special ceremonies (cf. Pss. 23; 83;
14).

Some of the psalms of Sion can be fitted, with a high
degree of probability, into a definite historical setting.
Psalm 23 was likely composed on the occasion of David's

solemn translation of the Ark of Jerusalem. Psalms 45, 47, and 75 would seem to celebrate the deliverance of Sion from Sennacherib in 701 B.C. or 688 B.C. The other three, of their nature, cannot be placed in a determined historical background: Psalm 83 extolls the Temple as the dwelling place of Yahweh and the center of the cult, while Psalm 86 looks to an idealized Sion as the spiritual capital of mankind. Psalm 121 is patently a pilgrim song.

6. THE KINGSHIP OF YAHWEH PSALMS

Israel's conception of God as the King of Israel is found early in sacred history: Ex. 15:18; Nm. 23:21; Dt. 33:5; Jgs. 8:22; 1 Sm. 8:7; 12:12. This God was enthroned in their midst, on the Ark of the Covenant; more precisely, he was seated between the cherubim, or upon them, above the Ark: "The Lord is enthroned on the cherubim" (Pss. 17:11; 79:2; 98:1; Dn. 3:55; 1 Kgs. 19:15). Yahweh said to Moses: "From above the mercy seat, from between the two cherubim that are upon the ark of the testimony, I will speak with you" (Ex. 25:22). Ex. 37:1-9 gives a description of the Ark: the "mercy seat" or "propitiary" was the golden cover of the Ark and the cherubim were the two sphinx-like creatures placed at either end of the cover; the whole resembled an elaborate throne. In the gloom of the tent of assembly and later in the darkness of the Holy of Holies, Yahweh was enthroned invisibly upon the Ark. Alternatively, the Ark is called the footstool of Yahweh (Ps. 131:7; cf. 98:5).

The *Sitz im Leben* of the psalms of the Kingship of Yahweh is found in the liturgical feasts of Israel. This, we have seen, is the setting of the hymns of praise, but these psalms, too, are hymns of praise. S. Mowinckel[5] has posited the existence of a New Year ceremony of the enthronement of Yahweh, on the model of the Babylonian annual enthronement of Marduk. The existence of such a feast in Israel cannot be demonstrated; it remains a hypothesis and, seemingly, a doubtful one. Others have suggested that, in celebrating the Kingship of Yahweh, the intention was to extol the universal kingdom of the future; the emphasis is eschatological.

The true position may be quite simply that the Kingship of Yahweh, acknowledged from the earliest history of the people, was spontaneously honored in the liturgical celebrations. The liturgy of Israel should be taken on three levels, for present, past, and future were united in one actual celebration. The Covenant of the past is regarded as still at work, and the present generation enters into it consciously and freely, while it looks already, full of confidence, to the full realization on the day when Yahweh will appear as King over the whole earth. It is, doubtless, in the background of such a liturgy that we must recognize the background of our psalms of the Kingship of Yahweh.[6]

7. OTHER GROUPS

1) *Wisdom Psalms*

It is to be expected that the Wisdom movement would have inspired some, at least, of the psalms. In fact, quite a large number are markedly sapiential in treatment. These psalms may be grouped according to their stand on the question of retribution.[7] Many of them take for granted, either more or less, the traditional position that virtue is rewarded and wickedness punished in this life. Other psalmists, like Job and Qoheleth, are painfully aware that this facile solution does not answer the problem, while a few seem to glimpse the true answer.

The greatest number of wisdom psalms represent the traditional teaching and thus do not really face up to the problem of retribution at all. In a second group the anomaly of the suffering of the just and the prosperity of the wicked is keenly felt, and God is asked to restore the equilibrium by punishing sinners and restoring well-being to the just. The psalms of a third group take a step towards the ultimate solution when they question the contentment of the wicked in their prosperity and when they underline the true good of the just: the possession of God, and his approval, despite their trials. Finally, three of these psalms

(36; 48; 72)—together with the supplication psalm 16—
reach, or at least very nearly attain, the ultimate solution.
It is seen that retribution is not a matter of prosperity or
the lack of it; it is not spelled out in terms of the things of
this world.

2) *Psalms of a Deuteronomical Liturgy*[8]

Five psalms (80; 94; 77; 104; 105) are closely related to
Deuteronomy (especially to Dt. 5-11) and appear to form
a special "liturgy."

It is notable that the same principal motifs recur frequently in Dt.; these are: (1) the observance of the statutes and ordinances (for example, Dt. 5:1 f.; 6:1-9); (2)
an admonition to fidelity to the true cult of Yahweh (for
example, Dt. 6:10-16; 8:11-18). The admonition is accompanied by threats (for example, Dt. 4:26-29; 8:19 f.),
and promises of easy conquest (for example, Dt. 6:18 f.;
7:16-24) and great fertility (for example, Dt. 7:13-15;
8:7-10); (3) commemoration of the events of the Exodus
(for example, Dt. 6:6-9; 11:18-21) by a "commemorative discourse."

This group of psalms not only reflects these motifs but
reflects also a liturgical function which gave concrete expression to the prescriptions of Dt. After an initial invitation to praise Yahweh (Pss. 80:2-4; 94:1 f.) the motifs of
Dt. recur:

1. Recall of the law and statutes (Pss. 80:5 f.; 77:5 f.;
104:8-10).
2. The "commemorative discourse" (Pss. 80:7 f.; 104).
3. The admonition (Pss. 80:9-13; 94:8-11; 77; 105).
4. The promises (Ps. 80:14-17).

The liturgical action suggested by these psalms fulfilled
the prescription of Dt. 27:32 (cf. Jos. 8; 24) that the
commandments should be reiterated and the events of the
Exodus, and the Covenant, should be recalled at an assembly of the people. In practice, this would have taken
place at the great feasts.

3) *Various Prayers*

Five of the gradual psalms (120; 122; 125; 132; 133) form a small collection of postexilic prayers. Though they might have been attached to some of the greater groups, it seems best to consider them apart. Psalm 120 treats of the continual and loving protection of God, while the theme of Psalm 122 is the humble expectation of mercy. The wonder and deep joy of the restoration are beautifully caught in Psalm 125. Psalm 132 would seem to reflect the first harmonious relationship of the returned exiles. The group is suitably rounded off by the invitation, to priests and levites, to praise the Lord in his sanctuary through the hours of the night.

8. DOCTRINAL ASPECTS OF PSALMS

1) *The Old Testament Notion of Thanksgiving*

When we turn to the Bible we soon perceive that the *Heilsgeschichte,* the salvation history, is throughout dominated by the realization of God's free choice of Israel and by the awareness that this was no isolated act but a continual grace which tends to fulfillment—fulfillment in Christ. And in the light of this awareness it is felt, more or less confusedly, that each particular gift of Yahweh, even his benefits to individual men, is a consequence of that choice and, in its own modest way, a moment of this great history. Therefore the Israelite spontaneously reacted to the divine generosity, towards the nation or towards himself, by wonder at the unbounded goodness of God, by praise and thanksgiving. Even beyond the horizon of Israel the biblical view is that any man who comes to the knowledge of God must react in the same way: it is the proper and the only reasonable attitude of the creature. Failure to act so was, in Paul's eyes, the capital sin of paganism: "Though they knew God, they did not honor him as God or give thanks to him" (Rom. 1:21).

Old Testament thanksgiving is never merely gratitude for past favors; it ever looks to the future and to a higher grace; and indeed, in the time of fulfillment, thanksgiving dominates the prayer of Christians, as we may readily learn from Acts and from the New Testament epistles. Yet gratitude does remain, in Israel, the distinctive feature of this prayer. Thanksgiving, we have noted, always goes along with profession of faith in God and with the recognition of his glory and of his goodness, because the acknowledgment of God inevitably gives rise to praise of him and calls forth gratitude for his generosity. Above all else, it is the merciful and saving work of God that fills the heart of the Israelite with overflowing gratitude. For him, thanksgiving is the public confession of determined divine acts; to thank God is to publish his greatness, to proclaim the marvels he has wrought, to bear testimony to his works.

It should be noted, however, that the psalms of thanksgiving by no means exhaust the Bible's stock of thanksgiving hymns. The attitude of thankfulness to God is, as we have seen, characteristically biblical, and once the distinctive literary form of the thanksgiving psalm had evolved it is natural to expect that it would have been rather widely exploited. An excellent representative of the form is the canticle of Hezekiah (Is. 38:10-20) and, significantly, it has an unmistakable liturgical suggestion: "The Lord will save me,/and we will sing to stringed instruments all the days of our life,/at the house of the Lord" (v. 20). We may cite as further examples the canticle of Hannah (1 Sm. 2:1-10) and the prayer of Jonah (Jon. 2:2-9)—this last is of special interest. Though obviously not placed in a liturgical setting—Jonah prays "from the belly of the fish"—yet it still looks to the Temple: "When my soul fainted within me,/I remembered the Lord; And my prayer came to thee/into thy holy Temple" (v. 7). This is surely an echo of the origin of such psalms, while at the same time it offers striking evidence that the Israelite, while maintaining that Yahweh could be adequately worshiped only in Jerusalem, nevertheless believed that he might pray anywhere and offer thanksgiving in any circumstance, and that his prayer would be heard. Nor is the thanksgiving psalm confined to the Old Testament. The *Benedictus* and *Magnificat* are much influenced by the form and, outside

of the Bible, we have the *Hodayoth,* the hymns of the
Essene community of Qumran.

We have remarked that the most significant feature of
the thanksgiving psalms is the relating of the benefit received, precisely because this was a manifestation of God's
goodness and redounded to his glory. Here we find that
close association of praise and thanksgiving so characteristic of the Bible. It is in his great works and because of
his great goodness that God appears worthy of all praise,
and it is for the same reason that he must be thanked.
This situation quite satisfied the Hebrews, but if we, in our
Western way, would like to be more precise (and Western
precision is not always an improvement on biblical language) we might say that praise regards God in himself,
whereas thanksgiving looks to his gifts.

An important element of the thanksgiving ceremony is
that the Israelite, by openly acknowledging the benefit received, bears witness to the goodness of God. He can point
to one more instance of God's solicitude for his people; it
is precisely because he is conscious of being one of God's
people that he feels urged to go up to the Temple and there
praise God with his brethren:

> "I will tell of your name to my brethren
> and praise you where they are assembled"
>
> (Ps. 21:23).

The man who has so experienced the goodness of the
Lord becomes a witness of that goodness, an apostle of his
fellowmen.

2) *The Kingship of Yahweh*

The nearness of God and the kingdom of God are the two
principal themes of the Kingship of Yahweh psalms.[9] The
end of all revelation is communion between God and man.
God wills to draw near to man, he wills to establish his
kingdom in the midst of humanity. God's dominion over
man is aimed at elevating man to communion with God
and hence, mercifully, the reign of Yahweh was progressively manifested. The earlier prophets visualized this kingship as the "Judgment" of Yahweh on Israel and on the

wicked. The more recent prophets contemplated a re-created world standing in the shadow of God's presence; while the authors of the apocalypses described the establishment of the kingdom in the scenario of a cosmic catastrophe. In the wisdom literature the kingdom of God was presented as the fruit and the progressive realization of the plan of the divine wisdom. The New Testament announced the kingdom as imminent, thanks to the death and resurrection of Christ, or as already come in his person, and put the accent on its essential interior character, founded on charity. Our Christian world lives in the expectation of the full manifestation of this kingdom at the end of time. All these aspects are covered by the one concept of "kingdom of God." There is no conflict between them, nor do they differ entirely from one another, though they are not the same. They go together, closely linked, one depending on the other as they constitute so many progressive realizations of that communion of life which God has willed to establish between himself and humanity.

The people of Israel first conceived the Kingship of Yahweh as an actual reality, valid for the present—though already it was vaguely felt that one day it would transcend time (Pss. 9:39; 28:10; 73:12; 102:19; cf. 5:3; 23:7 f.; 34:5; 144:1,11). Thus envisaged, the Kingship of Yahweh was linked to the destiny of Israel, for it was in his people that Yahweh was present. His presence was even localized in the Temple, above the Ark of the Covenant. It was this presence which gave Israel its cohesion and made it a people.

But this first community of God was only the prefiguration of another community, of a new kingdom of God, more interior and more universal. Not only will God be present in his people as a people, but he will henceforth be present to each of its members; more, he will be *in* them, under the regime of a New Covenant. Any man—and not only a son of Abraham—may henceforth be joined to him. It is in the crucible of the Exile that Israel acquired this new comprehension of her destiny: when the glory of Yahweh had abandoned the Temple (Ezek. 10:18 f.), when the Ark had disappeared, and when the Temple itself had been destroyed. In God's plan these bitter facts were a purifying trial destined to mature the mentality of the people in view of new graces and richer blessings. Before the ruins of the abolished monarchy, Israel gained a deeper understanding of the faithfulness and of the tenderness of Yahweh. A spiritual Israel was born, and grew in the awareness of a nearness to God that was more real than ever. Jeremiah, Ezekiel, and Second Isaiah prepared the people for the coming of a renewed and enlarged kingdom. Henceforth the Kingship of Yahweh appeared as a reality of the world to come, not limited to Israel but embracing all peoples (Jer. 31:31-34; Ezek. 37:26; Is. 60:2 f.; cf. Pss. 21:29 f.; 47:3; 67:30; 86:4).

The psalms of the Kingship of Yahweh have particularly underlined the future coming of the kingdom of God. It is Yahweh in person who will establish his kingdom on earth—no allusion is made to the Messiah. It is Yahweh who will reign, clothed in majesty; it is he who will come to judge nations. For the coming of Yahweh and the establishment of his kingdom will take the form of a terrible *judgment,* but the divine coming will signify at the same time *grace and salvation*: Yahweh will reign in justice, in peace, and in goodness. That is why, in these psalms, despite the awesomeness and the terror of his majesty, joy always accompanies the coming of Yahweh.

After centuries of preparation, the Jewish people lived at last in vivid expectation of the kingdom of God. Most often this expectation took a political turn: they looked for the restoration of the Davidic monarchy. But the more deeply religious visualized a reality that was essentially interior: in obeying the Law, "the just man took on himself the yoke of the kingdom of God." Therefore it is surprising, especially given the place which the preaching of the kingdom of God holds in the Gospel of Jesus, that we attach more importance to the proclamation of the Messiah-King than to the proclamation of the kingdom of God. It is surprising, seeing that Jesus is God and that in him God has come on earth, that one does not learn to find in him the accomplishment of the promises which proclaim the coming of Yahweh in order to establish his kingdom.[10]

[1] See Drijvers, *op. cit.*, pp. 49-55.

[2] See *ibid.*, pp. 101-11.

[3] See W. Harrington, "Thanksgiving," *The Furrow*, 14 (1963), 225-33.

[4] See Drijvers, *op. cit.*, pp. 57-69.

[5] *The Psalms in Israel's Worship*, trans. D. R. Ap-Thomas (Nashville, Tenn.: Abingdon, 1962), I, pp. 106-92.

[6] See Drijvers, *op. cit.*, pp. 154 f.

[7] See Castellino, *op. cit.*, pp. 729-31.

[8] See *ibid.*, pp. 677-81.

[9] See *ibid.*, pp. 155-59.

[10] See A. Gelin, "Messianisme," DBS, V, col. 1192. Throughout this chapter, by permission of The Grail (England), psalm-texts have been quoted from *The Psalms: A New Translation* (London: Collins [Fontana Books], 1963).

SIX

THE CHRONICLER'S HISTORY

1 AND 2 CHRONICLES
EZRA AND NEHEMIAH
THE MESSAGE OF THE CHRONICLER

We have seen that the deuteronomical school produced a great historical work, marked by a distinctive theological outlook. In the postexilic age another major historical work saw the light, one that reflects the priestly interests and that is also dominated by the theological views of its author. This unknown writer is conveniently named the Chronicler —after the title of the first part of his work.

1. 1 AND 2 CHRONICLES
1) The Book

TITLE It is generally agreed that 1 and 2 Chronicles, Ezra, and Nehemiah form one work. This is borne out, in the first place, by the language and style of all these books. Then too, the same intense interest in the Temple is found throughout, and a penchant for genealogies and statistics is evident from first to last. It is also significant that the closing verses of 2 Chronicles (36:22 f.) are reproduced in the introduction of Ezra (Ez. 1:1-3a)—this is a manner of indicating that Chronicles and Ez.-Neh. are one book.

The Hebrew name for Chronicles is *dibre hayyamim*, which means literally "the things of the days," that is "the events of the past." St. Jerome, in his *Prologus Galeatus*, comments that the work might well be called *Chronicon totius historiae divinae*, that is, "the chronicle of the whole of sacred history." In the LXX the title is *Paraleipomena* or "the things omitted," because the translators viewed the work as a supplement to Sm. and Kgs.; this view and name were adopted by the Vg. Chronicles is the last book of the Hebrew Bible and comes after Ez. and Neh. This position of the work seems to be indicated by Christ in Mt. 23:25 and Lk. 11:51 (cf. 2 Chr. 24:20-22): the murder of Zechariah is the last mentioned in Scripture, as that of Abel is the first.[1]

DATE In determining the date of Chronicles we must keep in mind the continuation of the work in Ez.-Neh.; consequently a date later than Ezra is certain—in other words, later than 428 B.C. The genealogy of the Davidic line given in 1 Chronicles 3:19-24 descends to at least six generations after Zerubbabel (that is, to c. 350 B.C.). The language of the work, the priestly preoccupations, and its position as the last book in the Writings all point to the late postexilic period. We may reasonably date the Chronicler's history about 300 B.C.

2) *Literary Form*

A comparison of Chronicles with Sm.-Kgs. carries the conviction that the Chronicler intends to write a history; a closer look at the work gives the further assurance that he has planned to set a religious doctrine in full relief. It becomes clear that, despite a wide material agreement, the outlook and object of the deuteronomical history and of the Chronicler are not the same. In the latter a constant tendency is manifest: to justify, from history, the solutions which, in the postexilic era, had been given to complex problems, and notably to refer back to David the basic element of the Jewish community. The writer desires to establish the continuity between the past and the present and to make the old relevant to the new.

His primary purpose is to write a history of the dynasty of David, to bring out what it achieved in the religious sphere, especially in matters of the cult, and to establish legitimate patterns of institutions and their personnel for the people of God. The Chronicler built his history and his theology around these fundamental points.[2] His work is a history, and a theology of history, quite independent of that of the deuteronomists.

3) The Purpose of Chronicles

The Chronicler is interested not only in the meaning of history but in the lesson of history and in the relevance of the pre-exilic age to his own time. His work may be more aptly described as a theology of history than as history, and he himself is a theologian rather than a historian. He has written for his contemporaries, not to present a summary of past events, but to offer them a reinterpretation of Israel's past. He has done this in order to bring them to an awareness of their status as God's people and to urge them to live in fidelity to God by obeying his Law and by rendering him true and meaningful cult.

This is not to say that the data brought forward by the Chronicler, beyond those furnished by his canonical sources, lack historical reliability. We have to examine each item of this additional material on its merits, while noting that recent archaeological discoveries and historical investigations have repeatedly vindicated the trustworthiness of the author.[3] But keeping in mind the literary form he has adopted, we must also acknowledge that, by studied selection and by deliberate insertions and omissions, he has consciously modified the picture of events drawn in Sm.-Kgs. He selects material that would emphasize certain aspects of the tradition, as for instance, those actions of the kings of Judah which affected the religious life of their people and their attitude towards the Temple. A notable addition is the long account of David's preparations for the building of the Temple and the organizing of its services (1 Chr. 22-29). Events had shown that God's plan would be fulfilled in the Davidic line and in Judah; thus the author omits altogether the history of the Israelite kings. Modifications are usually inspired by a more refined theological insight: in 2 Sm. 24:1 Yahweh moved David to number Israel, whereas in 1 Chronicles 21:1 the action was instigated by Satan; 1 Chronicles 17:11-14 deftly adapts the dynastic oracle of 2 Sm. 7:12-16 to fit the later stage of messianic expectation.

In short, the author is "a theologian who in the light of the experiences of the past and especially of the Davidic experience, 'thinks' the conditions of the ideal kingdom. He brings together in one synthesis past, present, and future; he projects into the age of David the whole cultic organization of his own time while he omits everything that might lessen the standing of his hero, now become the type of the messianic king for whom he yearns. Apart from some additional information whose reliability can be checked his work is less important as a reconstruction of the past than as a picture of the situation and of the preoccupations of his own epoch."[4]

From his study of the past and his knowledge of the postexilic situation, the Chronicler was fired by one dominating conviction: Israel was called to be a holy community. He had read the deuteronomists aright and had imbibed the spirit of Ezekiel and the priestly writers. The true Israel, brought into being by God, was an Israel gathered about one central shrine, a "kingdom of priests and a holy nation" (Ex. 19:6); a people "whose whole life was to be a 'liturgy' or divine service."[5] In practice, this meant a community which had its center in the Temple where priests and levites assured that fitting cult would be paid to God on behalf of his people.

The Chronicler was anxious to demonstrate that the community, living in the spirit of the reforms of Nehemiah and Ezra, was in fact the kind of community that God had willed from the beginning. He wanted to show that the Exile had not meant a break and had not led to the emergence of something entirely new. After all, it did look like that: the monarchy had been the accepted shape of Israel's life for centuries and the new state of Judah had been built on different lines. So he looked again at the past and found in it the seeds of the future—he saw fulfillment, not rejection. Forms were different, but the essential features of God's people had persisted.

He took his stand on the Nathan prophecy (2 Sm. 7) and on the divine choice of the Davidic dynasty. From this standpoint he viewed the political schism as a rebellion against the divine plan: the Northern Kingdom had broken with the divinely-chosen king and had turned its back on the one shrine where legitimate worship might be offered to God. Jeroboam and his people had cut themselves off from the Covenant—logically, they may be left aside. It is no more than a development of the judgment passed on the Northern kings by the deuteronomists. The author's stand on the choice of the Davidic Dynasty also explains his idealization of David, while his preoccupation with the cult leads him to exaggerate the cultic role of his ideal king. Basing himself on David's bringing of the Ark to Jerusalem, on his desire to build a Temple, and on his reputation as a psalmist, the Chronicler has given him credit for drawing up the plans of the Temple, for making all necessary preparations for its construction, and for organizing the liturgical worship of the nation. This is a striking way of bringing out the essential link between the kingdom of David and the little Judaean community. The monarchy has gone, but the work begun by David has developed: Judaism is a worshiping community gathered around a central shrine and living in expectation of the coming of a new David.

History had demonstrated that the Lord's people were in fact narrowed down to those for whom Jerusalem, the Temple, and the Davidic line were central to their loyalty. To deny this was apostasy. Not to know this was heathenism. For these were of Yahweh's choosing, and through their media his people acknowledge his rule. Yet it is an important element of the Jewish faith, as reflected in this book, that the apostate might return and the heathen acknowledge the one true God, the sole ruler of all history who is known in his dealings with his Chosen People. All historical success or failure are the direct product of Divine reward for loyalty to the Torah or punishment for apostasy.[6]

The Chronicler has brought about the marriage of dynastic messianism with the priestly ideal of Ezekiel. His

David, king and priest, is not only an idealization of the historical king, he is the ideal David of the future, the Messiah. Unhappily, his stress on the primacy of the spiritual and on the essentially religious nature of the kingdom of God did not have the impact it deserved and a more materialistic outlook prevailed. But the Chronicler was vindicated by the King he had dimly foreseen, by him who declared: "My kingship is not of this world" (Jn. 18:36).

2. EZRA AND NEHEMIAH

We have noted that the Chronicler did not lay down his pen at the close of 2 Chronicles. Although in modern versions Ezra and Nehemiah constitute two books (in the Vg. they are 1, 2 Esdras) they are really sections of the Chronicler's one work. The position of Ez.-Neh. before 1, 2 Chronicles in the Hebrew indicates that it was the first to be regarded as Scripture, probably because Chronicles seemed to be no more than a summary of the earlier histories.

CHRONOLOGY One of the most perplexing problems in the history of Israel is the relationship of the careers of Ezra and Nehemiah. Happily, we do not need to go into the matter here since we have examined it sufficiently in an earlier chapter. On the basis of the hypothesis which we regard as the most satisfactory we reconstruct the order of events as follows:[7]

1. 538-520 B.C. Several caravans of returning exiles arrived in Jerusalem. The first of these was led by Sheshbazzar, prince of Judah, who restored the altar of holocausts and laid the foundations of the Temple (Ez. 1:1–3:13).

2. 520-515 B.C. The rebuilding of the Temple, a work encouraged by Haggai and Zechariah (Ez. 5:1; cf. Hag. 1-2; Zech. 2:5-17) was completed by Zerubbabel; the Temple was consecrated and the Pasch celebrated (Ez. 5:1–6:22).

3. 515-445 B.C. The Samaritans successfully impeded

the restoration of the fortifications under Xerxes I (486-465 B.C.) and Artaxerxes I (465-424 B.C.) (Ez. 4:6-23).

4. 445 B.C. (twentieth year of Artaxerxes I). Beginning of the first mission of Nehemiah. The walls were rebuilt and the fortifications were dedicated (Neh. 1:1-4,17; 6:1-73a; 11:1-20,25a; 12:27-32, 37-40,43).

5. 433 B.C. (thirty-second year of Artaxerxes I). Nehemiah, after twelve years of governorship (Neh. 5:14), went back to Susa. He returned on a second mission before the death of Artaxerxes (424 B.C.)—most likely before the mission of Ezra (Neh. 13:4-31; 10).

6. 428 B.C. (thirty-seventh year of Artaxerxes I). Arrival of Ezra who busied himself with the organization of the religious life of the community (Ez. 7:1—8:36). He read the Law to the people (Neh. 7:73b—8:12), presided at the Feast of Tabernacles (Neh. 8:13-18), sought to suppress mixed marriages (Ez. 9-10), and moved the people to true repentance (Neh. 9:1 f.).

Despite the uncertainty of the chronology, the data of Ez.-Neh. are worthy of every respect. The main sources go back directly to the two great figures of the epoch and, in fact, the accuracy of many of the details can be checked. We find that the administrative organization of the Persian state is correctly presented, even to precise references to the relations of governors among themselves and with the king (Ez. 4:7-23; 5:3-17; 6:1-13). The description of events and circumstances in Judah fits in with what we happen to know of the situation. Apart altogether from his contribution to our historical knowledge of these times, we are grateful to the Chronicler for the glimpse he has given us into the formative stage of Judaism.

FATHER OF JUDAISM Perhaps we today would be inclined to follow ben Sirach who eulogized Nehemiah ("The memory of Nehemiah also is lasting; he raised for us the walls that had fallen" [Sir. 49:13]) but did not mention Ezra; for it does seem that Ezra's contribution would not have been possible without the long and careful preparation of the other. But we can be certain that the Chronicler would not have shared our view. For him Ezra

is the father of Judaism; and his judgment has the support
of later Jewish tradition which witnesses to a continual
growth in the stature of Ezra. The Chronicler could evaluate the contribution of the man more accurately than we.

Ezra brought with him from Babylon "the book of the
Law of Moses" (Neh. 8:1). It seems certain that the title
designates the Pentateuch in its final form, or in something very nearly its final form. This "Book of the Law"
was accepted by the people as the law of the community,
and Ezra, by his cultic and moral reforms, brought the
life of the community into conformity with this norm.
From his time the life and religion of Jews was directed
and moulded by the Torah and Judaism assumed its distinctive characteristic of strict adherence and fidelity to the
Law.

This does not mean that Ezra is responsible for the often extreme legalistic outlook of pharisaism; though it is
not altogether surprising that his reform should have led
to legalism and isolationism—it is not easy to maintain a
balance in such matters. If we are to judge Ezra's role
aright, we shall need to make certain observations.[8] Ezra
did not introduce the emphasis on obedience to the Law:
this went back to Moses and the Sinai tradition. Then there
is Israel's attitude to the Law to be taken into account: the
Torah was not regarded as a code to be obeyed, a long
list of commands and prohibitions. Rather it was seen as
the expression of the will of a Lawgiver who is the Redeemer of Israel; the goodness of this God moved the Israelite to serve him freely and to obey him gladly. It follows that the Law was not counted as a burden: it was a
gracious gift of God and a source of delight (cf. Pss. 1;
19 [18]:7-14; 119 [118]). Nor does attachment to the
Law conflict with the prophetic outlook and spirit. The
long prayer of Ezra (Neh. 9) shows that the postexilic
priestly view was quite in sympathy with the prophetic
demands.

In the light of these observations we may appreciate
Ezra's attitude to the Law and to the cult and realize the
true place of the Torah in Judaism. If for many the elaborate Temple ritual became an empty form and if devotion

to the Law lapsed into legalism, these deviations were due to the weakness of Judaism, to the weakness inherent in any community of men. But to lay later abuses at the door of Ezra is no more justified than to blame the Founder of Christianity for the failure of Christians.

3. THE MESSAGE OF THE CHRONICLER[9]

Chronicles is a history of the theocracy. The genealogies of the opening chapters lead to David, but the emphasis is not so much on him as on the plan of God in which he plays a role. God will establish a kingdom, a kingdom of which he is King and in which the king of Judah is his vicar (1 Chr. 17:14,22). The first recorded event of David's reign is his capture of Jerusalem (1 Chr. 11:4-9), the dwelling place of God. The transport of the Ark (chapter 13) heralds the building of the Temple and opens the way for the prophecy of Nathan (chapter 17). The close of 1 Chronicles (chapters 21-29) is concerned with preparations for the building of the Temple and with the organization of the cult and clergy by David; the principal act of the reign of Solomon is the building of the Temple (2 Chr. 1-9).

The break-up of the united monarchy on the death of Solomon was more than a religious schism, it was an apostasy on the part of the Northern Kingdom. Judah had remained faithful to the ideal of the theocracy founded on Jerusalem, the Temple, the levitical priesthood, and the Davidic Dynasty. Israel, by turning its back on all this, had placed itself outside the pale of sacred history, and in the discourse of Abijah (2 Chr. 13:4-12) the Chronicler justifies his exclusion of Israel from his history. But he has to admit that most of the successors of David were little better than the kings of the North. In fact only three (Jehoshaphat, Hezekiah, and Josiah) walked in the steps of David and Solomon. Yahweh was at last forced to punish his ungrateful people (2 Chr. 36:14-16).

It is chastisement, not destruction, for God must be faithful to his promises. Just as he had moved Nebuchadnezzar to chastise his people (2 Chr. 36:17 ff.) he will raise up the king of Persia to deliver them and to permit them to return to the holy land (2 Chr. 36:22 f.; Ez. 1:1-4). Ez.-Neh. tell the story of the return, the reconstruction of the Temple and of the walls of Jerusalem; they tell of the religious formation of the new community that is yet the prolongation of the old, firmly linked to it by bonds of blood and by the same faith. But the Chronicler is aware that this re-establishment of his people is not the full realization of the prophecies (Neh. 9:36). Israel is still subject to foreign nations and the house of David has not been set up again at the head of the people. Hence there is an attitude of expectation in a spirit of hope and faith; in the time of waiting, Judah, a people separated from other nations, must group itself around the Temple and live according to its own Law.

The Chronicler has wished to present a history of the theocracy, but he has done so in a literary form that does not quite square with our modern notion of history. Indeed, his work is more truly a theology of history and to his religious teaching everything else in his work is subordinated. Even the historical facts themselves, whether he has found them in the Bible or in extrabiblical sources, are pressed into the service of his teaching. In his great work he brought to life again before the eyes of his contemporaries the history of the Davidic theocracy, both in its vicissitudes before the Exile and in its restoration, and he did so as a lesson for his readers. The recalling of the glories and of the woes of the Davidic Dynasty would help them to ponder on their vocation and on their standing as God's people. The story of the historical restoration, coming after the disastrous failure of the monarchy, would show how God had remained faithful to his promises; as a new beginning, it would turn their hope towards the perfect establishment of God's kingdom.

The Chronicler's recourse to history is not unlike that of ben Sirach and of the Book of Wisdom. Like the eulogy of the ancestors of Israel (Sir. 44-50) the passages of Chronicles consecrated to David and to the faithful kings have a generous element of idealization; and like Wis. 10-19 the Chronicler, despite his great respect for and his vast knowledge of the biblical writings, does not hesitate to draw new interpretations from their text. The parallel with Wis. is particularly striking since, as we have seen, Wis. 10-19 is a *midrash*. All three authors are concerned with instructing and edifying their readers.

The Chronicler has adopted a literary form in which historical facts are subordinated to the presentation of doctrine and to moral exhortation. We should not thereby conclude that the work has nothing to offer the historian —we have made this point before, but it bears repetition. In Chronicles the author has added many details which give every guarantee of historicity. The books of Ez.-Neh. are based on the narrative of Ezra and the memoirs of Nehemiah—immediate and even firsthand sources. If we wish to grasp the message of the Chronicler in its entirety we must pay attention to the contributions of great historical value which his work contains. He has traced the progress of sacred history from the Exile to the beginning of the fourth century B.C., and he has also preserved many details of the earlier phases of that history. But his work, with its definite purpose and its distinctive theological outlook, is anything but a *paraleipomena*—a mere supplement.

The Chronicler has taken his stand on the past—the Davidic Dynasty—and is concerned with the present—the contemporary postexilic community—but his eyes are ultimately fixed on the future. Though not himself a prophet (in the classic sense), he is the heir of the prophets and has learned from them. More than any other of the Old Testament historical books, the work of the Chronicler turns the eyes of his readers toward him whom Ezekiel called the "one shepherd," "my servant David" (Ezek. 34:22), and Jeremiah the "righteous Branch" (Jer. 23:5). He turns their eyes towards Christ, the final term of Israel, who by his life and by his death laid the foundation of a theocracy which no adversary can ever henceforth destroy.[10]

---

[1] See A. S. Herbert, PCB, n. 309 a.

[2] See D. N. Freedman, *The Chronicler's Purpose*, C.B.Q. 23 (1961), 436-442.

[3] See W. F. Albright, *From the Stone Age to Christianity* (New York: Doubleday, 1957²), pp. 273 f.

[4] Roland de Vaux, BJ, p. 404.

[5] B. W. Anderson, *Understanding the Old Testament* (Englewood Cliffs, N.J.: Prentice-Hall, 1957), p. 437.

[6] A. S. Herbert, *op. cit.*, n. 310 b.

[7] Cf. Lusseau, *op. cit.*, pp. 713 f.

[8] See Anderson, *op. cit.*, pp. 457-60.

[9] See A. M. Brunet, "Paralipomènes," DBS, VI, cols. 1256-1260.

[10] Cf. A. Noordtzij, "Les intentions du Chroniste," RB, 49 (1940), 168.

SEVEN

THE BOOKS OF THE MACCABEES

1 MACCABEES
2 MACCABEES

The Books of Maccabees take their title from the name Maccabaeus, the surname of Judas the leader of the revolt against Antiochus IV. The meaning of the name is uncertain; it is frequently explained as a derivative of *maqqabah*—"hammer." Judas is by no means the only hero of these books and 1 Mc. covers the whole of the Maccabaean movement to the accession of John Hyrcanus I.

Though 1 Maccabees was written in Hebrew it has come to us only in a Greek version; 2 Maccabees was written in Greek. Both books are represented in A (Codex Alexandrinus—5th cent.), V (Venetus—8th cent.), and a great number of minuscules; S (Sinaiticus—4th cent.) has 1 Maccabees only; B (Vaticanus—4th cent.) has neither. The Old Latin versions are important—the Vg. text is a mediocre representative of the Old Latin.

The Books of Maccabees are deuterocanonical, and theirs is the common history of the deuterocanonical writings.[1] Besides there are two apocryphal books of Maccabees. 3 Maccabees is a pseudohistorical account of a persecution of Alexandrian Jews in the reign of Ptolemy IV (221-204 B.C.). It is the work of an Alexandrian Jew and dates from about the beginning of the Christian era. 4 Maccabees was written by a Jew imbued with Stoic ideas who wished to prove that reason guided by piety can control the passions. He illustrated his theme by the example of Eleazer and the seven brothers of 2 Maccabees. The date is first century A.D., before the year 70.

1. 1 MACCABEES

1 Maccabees covers the period from 175 to 134 B.C., that is, from the beginning of the reign of Antiochus IV to the death of Simon, the last of the sons of Mattathias. In other words, it is the history of the Maccabaean revolt up to the establishment of the Hasmonaean Dynasty.

The eulogy of the Romans (chapter 8) proves that the book was written before 63 B.C., the year in which Pompey took Jerusalem and which marked the beginning of a bitter hatred of Rome. The closing formula, 1 Maccabees 16:23 f., modeled on the formula which closes each reign in Kgs., indicates that the author wrote after the death of John Hyrcanus I (134-104 B.C.). A date early in the reign of Alexander Jannaeus (103-76 B.C.) seems most likely; the book was written during the promising years of the king in order to glorify the ancestors of the dynasty.

The author is unknown. All we can say is that he was a Palestinian Jew, well versed in the Scriptures, who wrote in Hebrew, the sacred language, and was concerned to a notable extent with contemporary events. He was an ardent supporter of the Hasmonaeans and he was convinced that they alone could lead Israel along the right road. He has no difficulty about accepting the fact that these princes, though not of the Aaronitic family, should be high priests as well as civil rulers. It does seem that his outlook was close to that of the later Sadducees.

The author has consciously imitated the literary forms of the older historical books (Jgs., Sm., Kgs.). His history too is fragmentary; it is concerned with certain episodes rather than with providing a continual sweep of events. Such statements as "not even one of them was left" (1 Mc. 7:46), "not one of them had fallen" (1 Mc. 5:54), and the grossly exaggerated numbers are to be seen as echoes of a traditional style and should be evaluated accordingly. This is not the language of a modern historian, anxious about exact figures and details, but testifies to a vivid impression of events that are still fresh, balanced by a familiarity with traditional historiography.

The author has reproduced documents where these were available to him. On the other hand he has not hesitated to put speeches in the mouth of his heroes; this, most likely, indicates a certain Greek influence, though the procedure is by no means unknown in earlier biblical writings (cf. Gn. 49:1-27; Jos. 23). Again true to his scriptural background he has striven to bring out the religious meaning of events. We may say, in short, that 1 Maccabees belongs to the same historical literary form as the deuteronomical history and Ez.-Neh. Though the name of God is not mentioned (a reflection of the growing postexilic tendency to avoid pronouncing the Holy Name) 1 Maccabees is a religious history. The course of events is governed by divine Providence, and God himself is spoken of under the titles Savior of Israel (1 Mc. 4:30), Heaven (1 Mc. 3:18 f., 60), or is indicated simply as "He" (1 Mc. 2:61; 3:22). The Jews turn to God for help before battle and thank him for victory (1 Mc. 4:24,33; 13:47,51). His interventions in the past (1 Mc. 4:9,30; 7:41) are a firm foundation of hope.

The author has been influenced not only by the style of the deuteronomical history, he has also been inspired by the same outlook towards the Law and its observance. In his history too the Law is the center of everything; it is that which divides men into two camps. "The struggle is not between Seleucids and Hasmonaeans, nor even between pagan kingdoms and the Jewish state; it is between the upholders of the Law and its adversaries." The sons of Mattathias are not less zealous than their father and do not betray his last testament when they treat with pagan princes; they are conscious that such action will effectively guarantee the free observance of the Law. On the other hand, confidence in the unfailing promise of God must not end in quietism. The author is not in sympathy with the attitude of those who allowed themselves to be massacred on the sabbath (1 Mc. 2:36-38); and he manifestly approves the decision of Mattathias that it is a far better thing to fight for the Law on the sabbath (1 Mc. 2:42-48); the greatest glory is to die, sword in hand, for the Law (1 Mc. 2:50,64). "This history exalts, at one and the same time, human values and supernatural values: faith engenders heroism and service of the fatherland becomes one with service of the only God."

Yet, when all is said and done, it is plain that 1 Maccabees does not attain the religious stature of the earlier biblical histories. Here there is no influence of the prophets; we note instead a further step towards a legalism that will eventually become excessive; already the Law seems to be more important than God himself. The victory of the Maccabees seems to satisfy the aspirations of the people and the eulogy of Simon is almost messianic in tone. Then there is the fact that the revolution was so soon betrayed —by the immediate successors of John Hyrcanus I—and so utterly; the seeds of thàt betrayal must have been planted at an early date.

On the other hand, despite these shortcomings, the message of 1 Mc. remains valid and its appeal persists. We are shown what faith and confidence can achieve and we once again witness an intervention of God on behalf of his people. And knowledge of the subsequent history of the Hasmonaeans warns us that success and power can corrupt with devastating ease. Where persecution had engendered heroes and martyrs, worldly success had brought a decline in religious fervor. The book continues to utter its message of hope, and the failure of men to remain true to the faith on which that hope was built continues to be a warning to us.

2. 2 MACCABEES

The Second Book of Maccabees is not the sequel of the first. It deals in part with the same history—from 176 B.C. to the victory of Judas Maccabaeus over Nicanor in 160 B.C.—and is a résumé of a work in five volumes by Jason of Cyrene.

The opening letter is dated 124 B.C., and this letter—an invitation to the Jews of Egypt to celebrate the Feast of Dedication—seems to have led to the composition of the work. We may date 2 Maccabees to the last quarter of the second century B.C.—and hence a little before 1 Mc.

The author has not named himself. Since he wrote in Greek and used a Greek history as his source, it is likely that he was an Alexandrian. Unlike the author of 1 Mc. he is no champion of the Hasmonaeans; Judas is for him the man who saved the Law and purified the Temple, and he does not follow the later fortunes of the family of Mattathias. His outlook and his theology also serve to mark him as one who, if not a Pharisee, was in that tradition. We know nothing of Jason or of his work apart from the references of this book.

In his preface the author has stated that the history of Jason has been his main, and seemingly his exclusive, source: "All which has been set forth by Jason of Cyrene in five volumes, we shall attempt to condense into a single book" (2 Mc. 2:23). The letter of 2 Maccabees 9:19-27 and the four letters of chapter 11 most likely came by way of Jason. The two introductory letters, however, were originally written in Hebrew or Aramaic and were probably translated by the author of 2 Maccabees.

The purpose of the author was to persuade his fellow Jews to celebrate the Feast of the Dedication of the Temple; hence each of the five tableaux of his work is composed in oratorical style: the whole is meant to move the reader and give him a sense of involvement. In the first episode we taste something of the peace and joy of the Temple service under the saintly Onias; we share the anguish of the high priest when the sacred place is threatened and again rejoice with him when Heliodorus is compelled to acknowledge the holiness of the God who dwells there. The next two episodes form a contrast. Impiety develops from Jason to Menelaus—from the pillage of the Temple to its profanation, from a massacre of the inhabitants of Jerusalem, to a general violent persecution of Jews. But, in the third discourse, the death of the martyrs, a sacrifice of expiation, turned aside the divine anger and Judas rescued his people and purified the Temple. We feel that hopelessness has given place to hope and confidence. The fourth discourse strikes the same optimistic note and dwells on the further successes of Judas. The last discourse is particularly dramatic and builds up to a climax: the death of Nicanor and the establishment of a commemorative feast.

It is clear that 2 Maccabees belongs to a literary form then popular in the Hellenistic world and known as "pathetic history"; its characteristic was its appeal to the imagination and emotions of the reader. Impassioned discourses, forceful language, enormous numbers, contrived contrasts, flowery style—all are part of the form and all are typical of 2 Maccabees. The intention is to move the reader and the means employed are accepted literary conventions. Therefore the author of 2 Maccabees seeks to bring out the significance of the events he relates, but he neglects the details that scientific history would demand. Chronology yields to oratorical expediency and the orator reserves the right to choose, and to magnify, certain aspects. The "help which comes from Heaven" (1 Mc. 16:3) here takes the form of celestial manifestations (2 Mc. 3:24-26; 10:29 f.; 11:8; cf. 12:22; 15:11-16). The apparition of gods come to aid warriors in battle was a current feature of pathetic history; the Jewish author simply substituted angels for the gods.

The author of 2 Maccabees is more interested in theology than in history (or, rather, in politics); hence in religious stature and in doctrine this book far surpasses 1 Mc. The issue is not clouded by political motives; the struggle is a stark combat of Judaism (the word appears for the first time [2 Mc. 2:21; 8:1; 14:38]) with Hellenism, and it is war to the death. Compromise can lead only to ruin (2 Mc. 4:7-17) and it is unthinkable that the high priesthood should be obtained by the favor of a pagan king (2 Mc. 11:2 f.).

Though fidelity to the Law is inculcated at all times, the legalistic tendency of 1 Mc. has been avoided; this has been achieved by insistence on the holiness of the Law and on its interior aspect. It is this deeper appreciation of the Law that saves the author from the consequence of a seemingly intransigent attitude. Thus, for instance, the sabbath rest may never be transgressed—not even in view of self-defense (2 Mc. 5:25; 6:6; 15:3). He has also linked the sanctuary, the holy place, with observance of the Law.

The "holy One, Lord of all holiness" (2 Mc. 14:36) can tolerate no defilement of his land, his city, his dwelling, no stain on his holy people. That is why the piety of Onias can guard the Temple more effectively than an army, and that is why the impious Jason and Menelaus bring disaster on the holy place. In the dream of Judas the avenging sword which he received from Jeremiah was given to him at the prayer of Onias (2 Mc. 15:16); the intercession of the just high priest was the means of victory over Nicanor.

This religion of the Law and of the Temple is firmly centered on God. It is significant that 2 Maccabees (unlike 1 Mc.) names God continually; he is the Creator of the universe, the All-Powerful, the Lord of the World, and the King of kings; he is the "Lord who has manifested himself" (2 Mc. 15:34); this last title, at the close of the book, is a deliberate challenge to the arrogant claim of Antiochus Epiphanes. Yet this great God is near his people, ready to help them; the earnest prayers illustrate the point in a striking way. There can be no doubt that the spirituality of 2 Maccabees is profound and living.

One point perhaps more than any other serves to underline the difference in outlook of these two books: it is their attitude towards the martyrs. For the author of 1 Mc. their death is a result of the divine anger that has fallen on Israel (1 Mc. 1:64); it has no positive significance. The divine anger is averted by armed resistance, by the resolute action of Judas (1 Mc. 3:8). For the other writer, though the sufferings of the martyrs are still a chastisement, their willing acceptance is an expiation which turns aside the anger of God. If Judas wins victories it is because God has accepted the sacrifice (2 Mc. 7:36; 8:5).[2]

An important feature of 2 Maccabees is its confident teaching on the afterlife. Here the influence of Dn. 12 is manifest and the contrast with 1 Mc. is sharp—a contrast that reflects the Pharisaic and Sadducean tendencies of the two authors (cf. Mt. 22:23; Acts 23:6-8). We learn that the living can pray for the dead and make sin-offerings on their behalf (2 Mc. 12:42-45); this is the scriptural basis for the doctrine of Purgatory. On the other hand, the just who have passed beyond the grave can intercede for those who still live on this earth (2 Mc. 15:11-16). Here we have for the first time, explicitly stated, the doctrine of the communion of saints. It is not surprising that the resurrection is taken for granted (2 Mc. 7; 14:46). These doctrines are the climax of the sure faith and unswerving hope that characterize the book; at the same time they highlight the loving mercy of God and his care for those who are faithful to him.

---

[1] See Wilfrid Harrington, *Record of Revelation: The Bible* (Chicago: The Priory Press, 1965), p. 64.

[2] Lefèvre, *op. cit.*, p. 762.

EIGHT

THE WRITINGS

RUTH—JONAH
TOBIT—BARUCH
DANIEL—ESTHER
JUDITH

In the Hebrew division of the sacred books the third grouping, after the Law and the Prophets, is that of the *kethubhim*, the Writings. The title of this chapter does not refer to that collection of inspired books and is not meant to have a precise technical sense. It is obvious indeed that *kethubhim* is a deliberately broad designation, calculated to accommodate a variety of books that do not belong in the other categories. In a similar fashion the works that fall outside the determined groups we have studied may be gathered here under the same vague title. The advantage of this procedure is that miscellaneous writings can be treated in a single chapter, while the question of literary forms is not begged in advance.

1. RUTH

1) The Book

The Book of Ruth, one of the shortest of the Old Testament writings, takes its name from the Moabitess whose story it relates. In the Hebrew Bible it is found among the *kethubhim* and is the second of the five festal *megilloth* or "rolls"; it was read at the Feast of Pentecost. In the LXX and Vg., Ruth comes immediately after Judges. It is quite unlikely that, if Ruth had ever formed part of the Former Prophets (Jos.-Kgs.), it would have been detached and inserted in the later collection of Writings. It is noteworthy that the book shows no signs of editing in a deuteronomical sense. We may take it that Ruth originally took its place in the Bible among the Writings. Its position (in the LXX and Vg.) between Judges and Samuel is explained by its opening words: "In the days when the judges ruled" (Ru. 1:1).[1]

While it is reasonable to suppose that Ruth is based on a pre-exilic tradition, a study of the writing convinces one that its literary form is close to that of the modern novel.[2] The author, skillfully and with charm, presents an idyll of simple family devotion and of country life. We see that the virtues of generosity and piety are rewarded and we discern the guiding hand of divine Providence over all. The very names suggest that the writing is fiction: Naomi—"my gracious one"; Mahlon—"weakness"; Chilion—"pining"; Orpah—"stiffnecked"; Ruth—"friend." Still, the existence of a tradition that David's ancestress was a woman of Moab is significant; and David's care to seek asylum for his family in Moab (1 Sm. 22:3 f.) perhaps points to a family link with that country.

2)   *The Message*

The author of Ruth cleverly exploited the ancestry of David to make a point that had special relevance to the postexilic Jewish community. In the tiny Jewish state the struggle to preserve national identity was a painful one. Some came to regard mixed marriages as a mortal danger to the continued existence of the people as the people of God; an excessively nationalistic and exclusive outlook tended to develop. The author of Ruth (like the author of Jon.) struck a blow on behalf of a more liberal and more universalist outlook. (It is noteworthy that both of them are unusually gifted writers.) Ruth the Moabitess (this foreigner) had accepted Yahweh as her God (Ru. 1:16) and had entered so wholeheartedly into the Jewish way of life that she is lauded by Boaz for her earnestness in seeking the one kind of marriage that would perpetuate the family name (Ru. 3:10). Her attachment to Naomi is beautifully touching. The divine favor had come upon

her; she had become an ancestress of David, an essential
link in the messianic line.

Ruth brings out two complementary truths: the revelation which the Jewish people had received from God must
be carefully preserved from contamination and must, at
the same time, be made available to all. The danger was
that, in the effort to maintain the purity of Judaism the
door should be firmly barred to the Gentiles. Here is a reminder, and a striking one, that the Gentiles too should
be received into the community of Israel (cf. Is. 2:3 f.;
45:22 f.). The known Moabite ancestry of David adds
point to the story of the Moabitess who recognized the God
of Israel and entered wholly into an Israelite family.

2. JONAH

The Book of Jonah, though listed among the twelve minor
prophets, is not a prophetical book. The realization of this
fact and the establishment of its true literary form and its
purpose set the little writing in its proper light and underline its real significance.

The Message

The milieu in which Jonah was written would have been
the same, or much the same, as that in which Ru. took
form. It is understandable that, among the returned exiles,
in view of all they had gone through and were still suffering, a certain exclusiveness should have appeared—at least
in some circles. Those who shared this outlook wished to
cut themselves off from contact with other peoples and
looked with impatience for the vengeance of God on the
Gentiles—for they were the Chosen People and all others
were accursed. Jonah is nothing other than a criticism
of this view and a bold declaration that God is the God
of all peoples. It is no naïve collection of improbable miracles, but it is a highly-sophisticated writing, a brilliant
satire. For all its brevity it is one of the masterpieces of
literature and, from the point of view of doctrine, it is in
advance of its time, for its universalist outlook anticipates

that of the Gospel. We can understand this if we glance again at the contents of the book.

Jonah is presented as an authentic prophet of the Chosen People, one entrusted with a divine mission. This mission is to preach to the Assyrians, the hated oppressors of his people. The Prophet well knows the mercy of God and he suspects that, in fact, the Assyrians will repent and God will not carry out his threat against them. The thought of the divine mercy extended to the great enemy is more than Jonah can stand. Hence, instead of setting out for Nineveh in the east, he flees to the west (Jon. 1:1-3).

With splendid artistry the author contrasts the narrow, unforgiving disposition of the Israelite Prophet with the open and sympathetic attitude of the other characters of his story—all Gentiles. The pagan sailors are horrified to learn that anyone can bring himself to disobey a divine command (Jon. 1:10) and they are loath to cast him into the sea (Jon. 1:13). The king of Nineveh and his people at once believe the word of the Prophet and are converted and do penance (Jon. 3:6-9). The irony is unmistakable: the preaching of the reluctant Jonah meets with an immediate and universal response in the pagan city, whereas the great prophets had, over the centuries, preached to the Chosen People in vain!

God did accept the sincere conversion of the Ninevites; but what of Jonah? "It displeased Jonah exceedingly, and he was angry" (Jon. 4:1). However, he did not give up hope that the Lord might yet change his mind, and so he sat outside the city, waiting for the longed-for destruction (Jon. 4:5). Then God, who was all patience and mercy even towards his stubborn Prophet, taught him a lesson in a gentle but effective way. He caused a plant to spring up and give shade to Jonah, and then he permitted it to wither just as quickly—and this angered the Prophet (Jon. 4:6-9). Now the moral of the story becomes clear: If Jonah felt that he had a right to be annoyed because the plant had withered up, should not God pity Nineveh in which there were more than 120,000 helpless infants ("who do not know their right hand from their left" [Jon.

4:11])—and so necessarily innocent—as well as many animals, and not seek to destroy it? The loving mercy of God extends to all peoples and to all his creatures.

Understood in this way the Book of Jonah makes delightful reading. The miracles are no longer an embarrassment, but serve to embellish the story, leaving us free to appreciate its satirical humor. At the same time, however, we must not forget the sublime teaching of the book, a doctrine that is valid for all time, even though it was largely overlooked in the following centuries until it was emphatically restated by Christ.

There is perhaps one point that may appear to conflict with our presentation of Jonah as a work of fiction. In Mt. 12:41 and Lk. 11:29-32 Jesus brings forward the conversion of the Ninevites as an example; and in Mt. 12:40 he presents Jonah in the belly of the fish as a type of his own sojourn in the tomb. But these references are to the *Book* of Jonah: the Ninevites, as there described, are an example; and Jonah, as there represented, is a type—it does not follow that they or he are historical. The argument is strictly scriptural; it is confined to the biblical Jonah and to the Ninevites as portrayed in this one writing.

It is not surprising that our Lord referred to Jonah, for it was he who brought to fulfillment the sublime doctrine of that book. Jonah had declared that God was the God of all peoples, a merciful God who had pity on his creatures; St. John is able to go far beyond that and can assure us that God "so loved the world that he gave his only Son" (Jn. 3:16). And this Son tells us that he is the Shepherd who desires to gather all his scattered sheep into one flock (Jn. 10:16).

3. TOBIT

The charming story of Tobit has been largely inspired by biblical models, especially by the patriarchal narratives of Genesis: Abraham and Sarah; Isaac and Rebekah; Jacob and Rachel. The portrayal of Raphael, for instance, is based on Gn. 24:40: "He [Abraham] said to me: 'The Lord, before whom I walk, will send his angel with you to prosper your way; and you shall take a wife for my son from my kindred.'" This example also shows with what freedom the author handles his sources in order to build up a new composition.

This obviously resembles the *midrash* technique; but there is no suggestion in the story that Tobit intended to be a rewritten story of the patriarchal age brought up to date. It is a matter of simple borrowing of details and is no different from other borrowings in Tobit. The author has written freely, but with an eye to the biblical parallels. Nor is he worried about precision in topography or chronology. Thus Tobit 5:6 (S) sets Rhages in the mountains and Ecbatana in the plains and has them only two normal days' walk apart. In fact, Ecbatana is nearly 3,000 feet higher than Rhages and they are about 250 miles apart. Tobit could not have been a witness of the beginning of the schism in 931 B.C. (Tb. 1:4) and have been deported in 734 B.C. (Tb. 1:10). His son, born before the deportation (Tb. 1:9), can scarcely have heard of the destruction of Nineveh in 612 B.C. (Tb. 14:15). This is enough to indicate that Tobit is not historical; indeed it approximates more closely to the wisdom literature. We may well describe the book as a novelette; we do in fact find it surprisingly modern.

Its date is difficult to establish. There seems to be no reason why it might not have been written in the fifth century B.C., though a date even as late as the third century B.C. cannot be ruled out.

The Message

The proverbial maxims of chapters 4, 12, 14 are little more than ornaments attached to the main narrative. That narrative is concerned with a double case of the just sufferer: Tobit, a model of observance and of charity, is the victim of an unfortunate accident; Sarah, an innocent girl, is grievously afflicted through no fault of her own. Both become the butt of bitter tongues (Tb. 2:14 [22]; 3:8) and, as a result, both seek to die (Tb. 3:7,15). Here we have the problems of the wisdom writers: Is virtue re-

warded? Is life worth living? The key to the book is found
in Tobit 3:16 f. [24 f.] and 12:12-15. The prayer of the
two unhappy ones is presented to God by Raphael—and
the angel receives the mission to help them; Azarias is
indeed the instrument of God's providence. The author of
Tobit has not only borrowed from Genesis the elements of
his narrative, he has also read there the striking texts which
show God's providence drawing forth good from evil (Gn.
45:4-8; 50:19-21). In the light of these he can show that
suffering may be meaningful and he can present an optimistic view of life.[3]

Tobit obviously extols family virtues. The older couples,
exemplary in their own lives, have brought up their children well; it is clear that the only son and only daughter
motif suits the demands of the plot. Tobias and Sarah, in
their turn, have a lofty ideal of marriage and show themselves keenly aware of their obligations to their parents.
Great store is set by generous almsgiving; and an atmosphere of faith and trust in God—and joyful thanksgiving—
is all-pervasive. This little romance needs no one to plead
its cause; it has its honorable place in God's library and
marks an important step in the direction of the fuller
Christian ideal.

4. BARUCH

The manuscripts of the LXX have Baruch, Lamentations,
and the Letter of Jeremiah after the Book of Jeremiah. In
the Vulgate the Letter of Jeremiah becomes chapter 6 of
Baruch; however, the long title of the Letter clearly marks
it off as a separate writing. St. Jerome did not translate
Baruch, hence the Vulgate text is really Old Latin; indeed,
many good manuscripts of the Vulgate do not carry the
book at all. It is undeniable that the writing is later than
Baruch (the disciple and secretary of Jeremiah), and that
the attribution of it to him is in accordance with the practice of pseudepigraphy—the deliberate attachment of a
writing to a notable personage of the past—much in vogue
in the third century B.C. and after.

The Message

Baruch helps us in some measure to grasp the reasons that explain the endurance of the communities of the Diaspora. These were, notably: the link with Jerusalem, maintained by means of letters, collections, and communion of prayers; the synagogue prayer nourished on the vivid memory of the past; the reading of the Sacred Books (especially Dt., Jer., and Second Isaiah); the cult of the Law; a profound sense of sin and a desire of conversion; finally, resistance to any form of idolatrous cult.[4]

The writing offers a deep analysis of sin. Sin is a perversion of a moral order based on God's justice (Bar. 2:12); it is a proud rejection of wisdom (Bar. 3:9 ff.), manifested in rebellion against the Law and in indifference to the warnings of the prophets (Bar. 1:18,21; 2:5,10,24). The antidote to sin is a humble return to God, the source of all good (Bar. 2:8; 30 ff.; 4:28) and the observance of the Law. In the Law Israel will find life (Bar. 4:1).

In the discourse God is named the Everlasting (Bar. 4:10,14,22,24)—a title found nowhere else in the Bible. He is the source of wisdom (Bar. 3:12,32); he is the Holy One *par excellence* (Bar. 4:22,37; 5:5). He is the only deliverer of the exiles (Bar. 4:18,23,29), for his characteristics are justice (Bar. 1:15; 2:6,9; 5:9) and mercy (Bar. 2:27; 3:1; 5:9). Salvation comes from the Everlasting God (Bar. 4:8) who has been offended but who manifests his glory, first by chastening and then by saving sinners. In short, Baruch is a drama of sin, of conversion, and of salvation.

5. DANIEL[5]

1) The Book

In the Hebrew Bible, Daniel is found among the Writings, between Esther and Ez.-Neh. The LXX and all other versions place it among the prophetical books, immediately after Ezekiel. In the LXX and the versions based on it the text of Daniel has certain additions not found in the Hebrew; these constitute the deuterocanonical[6] parts of the book. As they stand, they form a supplement to the original work and we shall leave them aside until the close of this section.

Daniel is written partly in Hebrew (Dn. 1:1—2:4a; 8-12), partly in Aramaic (Dn. 2:4b—7:28), and partly in Greek (Dn. 3:24-90; 13-14). (The passage Daniel 3:24-90 is inserted between 2:23 and 3:24 of the Hebrew.)

There is no particular difficulty in the use of Greek for the deuterocanonical parts: they are present in the LXX only. On the other hand the juxtaposition of Hebrew and Aramaic in the rest of the book is a riddle. Daniel starts in Hebrew and abruptly, at Daniel 2:4b, switches to Aramaic. Chapter 8 changes back to Hebrew and the book concludes in that language (chapters 13-14 form an appendix). None of the many proposed solutions of the problem is convincing, because the stubborn fact is that the distinction of language breaks across the natural twofold division of the book. To this must be added the other fact that the book is the work of a single author; we simply do not know why he decided to use two languages.

2) *The Literary Form*

Traditionally, Daniel is a prophetical book: it was written by the prophet Daniel towards the close of and immediately after the Babylonian exile. Jewish and Christian tradition is unanimous in this respect. But here again, as in the case of Second Isaiah, the traditional attribution of the book to Daniel and to the sixth century B.C. does not purport to settle a problem of literary and historical criticism. And the literary and historical criticism of Daniel make it quite clear that the book was written in the second century B.C. This immediately raises the question of the literary form of the book. We must consider separately the two parts of Daniel because, corresponding to these parts, the book is a combination of two literary forms: the first part (chs. 1-6) is a *haggadah* (though ch. 2 is largely apocalyptic); the second (chs. 7-12) is an apocalypse (though ch. 9 is *pesher midrash*).

THE HAGGADAH   We have noted above that there is a type of midrash called *haggadah*. However, this word covers more than an interpretation of non-legal biblical texts: it describes one of two categories of oral tradition (the other being *halakah*, the traditional interpretation of a written law). *Haggadah* itself is of two kinds: one being an interpretation of biblical texts—haggadic midrash—while the other is more varied and includes legends, proverbs and so on which have no bearing on Scripture. The first six chapters of Daniel belong to this kind of *haggadah*. They tell the story of a legendary hero, Daniel, in order to establish a basis for the visions attributed to him in the following chapters. *Haggadah* is here at the service of apocalyptic.

The author of these first six chapters has written for the benefit of his readers of the early Maccabaean period. Building upon traditional material, he represents the young Jewish nobleman as playing in Babylon the same role that his descendants are called upon to play in Palestine. Nebuchadnezzar and Antiochus are very much alike: both are profaners of the Temple (2 Kgs. 25:9,13-15; 1 Mc. 22-24,57-62); and Babylon, like Antioch, is ranged against Jerusalem, the city of the true God. Daniel and his companions are scrupulously faithful to the food prescriptions of the Law (Dn. 1:8-16); the three companions refuse to adore the statue of the king (Dn. 3:12-18); the edict of Darius cannot prevent Daniel from praying to his God (Dn. 6:11)—all of these are apt lessons for Jews who are face-to-face with the persecution of Antiochus.

Furthermore, the resistance of Daniel and his companions, and their God-given wisdom, contribute to the acknowledgment of the power of Yahweh (Dn. 1:17; 2:46 f.; 4:34; 5:14-16). On his part, God worked prodigies to save them from the danger they incurred for his name (Dn. 3:49 f.; 6:22); the same will happen when the persecution of Antiochus will have exhausted the measure of God's patience.

The aim of these chapters is not merely, or principally, to describe who Daniel was or to narrate certain incidents in his life; it is, more especially, to magnify the God of Daniel by showing how he frustrates the purposes of the proudest monarchs while he defends his servants who trust in him. This is the author's message, of hope and confidence, to his suffering countrymen: If they are true and steadfast like Daniel the Lord will surely vindicate them. Given this purpose the historical inaccuracies are no problem. If Nebuchadnezzar is named instead of Nabonidus is it not because the former resembles Antiochus? The parallel is more striking and the message clearer when the villain of the piece is the great traditional enemy of Jerusalem. The author is interested in the trying and stirring times of Judas Maccabaeus and he has written to encourage his people in their struggle; his work is not, and was not meant to be, a history of Daniel and his times. He has exploited to the full the old traditions, but his only concern is to insure the fidelity and steadfastness of his persecuted brethren.

PESHER MIDRASH

Daniel 9 offers a typical example of *pesher midrash*. The seventy years of Jeremiah's prophecy regarding the end of the Exile and the restoration (Jer. 25:11; 29:10) are interpreted in a manner that makes them applicable to the Maccabaean period. The method is ingenious: the seventy years become *seventy weeks* of years and the period thus obtained is divided into three parts in order to work in the application. Despite the artificiality of the technique, the argument is theologically valid: this is another crisis in the history of God's people and the oracle of the Lord has lost nothing of its force. The God who brought back his people from Exile will deliver them from Antiochus; and this deliverance, too, is a presage and a guarantee of the final deliverance of messianic times. When Jeremiah (Jer. 25:11; 29:10) sets seventy years as the duration of the Exile he probably referred to the space of a man's life; his figure is not to be taken mathematically. The same must be kept in mind in Daniel 9:24-27.

Daniel 9:24 describes the blessings of the messianic age. In three expressions the writer tells how mankind will be reconciled with God: evil will come to an end; sin will be a thing of the past; guilt will be expiated and forgiven.

Then, in place of infidelity, the people of God will practice justice; and whatever has been seen in "vision and prophecy" concerning the day of salvation will come to pass. Lastly a "holy of holies" will be consecrated—either the Temple or the high priest (cf. 1 Chr. 23:13).

The period until the advent of messianic glory covers seventy weeks of years; these are divided into three unequal periods: seven weeks; sixty-two weeks; and one week. The starting-point is the "going forth of the word," that is, the moment of the prophecy of Jeremiah (587 B.C.). At the close of the first seven weeks (of years) an anointed prince arises: this was Cyrus the Great (cf. Is. 45:1), who permitted the exiles to return home. Between 587 B.C. (the date of the prophecy of Jeremiah) and 538 B.C. (the date of the edict of Cyrus), 49 years elapse (= seven weeks of years). During the second period of sixty-two weeks the rebuilding of the city is undertaken. In fact this was slow work, subject to many difficulties and much opposition; but sixty-two weeks is simply the number left over from the significant first seven weeks and the last week—it has no special relevance.

At the beginning of the seventieth week an "anointed one" was put to death (Dn. 9:26); he is obviously not the same as the anointed one (Cyrus) in verse 25. The high priest Onias III was assassinated in 171 B.C.; he would appear to be indicated. After this a prince appears who destroys city and sanctuary; he is Antiochus IV, as the next verse makes abundantly clear.

This prince will enter into an agreement with many, that is, with the Hellenistic Jews who supported him (Dn. 9:27). He will abolish sacrifice for "half of the week" and will defile the Temple with the "abomination of desolation" (that is, the dedication of the Temple to Olympian Zeus [cf. 2 Mc. 6:2]). The half week (that is, three and one-half years) during which sacrifices will cease is the equivalent of the "time, two times and half a time" of Daniel 12:7; 7:25 (cf. 8:14). In every case it is the approximate duration of the persecution of Antiochus IV which lasted just over three years. The persecution will cease when the "decreed end is poured out on the desolator."

This interpretation of verses 24-27 relates the literal message of verse 24 to the blessings of the messianic age, but finds the historical events of the Maccabaean period described in verses 25-27, events which the writer has himself experienced. The perspective is the same as in the visions of chapters 2, 7, and 8, the only difference being that, whereas these visions end with the messianic kingdom, the vision of the seventy weeks describes it first.

APOCALYPSE   The term "apocalypse" is from the Greek *apokalypsis* meaning "revelation" and indicates something revealed or disclosed to a select few. The name was given by Jews to a type of literature which was supposed to reveal the future and which was especially concerned with the last things. As a literary form the apocalyptic is closely related to the prophetical; it is, in fact, the child of prophecy. Many passages in the prophetic books deal with the far horizons of time; they have the eschatological interest that is a feature of the apocalyptic.

While pseudonymity is not an essential feature of apocalypse, an apocalyptic work is almost always attributed to a venerated figure of the past. The reputed author is supposed to receive, in a series of visions, a revelation of God's plan working out in world events—and this revelation is represented as having been hidden for many years, laid up in a "sealed book." History is unfolded in symbols and finds its term in the epoch of the true author. The language is sometimes precise, but more frequently it is designedly vague—this in accordance with the literary fiction, since it is supposed to be prophecy. The apocalypse closes with a prediction of the imminent eschatological judgment and the advent of unending happiness, in other words, with the advent of the messianic age. A notable feature is the frequent intervention of angels; it is they who usually explain the mysterious symbols.

It should be observed that the apocalyptic form does not exclude true prediction of the future, and Daniel is prophetic to a certain extent. The apocalypse looks beyond the age of the writer to the messianic age. The visions of Daniel close, not with the downfall of Antiochus IV, but with the "kingdom that shall never he destroyed" (Dn. 2:44). Reference to the death of the tyrant (Dn. 7:26; 8:25; 9:26 f.) and to the restoration of the Temple worship is also true prediction.

The object of apocalypse is to show the providence of God at work in history and thus to inspire the readers with hope and confidence. Apocalypse was born in times of crisis. As a literary form it flourished from the second century B.C. to the second century A.D. The popularity of the form should be taken into account when interpreting apocalypse: features that appear very strange to us were part of a widespread and familiar literary convention. This fact alone would, for people of these centuries, dispel much of the mystery that attaches to the form.

On the other hand, the fact that these chapters of Daniel would have been recognized as apocalyptic by their first readers may cause us to wonder what effect they could have had. After all, these people knew that this was not prophecy but history. Or, to put it another way, since they were aware of the literary convention and would have realized that the writing was pseudoprophecy, how could they have taken it seriously? The truth of the matter is that these chapters set out a comforting and an entirely valid lesson from history. The author invited his readers to look to the past; then he sketched before their eyes a succession of empires—each had appeared, had dominated the contemporary scene, and had gone, leaving no trace behind. They would note, in contrast to the ephemeral powers, one constant element: the people of God. They could also see that time and again this people was at the mercy of a great power and on the point of extinction, but each time God had intervened; the great power had disappeared but Israel remained. The reminder of these facts gave absolute grounds for hope in the present crisis. Besides, the readers of Daniel believed that in just such a crisis the intervention of God, the establishment of his kingdom, would come; they could hope that it would follow the end of this persecution.

The narrative section of Daniel is a prelude to the visions. The story of Daniel assures us that, in the providence of God, persecution cannot achieve its purpose. The visions of the four animals and of the ram and the goat clarify this message. Indeed the burden of these visions is already present in the interpretation of the dream of Nebuchadnezzar. The history of the East is unfolded, centered around the kings symbolized by animals; symbols disappear in chapters 10-11. In every case the series closes with and concentrates on a personage who is the persecutor *par excellence,* Antiochus IV Epiphanes. Both parts of the book are dominated by one outlook and are welded into a close unit. Daniel and his companions, deported to Babylon, were supported by God and overcame all trials. The same divine providence, through changing empires, continues to work for the coming of the kingdom of God; it continues to protect the people of God and insures its survival. The work of God is accomplished in the midst of trials, but its final realization is certain. The final vision of chapter 12 fittingly concludes the book by pointing to the messianic age that lies just beyond the time of trial.

3) *The Author*

In the period just before the Maccabaean revolt we can place the origin of a Jewish party called the *Hasidim* (the "Pious Ones"). Their characteristic attitude was loyalty to the Law at all costs and they vehemently opposed the spreading pagan influence. They wholeheartedly supported the Maccabaean rising (cf. 2 Mc. 14:6, where they are called Hasidaeans). However, they maintained their own viewpoint and standards and cut themselves adrift from the Maccabaean movement in its later stages when they judged it to have become a political movement and no longer a religious one. The Pharisees are the linear descendants of the Hasidim, with the Essenes (like those of Qumran) forming another branch.

The author of Daniel is clearly one of the Hasidim: he has the same deep-rooted aversion to Hellenistic ways and hatred of the tyranny which strove to impose these ways on faithful Jews, and the same unswerving loyalty to the Torah. His purpose was to bolster up the faith that was in danger of being stamped out by Seleucid aggression. He wanted to hearten his people and urge them to unyielding loyalty in the face of persecution. He based his summons to courageous faith on the affirmation that God ruled the course of history. "For when men believe that the issues are in the hands of God, rather than in human hands, they can act without fear of the consequences."[7] It is noteworthy that the prayers which reflect the Hasidim outlook candidly admit the failures of Israel and appeal solely to the gracious goodness of Yahweh (Dn. 9:4-19; cf. 3:26-45). In short, Daniel sets forth the theology of the Maccabaean rising and it has been well named "the manifesto of the Hasidim." Though we are unable to name its author, he is one of the great writers of the Old Testament. It is fitting that he should mark an important stage in the progress of revelation; for in Daniel 12:2 f. the doctrines of the resurrection of the body and of retribution after death are explicitly formulated for the first time.

4) *The Supplements*

The Book of Daniel has been supplemented by way of insertion and by additions. The Prayer of Azariah and the Canticle of the Three Youths (Dn. 3:24-90) have been inserted in chapter 3; the narratives of the Judgment of Daniel and of Bel and the Serpent have been added to the book.

THE SUPPLEMENTS OF CHAPTER 3 Both passages, though now extant only in Greek, were originally written in Hebrew. The lovely prayer (Dn. 3:26-45) is a splendid testimony to Hasidim piety. It is a confession of the sins of the people with a view to obtaining God's mercy and is closely akin to the prayer of Daniel 9:4-19. Verse 38 indicates the situation under Antiochus IV. The Canticle of the Three Youths has three parts: (1) Daniel 3:52-56—a blessing; (2) Daniel 3:57-87—a hymn in praise of creation; (3) Daniel 3:88-90—a thanksgiving hymn of the three delivered from danger. The introductory verses 25 and 51 serve as titles.

CHAPTERS Though these chapters are now extant in
13-14 Greek only, it is agreed that they were originally written in Hebrew or Aramaic. The Babylonian
background of the narrative of Susanna is artificial. The
teaching is that of the late wisdom literature: Calumniated
innocence is divinely vindicated in answer to prayer, and
wisdom is a privilege not of age but of virtue.[8] The episodes of Bel and of the Serpent are manifestly satirical;
they are nothing else than a rather unkind "skit" on idolatry by a Judaism that is very sure of itself. The passage
Daniel 14:31-42 (Daniel in the den of lions) is surely a
doublet of Daniel 6:17-25. The two chapters, so markedly
different in style and content, give evidence of a rich fund
of traditional stories about Daniel.

5) A Theology of History

Daniel deals not with single empires but with a succession
of empires; it points out how their sequence is determined
by God and declares that, when the appointed limit has
been reached, they are destined to be overthrown by the
kingdom of God. In the author's view history follows a
timetable whose stages have been fixed by divine decree.[9]
History is purposeful and moves towards a goal, and all
of it is under divine control. We had occasion to point
out in *Record of Revelation: The Bible* that the sense of
God's activity in the events of history is often lost; here we
have, in a striking way, the typically Hebrew awareness of
that truth. The author of Daniel is convinced that
Antiochus is a puppet in God's hand; he has accepted the
persecution as God's punishment of a sinful people and
he is certain that the time is near when God will end
Israel's years of desolation. And, all the while, he looks forward to the final stage, the establishment of God's
kingdom.

He tells the story of the past in such a way that the
persecuted Jews may understand that their sufferings had
a place in God's purpose and may see that the tyranny of
Antiochus fell within God's plan. The situation has not developed by chance or in defiance of the divine decree.

Though the king may seem to succeed in his proud revolt against the Prince of princes, and may with impunity trample upon the people of the Prince, his triumph is illusory: "He shall prosper till the indignation is accomplished; for what is determined shall be done" (Dn. 11:36). And though it might seem that such emphasis on God's absolute control of human affairs must encourage a laissez-faire attitude, a directly opposite effect was intended and achieved. This confident assurance that history, divinely guided, moved towards a goal fixed by God, fired the tiny band of faithful Jews with indomitable hope when any hope seemed vain, and urged them to supreme effort where resistance seemed doomed to failure. Indeed, their plain duty was put before them in explicit terms: "The people who know their God shall stand firm and take action" (Dn. 11:32). This faith in God and firm confidence in his ways account for the exalted spirit and amazing success of the Maccabaean rising, especially in its first phase, the "three glorious years." Belief in the justice of their cause has sustained little nations and has, more than once, moved them to challenge empires. Even in our own century we have seen this happen and, whether we are personally involved or not, we must thrill that such things can be. And when we recall that over and above the deep-rooted instinct of a spirited people the Jews were conscious of their unique place in history and of their special role in God's plan for mankind, we can appreciate the effect of this powerful summons to fearless and resolute action. "If God was for them, what did it matter how many battalions were against them? And who cared how many battles were lost, as long as the saints were fighting on the winning side?"[10]

The book looks always to the final victory, to the time of the end, to the coming of the kingdom; the author sees the messianic age about to dawn, just beyond the "time, two times and half a time" of the persecution. Apocalypse is a child of prophecy and here the link with the prophetical writings is clear. The prophets before and during the Exile believed that the deliverance from Babylonian bondage would herald the Messiah's appearance, and the author of this book expected the great change to come with the death of Antiochus; in both cases we have the characteristic foreshortening of prophecy. The prophets have seen a vision and are overwhelmed by the majesty of it; and if the kingdom will not come as speedily as they had imagined, they are certain that it will come. God's victory over the world is assured, and those who serve him faithfully will have a glorious part in his triumph.

6) *The Son of Man* (Dn. 7:13-14)

The second part of the Book of Daniel (chapters 6-12) consists of visions which portray the movement of historical events towards the consummation, when God will overthrow the empires of men and establish his own kingdom on earth. Four successive empires are depicted: Babylonian, Median, Persian, and Greek; but the interest of the author always concentrates on one king (Antiochus IV Epiphanes), the persecutor of the Maccabaean revolt. In him evil has reached its term; his downfall will herald the messianic age.

In the first of these visions (chapter 7) Daniel saw four beasts rising out of the sea (the abode of things evil); an angel explained that these beasts were four successive empires (Babylonian, Median, Persian, and Greek [Seleucid]) or the kings who represented the empires. The "little horn" rising from the last of them is Antiochus IV; the phrase, "before which three of the first horns were plucked up," describes him as an usurper who had succeeded his assassinated brother Seleucus IV and supplanted the rightful heirs, his nephews Demetrius and Antiochus. The "mouth speaking great things" refers to his blasphemous arrogance (cf. Dn. 7:25; 11:36).

In a heavenly judgment scene the "Ancient of Days" (God) takes his seat; but other thrones are also set out, because God's saints judge with him. The "little horn" is condemned, while the other empires are no longer a danger since they have lost imperial power. Then, in contrast to the beasts, appears one "like a son of man" (that is, a human figure); again, in contrast to the beasts' origin from the depths of the sea, he appears "on the clouds of heaven"—"on" (LXX, Syr.) is a better reading than "with" (MT) (cf. Ps. 104 [103]:3; Is. 19:1). This "son of man" is presented to the Ancient of Days and receives universal and everlasting dominion. The phrase "son of man" is Aramaic idiom (*bar enash*) for "man"; the figure is "like" a son of man, to mark the symbolic character of the representation. As presented in these verses (13 f.) the figure certainly appears as an individual.

The difficulty is that, in the interpretation (vv. 26 f.), the kingdom, formerly given to the Son of Man, is now given to the "Saints of the Most High," that is, to the messianic people, the purified Remnant of Israel. Their everlasting and universal kingdom will be inaugurated after "a time, two times and a half a time" of the little horn, that is, after three and one-half years, the approximate duration of the persecution of Antiochus (167-164 B.C.). It appears that the "saints of the Most High" and the "Son of Man" must stand for the same reality, at once collective and individual. A study of the context justifies this interpretation.

In Dn. 7:17 we read that "these four great beasts are four kings who shall arise out of the earth." In verse 23 the fourth beast is interpreted as "a fourth kingdom"; hence the beasts represent both the kingdoms and their kings. We find the very same situation in chapter two of Daniel. The composite statue (Dn. 2:32 f.) represents the four empires (cf. 2:39-44); and yet the head of gold is Nebuchadnezzar (Dn. 2:37 f.), who stands for the Babylonian Empire. Again, after the other parts of the statue are interpreted in terms of empires, verse 44 speaks of "the days of those *kings*." It is sufficiently clear that, in Daniel, king and empire are interchangeable: the one symbol may stand for either. The king who incorporates and represents his empire, however, does not lose his own identity, his individuality. The head of gold may describe Nebuchadnezzar, insofar as he may be identified with the Babylonian Empire, but Nebuchadnezzar does not thereby become a mere symbol.

If we apply this reasoning to the Son of Man we find that both the individual and the collective senses indicated in Dn. 7 may be preserved. The Son of Man is certainly the representative of "the people of the saints of the Most High," but he is also an individual, with an identity of his own. "Saints of the Most High" and "Son of Man" are the messianic people and the Messiah who represents and contains them. It is clear from Dn. 7:13 f. that this Son of Man is no ordinary mortal; the reference to the "clouds of heaven" is sufficient by itself to prove this. Throughout the Old Testament, "cloud" occurs about one hundred times—in thirty cases it is the natural phenomenon. In all other cases it accompanies a theophany or an intervention of Yahweh. However, it would be going too far to argue that everything or everybody associated with this cloud must belong to the divine sphere. A New Testament text can be of help here: in Ap. 10:1 a mighty angel, entrusted with a very special mission, comes down from heaven "wrapped in a cloud"; he is a heavenly being and he has come from the presence of God, but he is not divine. Similarly the Son of Man comes, riding on the heavenly vehicle (cf. Ps. 104 [103]:3; Is. 19:1), into the presence of God. He is a heavenly figure, the leader of God's people, but the author of Daniel would not have regarded him as divine.

We may look at the Son of Man passage from another angle and see here two registers of the same tableau:[11] in the higher part, in heaven, the beasts are condemned by the Ancient of Days and dominion is given to the Son of Man (Dn. 7:13 f.); in the lower register we have the earthly repercussions of these heavenly events (Dn. 7:19-27)—the pagan empires are destroyed and the faithful part of the Chosen People (the Saints of the Most High) received the kingdom. In other words, while divine judgment has been passed on the beast and while the people of God are assured of ultimate victory, history must run its allotted span. After all, this is our own situation: by his death and resurrection Christ has won the victory over death and sin ("I have overcome the world" [Jn. 16:33]; the prince of this world is already judged [Jn.

16:11; cf. 12:31]) and yet Christians have to struggle with sin and suffer death. But ultimate victory is certain for those who are faithful to Christ.

Among the Jews, "Son of Man" never became a current messianic title, but probably in certain restricted circles a Messiah was awaited who was "Son of Man."[12] What is certain is that Jesus gave himself this title by preference, and, in using it, linked together the two notions of the great Judge of the world and of the Servant of Yahweh—notions that would seem mutually exclusive—and showed that both were united in his person.[13] For he, Son of David, is also the Suffering Servant, the Redeemer of mankind, and he is indeed the glorious Son of Man, Leader of the people of God, Head of his Body, the Church.

6. ESTHER

There is a notable difference between the Hebrew text and the Greek text of Esther. The latter has additions which make it one-third longer; these additional passages are given in italics in the text of *The Jerusalem Bible*.

We really have two editions of Esther, one considerably longer than the other. The question is further complicated by the fact that the Greek text has come to us in different forms: that of the great uncials; that of the Latin versions; that of the late revision of Lucian; and that which formed the basis of the Old Latin; in this respect, the Old Latin text is of first importance. It is nowadays generally accepted that the longer Greek text is later than the Hebrew. The editor wished to offer the Jews of the Diaspora "a work that would be more acceptable in a Hellenized milieu, more humane thanks to the suppression of traits too hostile to pagans (for example, Est. 9:5-19 [Heb.]), more religious also and showing more closely the action of Providence and the efficacy of prayer."[14] The supplements, taken together, form the deuterocanonical parts of Esther.

According to the last verse of the Greek version of Esther (11:3) the book was introduced into Egypt in

114 B.C. The Hebrew original must be earlier than that date but, it seems, not much earlier. The Persian background has a romantic coloring which suggests that the Persian Empire had long ceased to exist. According to 2 Mc. 15:36 the Palestinian Jews celebrated in 160 B.C. a "day of Mordecai"; this presupposes the story of Esther, but not necessarily the book. However, the Maccabaean period—after the persecution of Antiochus IV (167-164 B.C.)—seems indicated; perhaps about the year 150 B.C. The Greek edition (containing the "supplements") is somewhat later, but again certainly before 114 B.C.

Literary Form

The Book of Esther was written to justify the Feast of Purim, a feast that was not of Israelite origin and had no religious significance. "It was not held (at least directly) in honor of the God of Israel (whose name is not even mentioned in the Hebrew Book of Esther); it was not connected with the ancient history of the Chosen People; and it contained no cultic element at all. It was a foreign feast, but its origins are obscure."[15] If we are to understand the purpose of the book and if we are to appreciate its true literary form we must know something of that feast.[16] The name of the feast, "Purim," comes from the Akkadian *pûru* meaning "lot" or "destiny," but apart from Esther 3:7 and 9:20-32, there is no reference to the casting of lots and it appears that this was not a feature of the feast. It seems certain that the feast originated in the communities of the Eastern Diaspora, perhaps at Susa. It probably commemorates a pogrom (some time in the fourth century B.C.) from which Jews escaped in a seemingly miraculous manner. On the other hand, the feast preserves certain characteristics that appear to have been modeled on a Persian New Year feast. Babylonian influence is indicated by the names: Mordecai = Marduk; Esther = Ishtar—that is, the names of the god and goddess of Babylon. The feast gradually made its way into Palestine and to Egypt.

The Message

The Book of Esther is disconcerting. It is obvious that
the additions of the Greek text have in view the soften-
ing of the general impression; the Old Latin (an excellent
witness to the Greek text) omits Esther 9:5-19. Similarly,
whereas the Hebrew does not mention the name of God,
the additions (especially Est. 13:8—14:9) stress the power
of God and his readiness to help his people. Yet the sentiments of the book are an understandable reaction to the
hostility encountered by the Jews in the ancient world
because of their aloofness; this harsh nationalism is one
answer. The spirit of the book is not, and could not have
been, the Christian ideal.

We should not forget, however, that the author is not
describing historical events; the bloody massacre of enemies never did take place, and Jews living in ghettoes
throughout the Greek world were aware that it was not
so. Besides, the massacre is depicted as an act of self-
defense (Est. 8:10), since a decree of the Persian king
was unalterable (Est. 1:19; 8:5)—an idea suggested by
Dn. 6:9,13. If God is not mentioned, it is nonetheless true
that the events of the story are guided by Providence (cf.
Est. 4:13-17; 3:1; 4:16), and the actors of this drama are
aware that God does guide all the action. Ultimately the
message of Esther is that God does not abandon his people
but always comes to help them in distress.

7. JUDITH

Judith was written in Hebrew, but the original text is not
extant and all later versions are based on a Greek text.
The Vulgate is a revision by St. Jerome of the Old Latin
with reference to an Aramaic version known to him.

At first sight Judith seems to be the factual account of
a striking deliverance of God's people. On closer study we
find that the book shows "a superb indifference to history
and geography."[17] The story is set in the reign of Nebuchadnezzar "who ruled over the Assyrians in the great

city of Nineveh" (Jdt. 1:1), sometime after the return from the Exile and the rebuilding of the Temple (Jdt. 4:3). In reality, Nebuchadnezzar was king of the Babylonians and reigned in Babylon, while Nineveh had been utterly destroyed by his father, Nabopolassar. Furthermore, Nebuchadnezzar had taken Jerusalem and carried the Jewish people into exile; the return took place long after his death, under Cyrus the Great. Arphaxad, "king of the Medes," is a fictitious character; the name undoubtedly comes from Gn. 10:22. Holofernes and Bagoas were Persian officers of Artaxerxes III (358-337 B.C.)—two hundred years after the death of Nebuchadnezzar. The author's "presentation of Nebuchadnezzar, the Babylonian, as king of the Assyrians, waging war against Arphaxad, an unknown Median king, with an army commanded by the Persians Holofernes and Bagoas, is the equivalent of saying that Peter the Great, king of England, waged war against Arphaxad, the king of France, with an army led by Generals Eisenhower and MacArthur."[18] Judith is not mentioned in biblical history; significantly, her name means "Jewess." We find clear allusions to certain Greek customs (Jdt. 3:7 f.; 15:13) and to late Jewish customs (Jdt. 8:6). There is no trace of the monarchy, which was brought to an end by Nebuchadnezzar, and Judaea is ruled by a high priest as in postexilic times.

The geographical situation is no less confused. The route followed by Holofernes and his army (Jdt. 2:21-28) is "in defiance of geography."[19] Even when the Assyrians arrive in Samaria we are on no surer ground. Bethulia itself, the center of the drama, cannot be indicated on a map. The implication that it commanded the only route to Jerusalem (Jdt. 4:6 f.; 7:1-3) is, geographically speaking, nonsense. Instead of wasting time besieging a single fortress with his whole immense army (Jdt. 7:2), Holofernes could have left a contingent there and moved with the rest of his force along the coast, coming upon Jerusalem from the west, as Sennacherib had done (2 Kgs. 18:17).

We must presume that the geography of Palestine, at least, would have been familiar to the author and to those for whom he wrote. We cannot imagine that many Jews could have been ignorant of the respective roles of Assyria, Nebuchadnezzar, and the Persians in the destiny of Jerusalem. The only valid conclusion is that the author has deliberately multiplied the historical and geographical inaccuracies; and his object must have been to turn the attention of his readers from any precise historical context and bring it to bear only on the religious drama and its climax. He does not mean to teach a particular fact of Israel's history, but to present in a striking way the general sense of this history. In achieving this effect he has certainly been influenced by the apocalyptic form. We might even go so far as to regard his work as an apocalypse.[20]

At any rate it does appear that Holofernes is a synthesis of the powers of evil, and Judith (the "Jewess"), over against him, is an ideal representative of Judaism. The scene is set in the plain of Esdraelon (Jdt. 3:6), near the plain of Armageddon where John will place the eschatological battle (Ap. 16:16). Though the nation had seemed doomed God had brought about its triumph and the victory wrought through Judith was the reward of her prayer and of her scrupulous observance of the laws of ritual purity. Finally, the holy people went up in joyful procession to Jerusalem (Jdt. 15:12—16:20). The whole presentation is markedly apocalyptic.[21]

Judith was written in Hebrew, a fact that strongly suggests Palestinian origin. From the apocalyptic tone we might deduce that it was written to encourage Jews undergoing persecution. A likely background may be the persecution of Jews in Egypt by Ptolemy VII in the years following 145 B.C. Though we cannot be sure that this was its setting, it does seem reasonable to date the book to the end of the second or the beginning of the first century B.C.

The Message

Like Est. the Book of Judith describes a deliverance of the Jews by the intermediary of a woman. Judith, with her fidelity to the Law and her unshaken trust in God, becomes an instrument of God's justice. The prayer of Judith (chapter 9) is the key to the book: she calls on the God of her father Simeon who avenged the rape of Dinah (Gn. 34) to humble the Assyrians for their meditated rape of God's sanctuary. God will hear, the "God of the lowly, helper of the oppressed, upholder of the weak, protector of the forlorn, savior of those without hope" (Jdt. 9:11). He will act to save his people, for "there is no other who protects the people of Israel but him alone" (Jdt. 9:14). Judith, the ideal representative of her people, is another Daniel: a model of observance and an inspiration to boundless trust in God.

Though Est. and Judith meet in the common theme of deliverance by a woman, and though both illustrate the truth that God does not abandon his people, the two books are really very different in outlook. The former is candidly nationalistic and expresses something of the exasperation of the ghetto mentality. Judith, on the other hand, is universalist in perspective. Significantly, the salvation of Jerusalem is wrought not in Judaea but at Bethulia, in the land of the hated Samaritans. Even more striking, the religious issue of the conflict is brought out by Achior, an Ammonite (Jdt. 5:5-21), who is drawn to confess the true God (Jdt. 14:5-10). We have here an echo of Ru. and Jon., and already something of the atmosphere of that new age in which Jesus would hold up a Samaritan as a figure of Christian love (Lk. 10:30-37) and would, raised from the earth, draw all men to himself (Jn. 12:32).

---

[1] See H. Lusseau, IB, pp. 667 f.

[2] See BJ, p. 148.

[3] See R. Pautrel, *Tobie* (BJ), pp. 13 f.

[4] See A. Gelin, *Jérémie, Les Lamentations, Le Livre de Baruch* (BJ), pp. 283 f.

[5] See P.O Fiannachta-W.O h-Urdail (Harrington), *Leabhar Dhainéil* (Nenagh, 1965). The treatment of Dn. in the present chapter is a translation of my Introduction to this new Irish version of the book.

[6] See Harrington, *Record of Revelation: The Bible, op. cit.,* p. 64.

[7] B. W. Anderson, *Understanding the Old Testament* (Englewood Cliffs, N.J.: Prentice-Hall, 1957), p. 515.

[8] See A. Lefèvre, IB, p. 780.

[9] See Anderson, *op. cit.,* p. 526.

10 Anderson, *op. cit.*, p. 528.

11 See A. Feuillet, "Le Fils de l'homme de Daniel et la tradition biblique," RB, 60 (1953), 195.

12 See Pierre Benoit, *Exégèse et Théologie* (Paris: Cerf, 1961), pp. 133-40.

13 See W. Harrington, *Explaining the Gospels* (New York: Paulist Press, 1963), pp. 88-91.

14 Lefèvre, *op. cit.*, p. 779.

15 De Vaux, *op. cit.*, pp. 515 f.

16 See *ibid.*, pp. 515-17.

17 BJ, p. 493.

18 Ellis, *op. cit.*, p. 523.

19 BJ, p. 494.

20 Cf. Ellis, *op. cit.*, pp. 526-29.

21 See BJ, p. 494.

BIBLIOGRAPHY

This select bibliography has been restricted to works in English.

GENERAL

Albright, W. F., *From the Stone Age to Christianity*, New York: Doubleday, 1957².

———, *The Biblical Period from Abraham to Ezra*, New York, Harper & Row, 1963.

Anderson, B. W., *Understanding the Old Testament*, Englewood Cliffs, N.J.: Prentice-Hall, 1966².

Anderson, G. W., *A Critical Introduction to the Old Testament*, London: Duckworth, 1959.

Bauer, J. B., *Encyclopedia of Biblical Theology*, 3 vols., New York: Sheed & Ward, 1970.

Becker, J., *The Formation of the Old Testament*, Chicago, Franciscan Herald Press, 1972.

Black, M. and Rowley, H. H., eds., *Peake's Commentary on the Bible*, London: Nelson, 1962.

Buttrick, G. A., ed., *The Interpreter's Dictionary of the Bible*, 4 vols., Nashville: Abingdon, 1962.

Brown, R. E., Fitzmyer, J. A., Murphy, R. E., eds., *The Jerome Biblical Commentary*, Englewood Cliffs, N.J.: Prentice-Hall, 1968.

Cross, F. M., *Hermeneia. A Critical and Historical Commentary on the Bible*. Old Testament, Philadelphia: Fortress Press, 1972.

Davidson, R., *The Old Testament*, London: Hodder & Stoughton, 1964.

Dodd, C. H., *The Bible Today*, New York: Cambridge University Press, 1960².

Eichrodt, W., *Theology of the Old Testament,* 2 vols., Philadelphia: Westminster Press, 1961, 1967.

Eissfeldt, O., *The Old Testament: An Introduction,* New York: Harper, 1965.

Ellis, P. F., *The Men and the Message of the Old Testament,* Collegeville, Minn.: Liturgical Press, 1963.

Fohrer, G., *Introduction to the Old Testament,* Nashville: Abingdon, 1968.

———, *The History of Israelite Religion,* Nashville: Abingdon, 1972.

Fuller, R. C., ed., *A New Catholic Commentary on Holy Scripture,* London: Nelson, 1969.

Habel, N. C., *Literary Criticism of the Old Testament,* Philadelphia: Fortress Press, 1971.

Hartmann, L. F., *Encyclopedic Dictionary of the Bible,* New York: McGraw-Hill, 1963.

Jacob, E., *Theology of the Old Testament,* London: Hodder & Stoughton, 1958.

Kraus, H.-J., *Worship in Israel. A Cultic History of the Old Testament,* Oxford: Blackwell.

Leon-Dufour, X., ed., *Dictionary of Biblical Theology,* New York: Desclée, 1967.

Martin-Achard, R., *An Approach to the Old Testament,* London: Oliver & Boyd, 1965.

McKenzie, J. L., *The Two-Edged Sword,* Milwaukee: Bruce, 1956.

———, *Dictionary of the Bible,* Milwaukee: Bruce, 1965.

Power, J., *History of Salvation. Introducing the Old Testament,* New York: Alba House, 1967.

Pfeiffer, R. H., *The Books of the Old Testament,* New York: Harper, 1957.

Rad, G. von, *Old Testament Theology,* 2 vols., Edinburgh: Oliver & Boyd, 1962, 1965.

Rendtorff, R., *Men of the Old Testament,* Philadelphia: Fortress Press, 1968.

Rhymer, J., *The Covenant and the Kingdom. A Way Through the Old Testament,* Dayton: Pflaum, 1968.

Robert, A., Feuillet, A., eds., *Introduction to the Old Testament,* New York: Desclée, 1968.

Rowley, H. H., ed., *The Old Testament and Modern Study,* New York: Oxford University Press, 1952.

Rowley, H. H., *The Rediscovery of the Old Testament,* London: Clarke, 1945.

———, *The Unity of the Bible,* Philadelphia: Westminster Press, 1955.

Sheehan, J. F. X., *The Threshing Floor: An Interpretation of the Old Testament,* New York: Paulist Press, 1972.

Smart, J. D., *The Old Testament in Dialogue with Modern Man,* Philadelphia: Westminster Press, 1964.

Tucker, G. M., *Form Criticism of the Old Testament,* Philadelphia: Fortress Press, 1971.

Vaux, R. de, *Ancient Israel, Its Life and Institutions,* New York: McGraw-Hill, 1961.

Vriezen, T. C., *Outline of Old Testament Theology,* Oxford: Blackwell, 1958.

———, *The Religion of Ancient Israel,* London: Lutterworth Press, 1967.

Westermann, C., ed., *Essays on Old Testament Interpretation,* London: SCM, 1964.

Wright, G. E., *God Who Acts,* Naperville, Ill.: Allenson, 1958.

———, *The Old Testament Against its Environment,* Naperville, Ill.: Allenson, 1958.

Zimmerli, W., *The Law and the Prophets. A Study of the Meaning of the Old Testament,* Oxford: Blackwell, 1965.

CHAPTER ONE

Beegle, D. M., *Moses, The Servant of Yahweh,* Grand Rapids: Eerdmans, 1972.

Blair, E. P., *Deuteronomy, Joshua,* London: SCM, 1965.

Bright, L., ed., *Pentateuch. Scripture Discussion Commentary,* London: Sheed & Ward, 1971.

Driver, S. R., *Deuteronomy,* Naperville, Ill.: Allenson, 1951.

Hanson, R. C., *The Serpent Was Wiser. A New Look at Genesis* 1-11, Minneapolis: Augsburg, 1972.

Hargreaves, J., _A Guide to the Book of Genesis_, London: S.P.C.K., 1969.

Hauret, C., _Beginnings: Genesis and Modern Science_, Chicago: Priory Press, 1964[2].

Herbert, A. S., _Genesis 12-50_, London: SCM, 1971.

Hunt, I., _The World of the Patriarchs_, Englewood Cliffs, N.J.: Prentice-Hall, 1967.

McCarthy, D. J., _Treaty and Covenant_, Rome: Biblical Institute, 1963.

———, _Old Testament Covenant. A Survey of Current Opinions_, Richmond, Va.: John Knox Press, 1972.

McEvenue, S., _The Narrative Style of the Priestly Writer_, Rome: Biblical Institute, 1971.

McKenzie, J. L., _Myths and Realities_, Milwaukee: Bruce, 1963.

Noth, M., _Exodus_, Philadelphia: Westminster Press, 1962.

———, _Leviticus_, Philadelphia: Westminster Press, 1965.

———, _Numbers_, Philadelphia: Westminster Press, 1968.

———, _A History of Pentateuchal Traditions_, Englewood Cliffs, N.J.: Prentice-Hall, 1972.

Rad, G. von, _Genesis_, Philadelphia: Westminster Press, 1972[2].

———, _Studies in Deuteronomy_, Naperville, Ill.: Allenson, 1950.

———, _Deuteronomy_, Philadelphia: Westminster Press, 1966.

———, _The Problem of the Hexateuch and Other Essays_, London: Oliver & Boyd, 1966.

Richardson, A., _Genesis 1-11_, London: SCM, 1971.

Rowley, H. H., _From Moses to Qumran. Studies in the Old Testament_, London: Lutterworth Press, 1963.

Sheed, F. J., _Genesis Regained_, New York: Sheed & Ward, 1969.

Snaith, N. H., _Leviticus and Numbers_, London: Nelson, 1967.

Speiser, E. A., _Genesis_ (The Anchor Bible), New York: Doubleday, 1964.

Stamm, J. J., Andrew, M. E., _The Ten Commandments in Recent Research_, Naperville, Ill.: Abingdon, 1967.

Vaux, R. de, *Studies in Old Testament Sacrifice*, Cardiff: U. of Wales Press, 1964.

Vawter, B., *A Path Through Genesis*, New York: Sheed & Ward, 1955.

CHAPTER TWO

Ackroyd, P. R., *The First Book of Samuel*, New York: Cambridge University Press, 1971.

Bright, J., "Joshua," *Interpreter's Bible*, G. A. Buttrick, ed. Nashville: Abingdon, 1963.

Bright, L., ed., *Histories I, II*. Scripture Discussion Commentary, London: Sheed & Ward, 1971.

Cundall, A. E., Morris, L., *Judges, Ruth: An Introduction and Commentary*, Chicago: Inter-Varsity Press, 1968.

Gray, J., *I and II Kings. A Commentary*, London: SCM, 1964.

Hertzberg, H. W., *I and II Samuel. A Commentary*, London: SCM, 1964.

Maly, E. H., *The World of David and Solomon*, Englewood Cliffs, N.J.: Prentice-Hall, 1966.

Mauchline, J., *I and II Samuel*, London: Oliphants, 1971.

McKane, W., *I and II Samuel. Introduction and Commentary*, London: SCM, 1963.

Montgomery, J. A., *A Critical and Exegetical Commentary on the Book of Kings*, New York: Scribner's, 1952.

Rowley, H. H., *From Joseph to Joshua*, New York: Oxford University Press, 1950.

Soggin, A., *Joshua. A Commentary*, London: SCM, 1972.

CHAPTER THREE

Bright, J., *Jeremiah* (The Anchor Bible), New York: Doubleday: 1965.

Bright, L., ed., *Prophets I; Prophets II*, Scripture Discussion Commentary, London: Sheed & Ward, 1971.

Cunliffe-Jones, H., *Jeremiah. Introduction and Commentary*, London: SCM, 1965.

Heaton, E. W., *The Old Testament Prophets,* Baltimore: Pelican, 1958.

Heschel, A. J., *The Prophets,* New York: Harper & Row, 1962.

Kissane, E., *The Book of Isaiah,* 2 vols., Dublin: Browne & Nolan, 1960².

Knight, G. A. F., *Deutero-Isaiah. A Theological Commentary,* Nashville: Abingdon, 1965.

Lindblom, J., *Prophecy and Ancient Israel,* Philadelphia: Muhlenberg, 1962.

Mays, J. L., *Amos. A Commentary,* Philadelphia: Westminster, 1969.

McKeating, H., *The Books of Amos, Hosea and Micah,* New York: Cambridge, 1971.

McKenzie, J. L., *Second Isaiah* (The Anchor Bible), New York: Doubleday, 1968.

Mowinckel, S., *He That Cometh,* Nashville: Abingdon, 1956.

Rad, G. von, *The Message of the Prophets,* London: SCM.

Rhymer, J., *The Prophets and the Law,* Dayton: Pflaum, 1968.

Robinson, H. W., *The Cross in the Old Testament,* London: SCM, 1960².

Robinson, T. H., *Prophecy and the Prophets in Ancient Israel,* Naperville, Ill.: Allenson, 1953.

Rowley, H. H., *The Servant of the Lord and Other Essays on the Old Testament,* London: Lutterworth Press, 1952.

———, ed., *Studies in Old Testament Prophecy,* Naperville, Ill.: Allenson, 1957.

Scott, R. B. Y., *The Relevance of the Prophets,* New York: Macmillan, 1968².

Stuhlmueller, C., *Creative Redemption in Deutero-Isaiah,* Rome: Biblical Institute, 1972.

Vawter, B., *The Conscience of Israel,* New York: Sheed & Ward, 1961.

Ward, J. M., *Hosea. A Theological Commentary,* New York: Harper & Row, 1966.

Zimmerli, W., Jeremias, J., *The Servant of God,* Naperville, Ill.: Allenson, 1957.

CHAPTER FOUR

Beaucamp, E., *Man's Destiny in the Book of Wisdom*, New York: Alba House, 1970.

Geyer, J., *The Wisdom of Solomon. Introduction and Commentary*, London: SCM, 1963.

Glatzer, N. N., *The Dimensions of Job. A Study and Selected Readings*, New York: Schocken, 1969.

Gordis, R., *The Book of God and Man. A Study of Job*, Chicago: U. of Chicago Press, 1966.

Henshaw, T., *The Writings*, N.Y.: Humanities Press, 1963.

Jones, E., *The Triumph of Job*, London: SCM, 1966.

McKane, W., *Prophets and Wise Men*, London: SCM, 1965.

———, *Proverbs: A New Approach*, Philadelphia: Westminster, 1970.

Murphy, R., *Seven Books of Wisdom*, Milwaukee: Bruce, 1960.

Neiman, D., *The Book of Job*, Washington, D.C.: Consortium Press, 1972.

Paterson, J., *The Wisdom of Israel*, Nashville: Abingdon, 1961.

Pope, M. H., *Job* (The Anchor Bible), N.Y.: Doubleday, 1965.

Rad, G. von, *Wisdom in Israel*, London: SCM, 1972.

Rowley, H. H., *Wisdom in Israel and the Ancient Near East*, New York: Humanities Press, 1960.

———, *Job*, London: Oliphants, 1970.

Rylaarsdam, J. C., *Proverbs, Ecclesiastes, Song of Solomon*, Richmond, Va.

Skehan, P. W., *Studies in Israelite Poetry and Wisdom*, Washington, D.C.: C.B.Q., 1971.

Scott, R. B. Y., *Proverbs. Ecclesiastes* (The Anchor Bible), New York: Doubleday, 1965.

———, *The Way of Wisdom in the Old Testament*, New York: Macmillan, 1971.

Whybray, R. N., *Wisdom in Proverbs: The Concept of Wisdom in Proverbs* 1-9, London: SCM, 1965.

Wright, A. G., *The Literary Genre Midrash*, N.Y.: Alba House, 1967.

CHAPTER FIVE

Barth, C., *Introduction to the Psalms*, New York: Scribner's, 1966.

Crim, K. R., *The Royal Psalms*, Richmond, Va.: John Knox Press, 1962.

Drijvers, P., *The Psalms: Their Structure and Meaning*, London: Burns & Oates, 1965.

Eaton, J. H., *Psalms*, London: SCM.

Kissane, E. J., *The Book of Psalms*, 2 vols., Dublin: Browne & Nolan, 1953.

Mowinckel, S., *The Psalms in Israel's Worship*, 2 vols., Nashville: Abingdon, 1962.

Oesterly, W. O., *The Psalms*, New York: Seabury, 1953.

Rinngren, H., *The Faith of the Psalmists*, London: SCM, 1963.

Sabourin, L., *The Psalms, Their Origin and Meaning*, 2 vols., New York: Alba House, 1969.

Westermann, C., *The Praise of God in the Psalms*, Richmond, Va.: John Knox Press, 1965.

CHAPTER SIX

Batten, L. W., *Ezra and Nehemiah*, Naperville, Ill.: Allenson, 1949.

Curtis, E. L., Madsen, A. A., *The Books of Chronicles*, Naperville, Ill.: Allenson, 1952.

Dentan, R. C., *I & II Kings. I & II Chronicles*, London: SCM, 1965.

Kelly, B. H., *Ezra, Nehemiah, Esther, Job*, Richmond, Va.: John Knox Press, 1969.

Luck, G. C., *Ezra and Nehemiah*, Chicago: Moody Press, 1969.

Myers, J. M., *1, 2 Chronicles* (The Anchor Bible), New York: Doubleday, 1965.

———, *Ezra. Nehemiah* (The Anchor Bible), New York: Doubleday, 1965.

Torrey, C. C., *Ezra Studies*, New York: Ktav, 1970.

Vawter, B., *The Books of Ezra-Nehemiah With a Commentary*, New York: Paulist Press, 1971.

Welch, A. C., *The Work of the Chronicler: Its Purpose and Date*, New York: Oxford University Press, 1965.

CHAPTER SEVEN

Bright, L., ed., *Histories II. Scripture Discussion Commentary*, London: Sheed & Ward, 1971.

Corbishley, T., "1 and 2 Maccabees," *A Catholic Commentary on Holy Scripture*, Orchard, B., ed., London: Nelson, 1953.

Dancy, J. C., *A Commentary on I Maccabees*, New York: Oxford University Press, 1954.

Hunkin, H. A., "1 and 2 Maccabees." *A New Commentary on Holy Scripture*, London: S.P.C.K., 1928. Gore, C., ed.

Zeitlin, S., *The Second Book of Maccabees*, New York: Harper, 1954.

CHAPTER EIGHT

Charles, R. H., *The Apocrypha and Pseudepigrapha of the Old Testament*, New York: Oxford University Press, 1913. I.

——, *A Critical and Exegetical Commentary on the Book of Daniel*, New York: Oxford University Press, 1929.

Dancy, J. C., Fuerst, W. J., Hammer, R. J., *The Shorter Books of the Apocrypha*, New York: Cambridge University Press, 1972.

Gaster, T., *Purim and Hanukkah in Custom and Tradition*, New York: Schuman, 1950.

Heaton, E. W., *Daniel*, London: SCM, 1966.

Howie, C. G., *Ezekiel. Daniel*, Richmond, Va.: John Knox Press, 1962.

Lattey, C., *The Book of Daniel*, London: Longman's, 1935.

Luck, G. C., *Daniel*, Chicago: Moody Press, 1969.

Oesterly, W. O., *An Introduction to the Books of the Apocrypha*, New York: Macmillan, 1935.

Paton, L. B., *The Book of Esther*, Naperville, Ill.: Allenson, 1951.

Pfeiffer, R. H., *History of New Testament Times; With an Introduction to the Apocrypha*, London: L. & C. Black, 1963[2].

Porteous, N. W., *Daniel: A Commentary*, London: SCM, 1965.

Rowley, H. H., *Darius the Mede and the Four World Empires in the Book of Daniel*, Naperville, Ill.: Allenson, 1959[2].

——, *The Relevance of Apocalyptic*, New York: Association Press, 1964[3].

SEMITIC AND GREEK FORMS

al hag-gittith (H)—psalm direction; reference to Gath

al hash-sheminith (H)—psalm direction: "for bass voices"

al alamoth (H)—psalm direction: "for soprano"

Allelu-Yah (H)—praise Yahweh

'almāh (H)—young woman

ānî (H)—humble

'anawim (H)—the poor

apokalypsis (G)—revelation

Aram (H)—Mesopotamia

archisynagōgos (G)—an official who presides over a cult

archōn (G)—collective office

bar enash (H)—son of man

beneginoth (H)—psalm direction: "with stringed instrument"

berith (H)—covenant

biblos psalmōn (G)—book of psalms

darash (H)—to examine

deuteros nomos (G)—second law

diathēkē (G)—covenant

diaspora (G)—the Dispersion

dibre hayyamim (H)—events of the past (i.e., the Chronicles)

'edah (H)—a worshiping community

el han-nehiloth (H)—psalm direction: "to the flutes"

gahal (H)—church

gebirah (H)—"Grand Lady"

go'el (H)—champion

haggadah (H)—form of midrash

halakah (H)—form of midrash (legal)

Hasidim (H)—the "Pious Ones"

hesed (H)—steadfast love

hōzéh (H)—a visionary

karath berith (H)—to cut (make) a treaty (covenant)

kethubhim (H)—the Writings

khamseen (H)—sirocco

kōh 'āmar Yahweh (H)—"Thus says Yahweh"

lamnasseah (H)—psalm direction: "to the choirmaster"

le/al Jeduthum (H)—name of chief musician (Psalms)

maqqabah (H)—hammer

mashiah (H)—one who anoints

maskil (H)—type of psalm (sapiential)

massa (H)—burden

megilloth (H)—"rolls"

melek (H)—king

meridarchēs (G)—governor

mizmor (H)—accompanied song or hymn

midrash (H)—to research

miktam (H)—type of psalm (atonement)

nābâ' (H)—to pour forth

nābî' (H)—prophet

nābû (H)—to call

nāsî' (H)—prince

nb' (H)—to seek

ne'ûm Yahweh (H)—oracle of Yahweh

nomos (G)—law

Paraleipomena (G)—"the things omitted" (i.e., Chronicles)

pekah (H)—governor

pesher midrash (H)—type of midrash (research-prophetical)

phēmi (G)—to say, speak

prophētēs (G)—prophet

psalmoi (G)—psalms

psalterion (G)—a collection of sacred songs

pûru (H)—destiny

ro'eh (H)—seer

rosh (H)—prince

Selah (H)—psalm direction: "pause"

semereth (H)—top

sepher tehillim (H)—a book of hymns of praise

shiggaion (H)—type of psalm (lament)

shir (H)—type of psalm

shophetim (H)—judges

stratēgos (G)—military general

tehillal (H)—type of psalm (praise)

tehillim (H)—hymns of praise

tephillah (H)—type of psalm (prayer)

tôrah (H)—teaching given by God

wasfs (H)—wedding songs

APPENDIX

THE VALUE AND AUTHORITY
OF THE OLD TESTAMENT

1) *The Difficulties Encountered*

THE UNWELCOMED OLD TESTAMENT

Because of the very nature of the Old Testament, the 'authority' of the Old Testament and its place in the Christian's Bible have always been debated. Different solutions to the problem have been found in various forms throughout history. All of them have this in common: they take the New Testament as *the* point of orientation and evaluate the Old Testament from that perspective. Now although this does seem a reasonable procedure for the Christian to follow, and although all who have followed the lines of such solutions have done so in all good faith, yet the results have been unfortunate because the approaches have been misguided.

One major difficulty is classified by John Bright under the general title "Marcionism" after the second century heresy which, under Gnostic influence, devalued the Old Testament as the product of evil, of another and hostile god. Thus, "Marcionists" could be all those Christians who, because of the great differences in the Old Testament as compared with the New, would depose it or rank it as second-rate scripture. This Marcionist strain can be traced from those who overtly complain that there is so much in the Old Testament which is unedifying for Christians to those who practice Marcionism unawares (e.g. the layman or pastor who troubled by the Old Testament, treats it as if it were not in the Bible). There was an era in which theological courses offered in seminaries or elsewhere treated the Old Testament rather like an unwanted guest who could neither be sent away nor entertained properly. Rudolf Bultmann would be named among those who would accord a secondary value to the Old Testament. He saw it as a historical "miscarriage," a history of shattering failure yielding nothing but the great contradiction that belongs to human existence: to be called by God, yet to be bound to earthly and historical circumstance.

Bright summarizes this Marcionist fallacy thus: "wherever the law-gospel antithesis is pushed to the virtual equating of the Old Testament with law, wherever the discontinuity between the Testaments is stressed to the virtual exclusion of the continuity, wherever the Old Testament is accorded the exclusively pedagogical function of preparing man for the hearing of the gospel, the danger exists that the Old Testament will be reduced to a position of secondary importance."[1] The Church must continue to resist the Marcionist tendency not only by retaining the Old Testament, but by actively using it as a part of normative scripture. For, the Old Testament *was* authoritative scripture for Jesus himself, who knew no God save its God and who found in it the key to his own person. If perhaps it offends the feelings of some Christians, let them keep in mind that it did not seem to offend the "Christian" feelings of Jesus! Moreover, to loosen the bond between the Testaments always somehow results in damaging the gospel. For, the Old Testament binds the gospel firmly to history. It keeps it from being assimilated to alien philosophies and ideologies. The Old Testament restrains the gospel from flying into pure sentiment and other-worldly piety, or from disintegrating into solely individualistic interpretation.

LEVELS OF MEANING IN THE OLD TESTAMENT

Some have sought to "save" the Old Testament by reading a Christian meaning into all its texts. This began with the early Church Fathers, who resorted to allegory and typology in order to define the various levels of meaning.

Although patristic exegesis did manage to rescue the Old Testament (by making it a Christian book!), it strayed beyond control into a jungle of farfetched and imaginative interpretation. The Protestant Reformers objected to this quite rightly, asking what authority the Old Testament could have if each individual could read *any* meaning into it, and they defended the text in its plain meaning. Yet, they thought that this included a "prophetic sense" in the light of scripture as a whole (*sensus literalis propheticus*), and this too tended to become subjective. More recently, the trend in biblical scholarship has been to abide by the historical meaning of the text as the author intended it.

But can the Church really rest content with the plain historical meaning? Roman Catholics have taken a stand on the *sensus plenior;* christological interpreters and others feel that the Old Testament must be read beyond its historical sense. All these express the conviction that, on the one hand, the Old Testament is indispensable to the Church, while on the other hand she cannot be asked to "take it straight." Somehow, she needs it seasoned with a meaning over and above the plain, historical one. Yet, the text must be allowed to speak its own word. Typology or similar approaches are not to act as substitutes for straightforward exegesis, whose task is to make clear the precise meaning of the text. For, the text really has but one meaning—that intended by its author. And only one way can discover that meaning—the grammatico-historical method. There may be meanings, it is conceded, beyond the obvious sense of the Old Testament text: who can confine or limit the one God of both Testaments? However, this does not change the exegetical task. One can make an exegesis of texts, but not of the Holy Spirit's intention. For, as Jesus says, the Holy Spirit is like the wind, blowing where it wills (John 3:8), and cannot be probed by the exegete's tools. Interpretation must go beyond the historical meaning of the text, yes; but it must be controlled by that meaning.

Methods through which the New Testament writers related their message to the Old Testament included typology and allegory. But, whereas modern scholars can respect their processes and forms, they cannot maintain that they are mandatory for present biblical theology. This does not mean that the value of New Testament writings is lessened to the extent that allegorical exegesis has been admitted into it. Indeed, the real question does not even concern the Old Testament and its use in the New, but rather how *we* are to relate ourselves to the Old and its use in the New. Often, however, the relationship has not been adequately conceived in terms of biblical inspiration, so that the fuller sense approach has not been as successful as concentration on an adequate spelling out of the notion of promise/fulfillment. Properly understood, this means that the Old Testament contains the history of the promise which comes to fruition in the New Testament; the dynamic, historical life of Israel abides, even after its "fulfillment" in the New Testament. The Christian notion of fulfillment should not blot out the Old Testament reality, nor be an abstraction. We cannot simply overlook the concrete manner in which the Old Testament was understood by the early Church, and we should pay more heed to the meaning it had for the people of Jesus' day and age. Finally, the lines of continuity *and* discontinuity between the Testaments need delineating. We should not strive over much to give conceptual expression to biblical unity. For, the discrepancies between the different parts within the Old Testament or New Testament separately cannot be ignored, let alone the compounded problem when the Testaments are considered as joined.

THE CHRISTIAN INTERPRETATION OF THE OLD TESTAMENT

One of the solutions to the question of the Old Testament's authority is a kind of *via media* associated with liberal Protestantism. It consists of making a value judgment on the basis of New Testament teaching which is then imposed upon the contents of the Old Testament, separating the elements of abiding validity from those which are considered too old or "sub-Christian" or outdated to concern us. This liberalism, associated with Wellhausen, stressed the human aspect of the Bible and the social, moral aspects of its religion. It was seen as a historically conditioned book, as God's self-revelation progressively developing towards Christianity. Hence, all the Old Testament was to be evaluated according to the norm of its highest level: Jesus himself. But, this had two unfortunate results: large parts of the Old Testament were seen as irrelevant to the Christian and thus slipped into disuse, and what remained tended to be spiritualized or moralized. Granted, Jesus *is* the crown of revelation. But to test the *validity* of scripture by deriving a norm from him can easily become too subjective. In fact, to make such value-judgments leads to the breakdown of scriptural authority because, as a result, the individual formulates his own beliefs and practices. His own mind and heart become the final court of appeal. In reality, by contrast, the Christian faith is *not* what a given individual believes it to be by trying to isolate elements in scripture by value-judgments. It is a historical phenomenon, based on what *was*.

The relationship between the Testaments is complex. There are different levels on which the Old related itself to the New: the Old Testament text itself, the religious framework of later Judaism, Jesus' own understanding of himself and his work in terms of biblical patterns, and the apostles' understanding of Jesus and the authority with which he used the biblical text. When the New Testament quotes scripture it is imaginative and constructive in its choice and combination of passages. Because the New Testament writers were concerned less with methods than with results they used the Old in a way very different from "exegesis." Their object was to let the meaning of the text emerge by looking at every possible aspect of it.

And, as James Barr says,[2] the Old Testament *is* pre-Christian. It *was* written at a time in which Jesus had not yet come and should be understood as such. Jesus may have been the culmination of God's plan. But, this does not mean that Jesus must be the criterion for the meaning and fullness of what God did before he came. We need to do justice to the original setting of the texts, those real situations in Israel which did not need to be seen as prefigurations. We cannot really consider that Jesus is the "key" to the Old Testament, or that it is understood only in the "light of Jesus" or the "light of the New Testament." The apostles did not first understand Jesus, and then turn to the Old Testament. Rather, they turned to the Old Testament in trying to learn to know, explain, and understand him. The question we should ask ourselves, says Barr, is not how we can know the Old Testament from our understanding of Jesus, but rather: "Do we really know Jesus himself?"

Along these same lines, G. E. Wright[3] criticizes those christocentric theologies of the Old Testament which dissolve theology into christology and leave nothing to say about the independence of God. He calls this "Christomonism"—a "Unitarianism of the Second Person" which neglects to talk about God in favor of talking about Jesus. This fallacy of "Christomonism" takes an existential shape in Bultmann and plays a real role in his dehistoricizing of the Bible. For Bultmann, Christianity stands apart from the Old Testament religion as the faith which perceives in Jesus the revelation of God—thus, the idea that God is somehow accessible only in Jesus. Such a christomonistic standpoint affects the question of the significance of the Old Testament: it could be proclaimed in the Church as God's Word *only* when the Church finds in it what is already known from revelation in Jesus.

From all this, we may conclude that scholars would like to indicate the christological approach as the most obvious center of biblical unity and authority. However, they consistently must point out that such an approach used exclusively tends to eliminate the historical development of Old Testament material and reduce the validity of Old Testament thought to a "pale reflection of the Jesus-to-come." The only logical possibilities in answering the problem of the Old Testament's authority would *seem* to be those approaches which all take the New Testament as a point of orientation. But since, as we have seen, none of the approaches is entirely acceptable, we appear to have reached an impasse.

2) *Towards a Resolution of the Difficulties*

THE SERVICE OF BIBLICAL THEOLOGY

The question of the authority of the Old Testament does *not* end in an impasse but demands instead a retracing of steps, a reversal of direction. If we conclude that the Word of God addressed to Israel should be taken as it is and not be too hastily Christianized, we are also saying that "christocentricity" in biblical studies has no meaning without a prior "theocentricity." And this involves the entire realm of *biblical theology*. For, the reversal of direction is that we must begin with the Old Testament itself and progress with its line of history and structure of faith ahead to the New Testament. From there, we can then look backwards and understand the Old. The pivotal point in the thesis of scholars, especially of Bright, is that the key to the solution of the difficulties is to be found through the study of biblical theology—that is, in the theological structure of both Testaments in their relationship to each other. Although the Bible's unity has been questioned with the rise of the historico-critical method so that many different theologies within it have been proposed, yet biblical theology must press on behind the diversity to grasp the single structure of belief which underlies it.

What is the nature of this theological structure undergirding the Old Testament? There are recurrent themes: the uniqueness of Israel's belief, her distinctive God and singular understanding of history as the theater of his activity, her concepts of election, covenant, and promise-fulfillment. Behind all these manifold expressions lies a commonly-held structure of believing; in one way or another, Israel's normative faith underlies all parts of the Old Testament. However, the Old Testament *is* incomplete, and the fulfillment of the "promise" must always be spoken of in the future tense. Its salvation history is broken; it never quite arrives at salvation. Hence, the entire Old Testament asserts implicitly that Jesus Christ fulfills the redemptive purposes of God which began with Abraham, and this is the whole meaning of history. The Christian theologian must take the Old Testament seriously—not only as a historical document giving the background for later movements, but also as of vital import for life here and now. The Old Testament contains the history of a promise reaching fruition in the New, but Israel's dynamic and historical hope *abides* even after the New Testament has given it fulfillment. It is through the historical exegesis of Old Testament scripture that the modern Christian can affirm with certainty that Jesus did come from what had been done and prepared in Israel. The New Testament may have been arbitrary in its choice of Old Testament texts. However, it has been consistent in their general interpretation or in connecting the Old Testament with Jesus.

Thus, rather than taking Jesus as the given norm and arguing from him to the authority and meaning of the Old Testament, the proper strategy is to take the Old Testament as something we *have* in the Church. We can then ask in what ways the guidance it gives helps us to understand Jesus more truly. The Old Testament scholar must protest against "Christomonism" as a substitute for the only theology that can handle both Old and New Testaments together—namely, a theology of God's initiative in history. All who wish to keep in touch with the biblical understanding of reality must accept certain primary assumptions and assertions about God in the Old Testament (such as God as Creator, Lord, and Warrior). Wright feels that what is essentially biblical is a special political understanding of the universe. This is because human life is concerned with the means whereby humans relate to one another, and this takes place mainly on the socio-political level. In this perspective, certain repeated conceptions about God have an abiding relevance. The inspired writers, who collected and edited the traditions of Israel, already strove to bring out the existential value of past events by making them "present" to their contemporaries. There is a basic kerygmatic structure of event and commitment present in the Old Testament as well as in the New. For, the writers were not intent on merely accumulating material, but on inviting their readers to be converted and abide by the covenant. For example, the final form of the Pentateuch places all legislative material during the sojourn at Sinai. It represents the commitment demanded of Israel and her response to God's gracious acts on her behalf. Or again, the Deuteronomist brought out the kerygmatic spirit of this commitment through indicating the present significance of past events by means of a theological setting given to the traditions. As we shall see, to follow, this line already begun by the inspired writers will help us to see the Old Testament's value for *us*.

Yes, the key to Old Testament authority lies in its underlying theology. But, it must be the *whole* Old Testament that is considered "valid" or authoritative, just as is the New Testament, in order that then biblical theology can delineate this structure of faith and distinguish what is normative and central. There are indeed degrees of value, and not all parts of the Old Testament are equally important. But, *all is valid*. Since it is through their theology that passages speak to us, it is not a matter of designating certain passages as valid and disregarding others, but rather of grasping the theological concern that informs every passage.

THE OLD TESTAMENT WELCOMED

In contrast to our very first point about the rude welcome given by many to the Old Testament, we turn now to discuss its great *value* as contemporary scholarship has pointed it out for us. Firstly, there is the sheer literary value of the Old Testament—its great breadth of vision, its broad humanitarianism and sense of man as conveyed through the medium of literature. It portrays man as a free and responsible agent answerable to his God in history. The Old Testament manifests a joy in life, while at the same time being realistic in its awareness of pain and mortality. The specifically religious value of the Old Testament is not negated by such universal, human values but rather contained within them. The value of the Old Testament today is not primarily in what it teaches about God, man, and human destiny, but how it expresses the one abiding value: the meeting between God and man. The "eternal life" proclaimed in many forms throughout scripture is man's true life. Thus, the value of any scriptural text is measured by the extent to which it can guide a man's decisions towards a choice of that true life offered him by God.

This means that the Old Testament has an existential value for the Christian as one called to life in Jesus. It is the task of the exegete to reveal that value—which he knows through his faith that the Old Testament must have. He must point out in scripture a certain resemblance between his situation and that of the original hearers of the Word. As the authors of the New Testament could see, the Old Testament's men and events do have a real existential value in that they call to imitate God, they summon to decision, they advise conduct to be shunned. Episodes in the Old Testament can show us certain aspects of the mystery of Jesus whose claim on us would not otherwise be obvious. For example, even though the attitude of Jesus to his Father perfectly conveys the idea of the importance of faith, yet the New Testament writers have chosen not him but rather great figures of the Old Testament as models of the faith needful for salvation. How frequently the events of its salvation history have been seen as a divine education extending to the life of everyman. The Old Testament also helps us to balance the New Testament's possible impression of a lack of concern with temporal values or concrete needs of everyday life. The Old Testament is there to help us to take very seriously a human history which goes on and on and culminates in the total liberation of man.

Even the so-called "limits" of the Old Testament have an educational value: we learn that the limitations of revelation are not set by God, but come from human limitations. Israel's experience of God occurred in history and was subject to the contingencies of history. Thus, we can see that the only response which the people could give to its God was that response of which it was capable at each moment in its history. History and culture always conditioned Israel's experience of her God. "God as lawmaker" is emphasized in the Old Testament, but this is an imperfect human representation of him in our own language.

It was Israel's culture which kept her from finally reaching the Christian goals of love of enemies or the full dignity of woman. Such considerations make us more aware that concrete human conditions and cultural limitations *do* impose limits on man's experience of God and his translation of that experience into action.

If the limits of the Old Testament are so conceived, then ought not the Christian ask himself concerning the limits of New Testament revelation? Here, too, we are dealing with man's limitations, not God's. Does it seem that the human condition of the Christian has hampered a fullness of living Christ's life in the Church? Does it seem that Christians have not yet accepted fully the new dignity of the human person which the coming of Jesus has brought, and that we still define the human person in terms of secular values? If we answer in the affirmative, it must be because Christians have not fully accepted God or Jesus totally—because they have not totally accepted man. What a contradiction, seeing that the meaning of their new revelation is the incarnation!

The Church's constitution on revelation, *Dei Verbum,* emphasizes the abiding values of the Old Testament. Here, too, we read of how even its imperfect factors are turned to advantage. The Old Testament contains a "lively sense of God" and "sound wisdom on human life." It holds great theological wealth through its understanding of God and man in a unique manner. The New Testament is hidden within the Old, and the Old is made manifest in the New. But, all these things we have mentioned become actual only if we approach the Old Testament with reverence and intellectual humility, allowing it to speak for itself. The answers which the Old Testament gives concern ancient problems and situations which cannot always be made applicable to our own needs. However, the task of biblical scholars is to examine those ancient answers and discern the underlying theology expressed through them. With the guidance of the Holy Spirit, that theology may then be given new expression for the answers we are seeking today. That Spirit, promised by Jesus, has never failed to guide us aright.

For whatever was written in former days
was written for our *instruction,* that by
steadfastness and by the *encouragement* of
the scriptures we might have *Hope.*

BIBLIOGRAPHY

J. Bright, *The Authority of the Old Testament* (London: SCM, 1967).

G. E. Wright, *The Old Testament and Theology* (New York: Harper & Row, 1969).

J. Barr, *Old and New in Interpretation. A Study of the Two Testaments* (London: SCM, 1966).

R. E. Murphy, "A Christian Understanding of the Old Testament," *Theology Digest* 18 (1970), pp. 321-32.

J. L. McKenzie, "The Values of the Old Testament," *Concilium* 10 (December 1967), pp. 4-17.

F. Dreyfus, "The Existential Value of the Old Testament," *ibid.,* pp. 18-23.

---

[1] J. Bright, *The Authority of the Old Testament* (London: SCM, 1967), 72.

[2] J. Barr, *Old and New in Interpretation. A Study of the Two Testaments* (London: SCM, 1966).

[3] G. E. Wright, *The Old Testament and Theology* (New York: Harper & Row, 1969).